Program Design for Knowledge Based Systems

by

Graham Winstanley

SIGMA PRESS
Wilmslow, United Kingdom

HALSTED PRESS
a division of JOHN WILEY & SONS, Inc.
605 Third Avenue, New York, N.Y. 10158
New York • Chichester • Brisbane • Toronto • Singapore

First published in 1987 by **Sigma Press**
98, Water Lane, Wilmslow, SK9 5BB, England.

British Library Cataloguing in Publication Data

Winstanley, G.
   Program design for knowledge based systems.
   1. Expert systems (Computer science)
   2. ‑Programming (Electronic computers)
   I. Title
   005.3   QA76.76.E95

Library of Congress Cataloguing in Publication Data

Winstanley, Graham.
   Program Design for knowledge based systems.

   1. Expert systems (Computer science) I. Title.
QA76.76.E95W56 1987   006.3'3   87-14220

ISBN (Sigma Press)   1-85058-066-9
ISBN (Halsted Press)   0-470-20915-1

Distributed by

John Wiley & Sons Ltd., Baffins Lane, Chichester, West Sussex, England

Halstead Press, a division of John Wiley & Sons, 605 Third Avenue, New York, NY 10158, USA.

Printed in Malta by Interprint Ltd.

Typeset by Sigma Press

Acknowledgements:

The following are trademarks and/or registered trademarks:
IBM, CP/M, MSDOS, IQLISP, iLISP, TEXAS INSTRUMENTS EXPLORER, XEROX

Dedicated to
Christina, Lisa and James

Preface

Most problems, which can be well-defined, may be solved using algorithmic processes. The usual method would include stages of problem definition, algorithm developement and refinement, and finally, implementation in a highly-structured procedural computer programming language. The very nature of such problems would demand this approach and it is highly successful. However, there are realistic problems which are characterised by a certain amount of uncertainty or 'fuzziness', and in which the conclusions of any possible method of solution cannot easlily be predicted. In such cases, an approach is required capable of inference, assisted by experience and domain-specific knowledge. This technique relies ultimately on decisions arrived at through a variety of inference mechanisms, and is conveniently grouped under the anthropomorphic title of Artificial Intelligence.

Artificial intelligence is a relativley young subject and the opinion has often been expressed that it is too early to attempt to establish a definitive program design methodology. In particular, the more practical discipline of applications programming, is an evolving one capable of supporting a wide range of methodologies.

The underlying philosophy of this book is a system design methodology, using Lisp as the implementation language, and incorporating a mixture of formal design and 'rapid prototyping' techniques. In this way, the reader is guided through the text from initial concepts and problem definition, to the developement of a rule-based expert system. The latter chapters are concerned with alternative strategies; their usage and implications, and finally with the inevitable hardware developements required to realise embedded expert systems in the next generation of 'intelligent equipment'.

The reader is encouraged to follow the text from Chapter One to the end making use, of the function summary in Appendix One where appropriate. Although there are no tutorial examples, the program examples included in the book should be thoroughly tested and improved, and a well-documented system environment should be gradually developed. In various sections of the book, further system features are discussed without being explicitly developed. In these selected places, especially in the areas of information building and knowledge elicitation, the facilities outlined should be developed and incorporated.

Contents

Chapter 1

Problem-Solving Concepts and Choices

1.1 Introduction

Complexity, and the burden of complex problem solution has never imposed limitations on human endeavour. Indeed, by its very nature, complexity poses a challenge which inevitably attracts attention, and may result in advances in technology and understanding through its reduction and solution. Examples of man's almost fanatical quest to overcome the apparently insurmountable can be found throughout history, in all disciplines. As far as machine-implemented computational strategies are concerned, examples can be identified in the 1930s and 40s war time intelligence work on code breaking using an embryonic computer, to modern day experiences with space technology. Each new set of complex problems being solved, thereby producing more problems, which require more solutions, etc., etc. This iterative process which mankind is addicted to, is largely responsible for our technological development and innovation. Quite often, a complex problem cannot be solved without a significant development in available technology. A limitation such as this, however well understood, does not generally halt endeavour; it merely creates an atmosphere of frustrated research which ultimately leads to the sort of design breakthrough required.

In computer terms, these 'hurdles' can be identified. The first was the enabling technology itself, an automatic sequencing device capable of the storage and directed flow of data, numerical computation, and above all, decision making. The latter facility holds the key to all subsequent computational strategies. Natural human methods of problem complexity reduction, rely heavily on our ability to make certain assertions about the problem and its environment. Systems theory tells us that, for most problems, a system boundary can be constructed, capable of excluding certain factors which may cause minimal effects on the problem solution, but more importantly, would increase complexity to overwhelming proportions. Therefore, a problem, or set of problems may be enclosed within a 'closed system', and hence isolated in some way from the 'real world'.

This chapter deals with problem definition concepts, from a simple, but fairly realistic scenario, to a more formal treatment of the subject. It is vitally important not to bypass this process, or to underestimate its significance in the proceeding stages. Time spent in attempting to define, or even understand the problem in hand, can pay dividends later.

1.2 An Approach To Problem-Solving

In Section 1.1, the process of complexity-reduction was discussed. In that process, many non-significant factors pertaining to a viable solution, would be excluded. Having established a system boundary in this way, it is necessary to further reduce complexity by modularisation. As an example, consider the relatively uncomplicated task of interior decoration, or more precisely, the methodology of planning. There are some immediate problems to resolve. An ordered solution process will result, ultimately, in the optimal use of time, materials and manpower. Here are some of the most relevant points :

1. The building (and room within it) is occupied by a group of people. At least two of those people may hold strong views on the ideal outcome of the exercise; they would, most probably be conflicting.

2. There are options on the materials to be used, which have an influence on the final product. A rather incomplete list of these can be made:

    a) Paint or wallcovering materials; perhaps both. Apart from the obvious choice of colour, which perhaps should be part of point (1), what about quality and price ?
    b) Similar considerations for paintwork, plus the problem of which should be finished first. There are considerations here which could generate another (long) list.
    c) Some older buildings may be subject to cracks, as a result of the plaster ageing process. New buildings may acquire settlement defects. In the light of this, should one of the proprietary textured wall covering materials which have certain elastic properties be used? Several interdependences are apparent here (Point 1 and Point 2a). Perhaps this consideration can be placed outside our system boundary.

3. Should decoration be carried out at all? Perhaps the occupants intend to vacate the premises in the near future. In which case, the selling price may be affected by the result of the decoration process. Perhaps the decoration is only part of a much more involved modernisation programme, in which case decoration must be performed after building works but before carpet fitting.

This may appear to be a rather trivial example of a problem purporting to involve complexity, but it is a good general example of an everyday situation which requires some thought and can demonstrate the points made. For example :

1. A boundary has been placed. There are other factors which could be considered. For example :

    a) Toxicity of materials .
    b) Certain materials used in the manufacture of wallpaper can cause allergic reactions in some people .
    c) Fungicidal effects of material .
    d) Effects of damp on all materials .
    e) Length of time required to complete the task .
    f) Optimal time to start.

2. By answering the questions posed by the list, decisions can be made, perhaps collectively, in such a way that the final outcome is pleasing to all the occupants, in terms of appearance and financial outlay.

    The whole process of itemising and documenting information relating to the task in hand can be viewed quite simply as a structured approach to an understanding of the problem. It has been said that, with a full comprehension of any problem, the solution is obvious. This may be a rather sweeping statement, but there is an element of truth in it. The creation of an ordered list of considerations, deemed to be important in the closed system, is a peripheral aid to the thought process and is essential to an understanding of the reality of complex situations. It would be quite easy to include an initial stage in the program planning algorithm, which could appear as 'apply thought to the problem and decide on the feasibility of the solution '. Although the algorithmic stage of program structure planning involves a high feasibility study content, it goes almost without saying, that thought and discussion is necessary at a very early stage. Indeed, insight and creativity is probably at its highest level long before the mechanics of software design are undertaken.

    Each set of points in the list, or questions contained in them, would be further divided, perhaps subconciously, into more detailed 'lower level' or 'sub' questions which, by implication, require that certain tasks be carried out in the quest for a satisfactory conclusion. For example, take the quality/price consideration (point 2a, page 2). A higher priced material may be more cost-effective if it lasts longer or can be used in another job, in which case the material could be purchased in a more economical quantity.

    In conventional, or 'traditional' computer terms, the overall task would be implemented as a sequential process which involves periodic program flow direction decisions and can be represented formally in the familiar 'inverted tree' format. In the case of the room decoration task, the root of the hierarchy contains the overall problem definition, i.e. decorate the room. Sub tasks can then be identified in the complexity reduction process with decisions represented by branch direction options. Figure 1.1 illustrates such a tree.

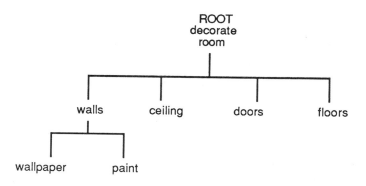

Fig.1.1 A job planning hierarchy

The design of a computer program which may be used to assist in the planning stage of the task would involve the implementation of the hierarchy shown in Figure 1.1. The process would involve the identification and classification of objects which are to be manipulated within the program, and all input/output requirements. In outline, the following stages would be found useful:

1. *The design of a general algorithm.* An overview and perhaps extreme simplification, but including enough generalities to render the structure recognisable. This process is useful in the initial problem definition stage and can provide information on the feasibility or practicality of the computer-based solution thought to be most suitable.

2. *The refinement of the general algorithm,* perhaps on the basis of further research and/or consultation and discussion.

3. *The expansion of the general algorithm* in order to add more detail. This process involves the identification of 'segments' which can be placed into almost independent modules and developed in isolation. Once modules have been identified, each must be treated as per general algorithm, i.e. identify objects to be manipulated in the 'local' environment and document all input/output requirements. In the process from (1) to (3), global and local variable details would be considered.

4. *The continual refinement of each sub-algorithm* to include all details considered to be relevant in the final implementation, and finally, the implementation in a highly structured high level computer programming language. At this stage, the transfer of detail from the final algorithmic stage to the coding stage

should be quite straightforward and result in very few problems later. In effect, coding is a result of a self-imposed structure on thought.

The very nature of such problems, as represented in the hierarchy diagram of Figure 1.1 demands the above approach. It may be viewed quite simply as a top-down design and implementation of a structured, closed- system problem, i.e. there exists a predefined and predictable set of conclusions. The general algorithm for the room decoration problem may appear as shown below :

Objects to be manipulated :

- MATERIALS
- TOOLS
- MANPOWER

Input/output requirements :

- TEXTUAL INPUT/OUTPUT INFORMATION VIA TERMINAL
- OPTIONAL INTERFACE TO EXTERNAL DATABASE OR TO
  SUPPORTIVE PROGRAMS SUCH AS COMPUTER-AIDED DESIGN
  PACKAGES

Algorithm :

BEGIN planning

    IF economical considerations are satisfactory
    THEN
        IF manpower is available
        AND materials are available
        THEN
            Decorate room

END planning

As the algorithm is expanded, sub tasks are identified and refined as independent modules, each with its own input/output requirements, governed partly by the real world problem in hand and also by the module-to-module interface requirements. Each module would have its own top-down structure and be capable of operating independently within any suitable environment capable of providing the specified interface, thereby successfully carrying out the required task with correct level of communication. Each module, therefore, would perform its function at a certain 'level' in the inverted tree hierarchy, with its communication channels rigidly fixed. At the final refinement stage, the algorithm should appear almost as a computer program in its own right, and the implementation should therefore be a simple process with very little oportunity for error. Errors apparent at this stage would be relatively easy to detect and correct by virtue of the rigorously imposed development procedure. Other beneficial results are :

1. Good, top-down documentation .

2. A modular format of the solution, which restricts the scope of a particular error to perhaps one module, thereby providing a means for speedy correction.

A highly structured language such as PASCAL would be the ideal implementation vehicle for this approach. It forces onto the programmer the sort of development discipline just outlined. For example, the program name always appears at the top, with all input/output streams explicitly declared and classified. All variables and data structures relating to objects which must be manipulated by the program must be declared immediately afterwards. The subsequent program conforms to the algorithm by virtue of its control structures and compound statement facilities. The availability and format of procedures and functions assist in complexity reduction by facilitating modularisation, and maintenance is eased. The structure of a PASCAL program to assist in the planning stage of internal decoration may be constructed in skeletal form and is shown in Figure 1.2.

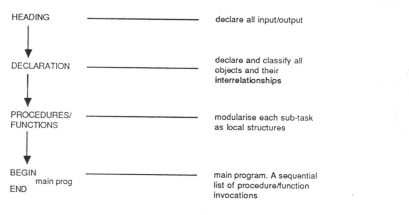

Fig.1.2 Structure of a PASCAL program

Figure 1.2 demonstrates the form of a structured program resulting from a rigid design methodology optimised for large system development. Each object must be declared and 'typed' at the beginning of the program. Whilst this is a deliberate strategy to force structure, it has obvious restrictions. Interrelationships which may be represented in the form of arrays, records and sets, for example, may not easily be modified. Indeed, each object and its relationships with others must be explicitly declared and must not be modified in ordinary circumstances. The whole point of the existence of programming languages like PASCAL is to place limits on possible 'esoteric' behavioural complexities of large systems. Such added complexity could render the final system illegible to future personnel, who may be given the unenviable task of system maintenance or documentation. In effect, flexibility in processing is made more complex by the rigidity of the implementation language and is determined largely by the success of the early algorithmic stages, where all possible variable entities should have been considered subsequent to a detailed study involving problem definition. Conventional control structures are available for the decision making processes, and these are used to direct program flow in predetermined directions, at definite logical positions. In addition, iterative processes are enclosed in specialised constructs.

The rigidity imposed by this highly structured strategy is typical of the so called 'program-driven' approach to processing. Structured programming concepts have evolved in response to the ever-increasing size and complexity of large software systems. The life cycle of such a system includes a large initial financial cost to the software developer, resulting from the manpower requirements of a development of this kind, and the amount of time required to bring the project from concept to conclusion. Development costs are always high, and of course, subsequent maintenance is a prime concern in the middle stages of the life cycle. Program designers have to be capable of understanding established software developed by other people, and implementing the required modifications and enhancements on a cost- effective time scale. The specifications for the design of programming languages like PASCAL involve considerations such as these, but are based on a set of problems existing in the real world, of which there is a predefined and predictable set of conclusions. Such problems could ideally be solved using a top-down, highly structured approach, with all objects and their respective interrelationships known in advance. The approach, both to program design and execution could be regarded as an inherently top-to-bottom sequential operation with known inputs and a known set of possible outputs. However, there are real world problems which do not fall into such a rigid classification: situations which human beings encounter and successfully manage every day, sometimes deliberately and sometimes subconciously. Most of these 'automatic' problem-solving feats, accomplished as a result of our interaction with the environment cannot be classified as analytical in the mathematical or pure logic sense, even on the odd occasion when a mathematical treatment would, in retrospect, provide a more conclusive result.

On the whole, we manage our lives with a mixture of correlation with previous or taught experience and a set of 'rules of thumb' or HEURISTICS. A mathematical approach to a particular problem is usually the result of a deliberate attempt to structure our thought processes to either solve a scientific problem beyond the scope of heuristics, or to justify our conclusions to other people. An example of the kind of problem which has traditionally relied on common sense brought about by experience can be found in the realms of project management. An industrial project may, once approved, involve the company in a large, almost prohibitive investment. The project could probably be conveniently partitioned into several discrete blocks :

- DESIGN
- PRODUCTION
- TEST

This very limited categorisation does not take into account other essential elements such as marketing, contracts, publicity, etc. Also, the relationship between each identified block is not indicated. In fact, the logical and physical interactions are extremely important to the success of the venture, as are the effects of personalities at all levels. Project managers have succeeded in structuring their approach to the job in hand by constructing graphical charts which display the project, and some of the most important variables, on a time scale. These devices are produced using CRITICAL PATH methods, and may be supported by hierarchy charts, bar charts and certainly by the common sense of the project manager, reinforced from regular 'project team' discussions. All of these methods (critical path methods, etc.) have limitations due to the necessary restrictive positioning of the system boundary, i.e. many variables must be excluded to prevent overwhelming complexity. Thus, traditional computer methodologies, when applied to this kind of problem, serve only to automate an essentially inefficient manual technique.

1.3 An Alternative Stratetgy

Before an alternative approach to an established convention is attempted, it must first be justified. In the true tradition of human development, the challenge must come first, the next obstructive wall to progress. This was apparent as far back as the early 1930s when Alan Newell and Herbert Soon attempted the LOGIC THEORIST, an artificial intelligence program based on a programming language developed by them specially for their work, concentrating on the processing of LISTS. The development of this specialised tool was a direct result of a new approach to a problem which could not be solved adequately with the currently available languages. The new language was developed at the Carnegie Institute of Technology (as its name was then) and was called IPL.

Some time later, Mc.Carthy developed a much more elegant list processing language which became known as LISP (LISt Processing). The impetus required for the birth of such a language, and the momentum required to carry the development to an advanced stage, was provided by a set of problems and ideas which could not (easily) be classified and solved by rigid, highly structured software methodologies, but rather had an element of UNCERTAINTY. Conclusions to these problems could only be achieved by recourse to the process of INFERENCE, using a variety of means. Data structures and logical constructs would have to be flexible. In essence, the computational processes were to emulate human thought. With this approach, the actual problem definition could remain 'fuzzy' and conclusions arrived at by a flexible mixture of mathematics, logic and heuristics. Probable solutions could be given, with some probabilistic values attached, and fashioned to simulate most human-derived conclusions, e.g. 'almost certainly, X applies'. Of course, just as with humans, an account of the deductive processes involved in achieving this somewhat less than definitive answer may well be required.

For this reason, most interactive AI systems, designed to provide conclusions, have some form of reasoning explanation facility incorporated. A simple, but widely used method of achieving this goal, involves an articulation of the decision methodologies used in arriving at a particular solution and the behaviour of the inference mechanisms in directing program execution. This is a very good facility for the program developer, but may be severely restrictive to the 'end user'. An explanation couched in computer-specific terminology may include more than enough information, but still requires a high degree of interpretation. Perhaps a separate intelligent system should be employed as a program-to-user interpreter interface, capable of giving clear, concise explanations and advice, at the level commensurate with the user's experience and knowledge. A system capable of 'filtering out' data not required to service a particular request for information and phrasing that information in the most optimal terms, based on KNOWLEDGE of the user's own level of experience and powers of comprehension.

1.4 An Alternative Structure

The conventional structures previously outlined can be used to explore the exciting idea of computation by INFERENCE - the idea of the computer-to-user response being modified by two-way communication as opposed to a rigidly imposed dialogue. It is useful to consider what we may want out of our eventual software system, highlighting in the process the deficiencies of conventional implementation languages, caused by their highly structured declarative nature. A simple example might be the decoration planner problem introduced earlier as a candidate for traditional treatment. A list can be drawn up to include some of the desired conclusions of the planning process. To simplify the situation for the purpose of example, we will close the system boundary around the painting sub goal, i.e. only consider this activity, even though we are aware that the interactions between other activities may well interfere to a large extent.

A list of considerations can be drawn up :

1. *A decision* must be made on whether to start the job at all. If so ... when ?

2. *Materials* must be chosen which are good enough to provide :

a) A pleasing appearance .

b) The right texture.

Expense is a major consideration. It can be sub-divided into :

a) A price per square unit of coverage .

b) The efficacy of cover (per coating) .

c) The ease of cover, related to the time required to finish the job.

3. *Manpower*. The number of people required and the length of time estimated to finish the job (two separate but highly interdependent considerations).

Each of these considerations is inter-related to at least one other. For example, material chosen to give optimal appearance would probably not be optimally priced. The job may be delayed for one reason or another, and price may increase beyond arbitrarily set limits, or even become unavailable. Ease of cover and price must be considered in relation to manpower. The problem begins to take on an unexpected degree of complexity, and with a certain amount of uncertainty. It would be easy to classify paint materials into price brackets, but a human would be highly influenced by previous experience with a particular manufacturer, either personally or by 'proxy' from a third party. Advertising has long been used to influence choices in this type of planning exercise. In essence, the various choices involved here could ultimately depend on pure heuristics, always assuming that an obviously large difference exists between a set of equally-motivated manufacturers plying for the same trade. A very hypothetical situation can be envisaged and Table 1.1 shows some possibly significant details.

1.5 Task Classification

The materials considerations are relatively static. The same list can be used for each and every job to be undertaken, as long as regular updating surveys are carried out. However, the interpretation and conclusions drawn from the use of Table 1.1 are very much dependent on other factors. One of the most important of these would probably be the nature of the task itself. Another table can easily be constructed, which includes information on manpower. An arbitrary classification can be made on the size of the prospective task, and the suitable number of persons required to be employed on the job. Notice that this classification has been made deliberately simple. The ideal number of people would realistically be influenced by various factors. However, in addition to this simplistic classification, data has been included on the number of individuals actually available at a given time in Table 1.2.

Table 1.1 Choice of materials

MATERIALS AND THEIR CHARACTERISTICS

MANUFACTURER	PRODUCT	ABILITY TO COVER	EASE OF COVER	PRICE CATEGORY
A	WW	1	1	1
B	XX	2	3	2
C	YY	2	2	3
D	ZZ	3	2	4

Where:

Price category:
1 - Very cheap (suspiciously !).
2 - Cheap .
3 - Reasonably priced .
4 - Expensive.

Ability to cover :
1 - Thin material, multiple coats required .
2 - Advertised as good quality .
3 - Guaranteed good quality.

Ease of cover :
1 - Difficult to work with. Requires high degree of workmanship and skill .
2 - Requires a certain amount of skill. Material tends to 'run' and 'drip' .
3 - Designed to be easy to use, with few 'mess' problems.

Given the information contained in Tables 1.1 and 1.2, the algorithmic expansion process can continue beyond the very general 'overview' to something which can lead to the modularisation stage. The resulting algorithm could be subsequently used in the design of a planning system. A part of such an algorithm is shown below.

Table 1.2 Personnel considerations

Job Classification	No. of People Ideally Required to Complete in a Reasonable Time	Time of Year to Commence Job			
		spr ing	*summmer*	*fall*	*winter*
small	one	1	1	2	1
medium	one	1	1	2	1
large	two	1	1	2	1
very large	more than two	1	1	2	1

Problem:

To decorate a room in an economical fashion, taking into account relevant factors, such as :

1. The 'real cost' of materials, i.e. longevity and cover potential ;
2. Manpower availability and cost ;
3. Collective preference.

Solution:

Using the information available, relating to manpower availability, cost and availability of materials, provide a 'reasoned' outline plan.

```
OBJECTS TO BE MANIPULATED: Wall-covering materials
                           Manpower
                           Time

END RESULT: A viable plan
```

```
BEGIN PLANNER
IF manpower is available THEN
   IF the preferred material is available in a suitable
      range of price/quality options
   AND IF manpower cost is not prohibitive
```

```
THEN
    Use the preferred materials and sufficient manpower
    to accomplish the task in the shortest possible
    time
OTHERWISE
    IF  . . . . . . . .
         .    .
         .    .
OTHERWISE  . . . . . . . .
```

                            etc. etc.

With some refinement of this algorithm, it should be possible to code the
solution into a PASCAL program quite easily. Objects to be manipulated would be
declared and 'typed' with their interrelationships explicitly declared. The table of
options may appear as arrays, and procedures would be designed to access and
manipulate them. A solution is possible therefore, using traditional sequential
methods, employing conventional representations and logical constructs.

The problems with this approach are highlighted by the number and repetitive nature
of the IF, AND-IF and ELSE-IF constructs. Another problem is execution
speed. The program, as it would appear as a logical consequence of the existing
algorithm, is constrained to test each logical construct in the sequence until the
appropriate test succeeds. In the simple case of the internal decoration problem, this
time penalty may be insignificant, but with a much more complex, multi-variate
problem such as the game of chess, an approach which includes a definitive list of
all possible combinations of play, could well result in computational times
measured in years!

There may be a better approach. A solution to the problem at hand can be arrived at
by breaking the problem down and using rules to arrive at intermediate solutions.
The tables (1.1 and 1.2) give us the information required to make conclusive
decisions, but knowledge is required to use that information sensibly. The
interrelationships or associations between objects can only be articulated through
knowledge, and knowledge is not a rigid device. The solution to a subset of our
problem (i.e. derived by the process of breaking down the problem) can be
represented as below:

        USE the material which is economically priced
        AND is suitable for the given task
        AND the required number of individuals is available

This is another way of representing the problems associated with choice of
materials. It is not as complete as the previous algorithm, in that
interdependences are not shown. The term economical infers financial considerations
which include the purchase price of the material, the longevity of the finish and the

manpower required to complete the task in a reasonable time. The remaining two considerations have their own interrelationships.

One of the main advantages of the latter form of representation is that it presents an easily-understood overview. It is presented as a set of logical entities which form the basis of the (sub) problem. If this were to be used, along with the 'aims' part of the algorithm to represent the problem to a third party, a good understanding would result. We could represent each separately-identifiable logical entity as a box in two dimensional space. Data can be extracted from the tables (1.1 and 1.2) and placed at 'levels' in the vertical axis, as shown in Figure 1.3.

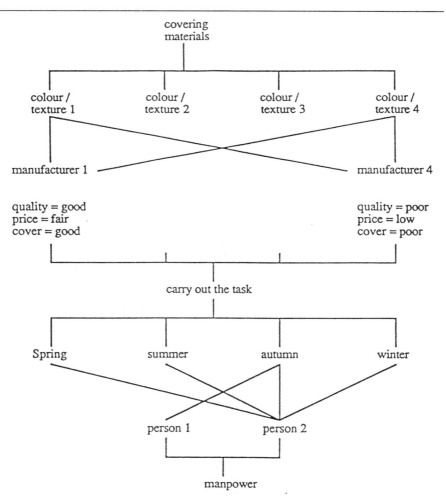

Fig. 1.3 Representation by hierarchy

Notice that all considerations relating to materials form a hierarchy with the root at the top, and all considerations relating to manpower are collected into another hierarchy with its root at the bottom. The effect of this structure is that all lowest level, or most detailed (less abstracted) factors appear in the middle, at the 'task' level. Ordered, top-down progression through the structure, ultimately leads to the level of detail required to perform the given task in the optimal fashion required. Interrelationships are included in the tabular representation and are shown diagramatically in Figure 1.3. Faced with relevant information in this form, and armed with a fairly simple set of rules, it would be possible to arrive at a good, well 'thought out' conclusion. A workable set of rules can be articulated, taking account of any order constraints there might be. These rules are :

1.   IF the material is of insufficient quality
        THEN
            do not use the material

2.   IF the cost of the material is unacceptable
        THEN
            do not use the material

3.   IF the material is not easy to work with, and therefore requires extra
        personnel
        AND those extra persons are not available
        THEN
            do not use the material

4.   IF none of these rules have 'fired'
        THEN
            use the material

Notice from these four simple rules, that the order in which they would be tested is relatively important, even though rules one to three would produce a conclusion in their own right. In some situations, it may be possible to structure the problem in such a way that order- independence of rules becomes a possibility. A great deal of thought is required to ensure that each rule, or the conditional part at least, is unique. Using these rules on the problem structure of Figure 1.3 eventually yields a combination of materials and manpower costs which satisfies a predeclared budget limitation. The program required to use these rules would use a control structure which is capable of accessing objects and attributes in the form of LISTS, the order of which would be unimportant. The rules would be applied to each entry in the list until a particular object (material in this case) satisfies them all.

There are some limitations to the rule-based strategy as presented up to this point, the main one being the particularly 'narrow' view taken by the control structure. The restricted set of simple rules, plus the extreme simplicity of the control structure, would result in an acceptable computational conclusion only if the materials list was arranged in a particular order, i.e. :

MOST PREFERRED --- NEXT MOST PREFERRED -- .... -LEAST PREFERRED

In this case, the chosen material could be regarded as the OPTIMAL selection as a logical progression 'down' the list. If, on the other hand, the list was arranged in a random fashion, optimality cannot be guaranteed. Indeed, for an optimal solution, an extended set of rules must be applied to the whole list. Of course, simple rules could initially be applied to operate on the random attribute list in order to 'pre-order' the contents in terms of quality (and perhaps price) in readiness for the 'main rule set'. For example, the rules below represent a bubble sort which could be employed to accomplish list ordering in terms of quality :

INITIALLY M=1   N=THE NUMBER OF ENTRIES IN THE LIST

```
1.   IF MATERIAL (M) IS INFERIOR IN QUALITY TO MATERIAL
     (M+1) THEN
         SWAP THE CONTENTS OF THESE TWO LIST ENTRIES
     M=M+1 ;

2.   IF M=(N-1) THEN
         M=1
```

A list of materials N entries long is to be ordered with the highest, and therefore most preferred quality, at the top of the list. The control structure would begin by setting the initial value of M (a temporary variable) to one, i.e. to 'point' to the first entry in the list. Rules one and two would be invoked in turn until a complete 'pass' of all data in the list has been made without a single data 'swap'. Such a condition would occur when the list had been successfully ordered. This constitutes a simple PRODUCTION SYSTEM in which a set of rules of the form :

```
     IF (CONDITION UNDER TEST IS TRUE) THEN
         SPECIFIED ACTION
```

is applied to a data base in such a way as to cause changes to be made to the information, or the representation of that information within the data base.

Another limitation of the rule based approach to our specific problem, at this stage, is the information required of the user on acceptable prices, acceptable qualities, cost and availability of manpower, etc. The various relevant attributes of the materials would be fixed and stored in a data base. In everyday life, many of these details are not definitely known. We may not know what a reasonable price is, or what the available manpower situation is likely to be at some given time in the future. A human solution to this type of uncertainty would be dominated by the following :

1. Experience of previous analogous situations, direct or third party- derived .

2. Calculations and comparisons, made possible by period of 'domain-specific' acquisition (market research) .

3. Rules of thumb, or heuristics (common sense).

The rule based approach allows us to continually improve the performance of our system by virtue of the facility to add more rules and make modifications to existing ones. The very nature of this strategy, its flexibility, allows us the possibility of dealing with incomplete data. A rule could be invoked of the form:

```
IF (SPECIFIC DATA ON X IS REQUIRED AND IS NOT
AVAILABLE) THEN
     INVOKE PROCEDURE Y
```

That is, if specific details on a particular subject (object) are not available, then attempt to gain that information as a result of some 'remote' procedural computation.

An example of this may be in the determination of quality of materials in the previous example. A list of facts relating to each material may be available in a data base in the form :

```
-  TEXTURE
-  LONGEVITY
-  AMOUNT REQUIRED TO PRODUCE ACCEPTABLE COVER
                      etc.
```

A procedure would be required to classify each material given these factors. Assessment would probably have to be based on comparison and a certain amount of heuristic information could be used, for example :

```
IF (COMPANY G RECOMMENDS IT) THEN
     IT MUST BE GOOD
```

Considerations such as these do not conform to the conventional 'wisdom' of traditional computer problem solving methodologies, but are certainly important in human reasoning. The advertising world is well aware of it!

In the discussion so far, conventional computer problem solving methodologies have been assessed and compared with an alternative approach which appears to provide the enhanced degree of flexibility required to attempt the solution of problems characterised by inexact or incomplete information. Traditional algorithmic processes provide a good means to enforce structure and are definitely not abandoned in the development of the far less rigid structures found in rule based systems. However, the latter strategy results in a rationalised solution with the facility for continual improvement. This facility is important in the solution of complex problems, where an initial 'attempt' can be made, based on a simplified set of rules. Continual, or INCREMENTAL development, usually takes place on the minimal system until it performs adequately. One of the characteristics of rule based systems is that :

THEY ARE NEVER FINISHED

Once an initial, fairly limited system is operational, new rules can be added to the list of rules at any time in the future to increase the sophistication and scope of the program. If the rule base is designed to be order-independent, then incremental development becomes a very attractive proposition indeed. In systems terms, the problem is initially represented in a much simplified form and a rule base and control structure is designed to conform to a simplified set of solutions. Once this has been accomplished, the system boundary can be expanded to include more and more extrinsic factors and peripheral interactions, in the form of relevant rules. With this program design philosophy, there is always scope for improvements and modifications indicated by EXPERIENCE and KNOWLEDGE ACQUISITION. Indeed, the philosophy introduced here tempts us with the possibility of MACHINE LEARNING, i.e. the capability of the program itself adding to its rule base, or making subtle modifications to existing rules on the basis of user-responses to knowledge-invoked stimuli.

An important feature of any problem solving strategy is the ability to arrive at conclusions on the basis of a given set of related information, i.e. INFERENCE. The most important method of human inference is DEDUCTION - the process of achieving a solution on the basis of LOGIC.

1.6 Inference Methodologies and Tools

The most important methods of inference are :

1. DEDUCTION - Logically correct inference

2. ABDUCTION -

$\left.\begin{array}{c} \\ \end{array}\right\}$ Logically inexact inference

3. INDUCTION -

1.6.1 Deduction and the Predicate Calculus

Deduction relies on a series of exact premises with which to test, in a logical manner, in order to arrive at an exact and true conclusion. For example :

IF (MOTOR CAR STOPS) AND (FUEL GAUGE READS EMPTY) THEN CAR NEEDS PETROL {URGENTLY}

This is a logical statement which requires two tests. Has the car stopped? What does the instrument panel tell us? The conclusion is one that has been deduced from a known set of facts and can be relied on to be exact and true. A formalisation of logical deduction is available to assist the computer programmer in the implementation of such inference, and is termed the PREDICATE CALCULUS. This rather grandiose, presumptuous and overweight name is attached to a useful set of tools, organised in such a way as to be suitable for computer implementation. A formal treatment of the predicate calculus will not be given in this text, but an excellent exposition of the subject may be found in a number of specialised texts referred to in Appendix two of this text.

In predicate calculus, a logical relationship between objects is called a PROPOSITION. A simple proposition, in 'plain language' might be :

FRED WORKS IN AN OFFICE

There are two objects in this proposition, Fred and office. Moreover, both of these objects have been explicitly defined, i.e. they can be regarded as CONSTANTS within the proposition. It would be quite easy to infer from this proposition :

X WORKS IN AN OFFICE

that X refers to a person who is probably an employee of the company whose work is carried out in the office in question. In formal terms, X is a VARIABLE within the proposition of, say, class employee. A similar proposition, therefore could be written in the form :

EMPLOYEE WORKS IN AN OFFICE

where all employees of that particular company would be assumed to be employed as some form of office worker. Employee in this case is a CLASS of person with a known set of attributes which might include :

- Requires regular payment
- Serves a useful purpose in the running of the business
- Contributes to company profits
- Works within the daylight hours 9.00 a.m to 5.00 p.m.
- Has a lunch break of one hour

etc.

A long list of the PROPERTIES of the EMPLOYEE class can be built up to define and describe a known set of facts which would be assumed to be constant, and can be applied UNIVERSALLY to any individual within that class. The objects within the proposition are also termed ARGUMENTS, and in addition to appearing as constants or variables, they may also be expressed as functions (in a similar way to the attachment of a procedure in one of the previous examples). For instance, the proposition :

FRED WORKS IN A (WORK-ROOM-WITHIN BUILDING-A)

would be evaluated by considering the workrooms of the specified building; building A. If this place is found to be an office block, then it may be assumed that Fred works in an office. In computer terms, it may be seen that the first term in the brackets invokes a separate function evaluation on the single argument, building A, in order that a conclusion to the proposition can be arrived at. Therefore, the OBJECTS or ARGUMENTS of the PROPOSITION of the predicate calculus can be one of :

1.   A constant definition of an object or class of objects .

2.   A variable which must become specified, or INSTANTIATED somewhere else in the program .

3.   A function definition, requiring further evaluation.

For historical reasons and reasons associated with the richness, and possible ambiguity of the English language, it is normal to arrange the proposition with the assertive definition or PREDICATE at the front, and the whole proposition delimited by parentheses. Using this notation, the previous example would appear as :

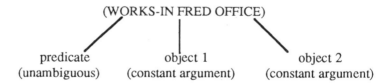

In this form, the order of terms within the brackets is very important and reads as before, i.e. FRED WORKS IN (AN) OFFICE. The predicate can be regarded as a named procedure with two arguments, and this formal representation of a proposition is ideally suited to program implementation. A proposition with one predicate is termed an ATOMIC proposition. A short list of atomic propositions is given below :

(WORKS-FOR FRED BILL)
(IS-A FRED EMPLOYEE SCOUT-LEADER POKER-PLAYER)
(HAS-PART BILL LEGS ARMS HEAD FINGERS)
(OWNS FRED CAR HOUSE COMPUTER)

Simple propositions such as these are useful to represent information on which rules, or knowledge can be applied. Deductive reasoning uses such relational information in logical tests to infer new propositions or definite facts. Therefore, in order to perform deduction, traditional CONNECTIVES are used. These are shown in Table 1.3. They CONNECT atomic propositions together in a logical structure to form new, COMPOUND propositions.

Table 1.3 Table of connectives

Connective	Symbol	Represents	Evaluation
AND	&	A & B	True if A AND B is true
OR	v	A v B	True if A or B is false
NOT	¬	¬	True if A is FALSE, false if A is true

The most important logical connective is not included in Table 1.3 because of its rather specialised nature and its requirement in any program designed to have the ability of reasoned decision making. The IF statement furnishes us with the facility to make IMPLICATIONS. A compound proposition can be constructed, initially in 'plain language' :

> IF (FRED IS AN EMPLOYEE) AND (FRED WORKS FOR BILL)
> OR (FRED SPENDS EACH DAY IN BULIDING A)
> THEN (FRED WORKS IN AN OFFICE)

The logical representation of Table 1.3 can be used to test the validity of this proposition and also prove the suitability of traditional logic. For example :

LET
    Fred is an employee = A
    Fred works for Bill = B
    Fred spends each day in building A = C
    Fred works in an office = D

This can be expressed more formally as :

    A = (IS-A FRED EMPLOYEE)
    B = (WORKS-FOR FRED BILL)
    C = (SPENDS-DAY FRED BUILDING-A)
    D = (WORKS-IN FRED OFFICE)
In symbolic terms :

    A & B v C > D

where the right arrow symbol conveys the meaning that :

IF A AND B OR C IS TRUE THE
THIS LEADS TO THE CONCLUSION THAT D IS TRUE

That is, the right arrow conveys the meaning IMPLY and corresponds to the IF...THEN logical construct.

Table 1.4
Alternative logical symbols

Connective	Symbol	Represents	Evaluation
AND	.	A . B	True if A AND B is true
OR	+	A + B	True if A OR B is true
NOT	—	$\overline{A}$	True if A is false, false if A is true

Basic laws:

a) $X . 0 = 0$ f) $X + X = X$

b) $X + 0 = X$ g) $X . \overline{X} = 0$

c) $X . 1 = X$ h) $X + \overline{X} = 1$

d) $X + 1 = 1$ i) $\overline{\overline{X}} = X$

e) $X . X = X$

Commutative laws:

a) $X . Y = Y . X$

b) $X + Y = Y + X$

Associative laws:

a) $(X + Y) + Z = X + (Y + Z) = X + Y + Z$

b) $(X . Y) . Z = X . (Y . Z) = X . Y . Z$

DeMorgan's theorem:

a) $\overline{X . Y} = \overline{X} + \overline{Y}$

b) $\overline{X + Y} = \overline{X} . \overline{Y}$

Distributive laws:

a) $X . (Y + Z) = (X . Y) + (X . Z)$

b) $X + (Y . Z) = (X + Y) . (X + Z)$

Fig. 1.4 Boolean manipulation rules

The theory of logical inference is quite well established and owes its foundations to people like George Boole. Boole devised a system for manipulating binary data, *i.e.* it could only have one of two values. The theories expounded by him are used in mathematics, but are particularly well suited to the design of digital electronics circuitry, including computers. The basic rules of manipulation, augmented by theorems introduced by De Morgan, are shown in Figure 1.4 which includes logic symbols according to the definition shown in Table 1.4.

In engineering, a typical starting point in the design of digital logic circuits is the construction of a TRUTH TABLE such as the one shown below:

A	B	Q
0	0	0
0	1	1
1	0	1
1	1	0

Where A and B would represent input to a logic circuit our purposes can represent atomic propositions. For example :

$$A = (WORKS\text{-}FOR\ FRED\ BILL)$$
$$B = (WORKS\text{-}FOR\ FRED\ JIM)$$

In the truth table above, Q represents the truth (1) or otherwise (false = 0) of both propositions in the appropriate row. The truth table can be expanded using another of Boole's theorems to produce a logical expression joined together by connectives. For example, an expansion of the truth table yields :

$$(\neg A\ \&\ B\ )\ v\ (\ A\ \&\ \neg B\ )$$

which, in logical terms represents an EXCLUSIVE OR function, i.e. exclusively A OR B. This may be made clear if the corresponding propositions were used, where the meaning would literally be :

(FRED WORKS FOR BILL) AND (DOES NOT WORK FOR JIM)

OR

(FRED WORKS FOR JIM) AND (DOES NOT WORK FOR BILL)

In other words, the propositions are MUTUALLY EXCLUSIVE. It would not be difficult to envisage a system where the compound proposition :

FRED WORKS FOR BILL OR JIM

could mean that Fred could, in some capacity, work for both employers. In actual fact, the logically-correct truth table for the OR function (as opposed to the exclusive OR function) is as shown below :

A	B	Q
0	0	0
0	1	1
1	0	1
1	1	1

Whilst this example has enabled us to infer some attributes of the employment details of Fred, and has indicated the results of building up compound propositions from simple atomic ones with the use of connectives, the process has been rather basic, requiring no further simplification. However, a computer program having the ability to infer by deduction may be presented with a large number of propositions, relating to a particular problem, which it must deal with. In this case, considerable simplification may be necessary with the aid of the predicate calculus.

Consider a further example, resulting from the 'connection' of three atomic propositions X, Y and Z. Such a compound proposition may be the result of logical computations:

$$\neg\,(\neg\,X\,\&\,(\,Y\vee\neg\,Z\,))\,\&\,(\,X\vee\neg\,Y\vee Z\,)\,\&\,\neg\,(\neg\,X\,\&\,\neg\,Y\,\&\,\neg\,Z)$$

This rather overweight connection of propositions could be the starting point for subsequent inference by deduction. Faced with such an apparently meaningless list of information, the program might make use of the manipulation rules of Figure 1.4 in its complexity-reducing operations.

The actual simplification process leading to a logical conclusion is shown in Figure 1.5. By progressively using the given rules in the appropriate order, a logically correct conclusion is made. The 'end result' is :

$$X\vee(\neg\,Y\,\&\,Z\,)$$

If we now examine the actual atomic propositions, using meaningfully named predicates and objects, the result becomes more clearly correct to us :

X = (HAS-ACCESS-TO FRED CAR)
Y = (OWNS-VEHICLE FRED CAR)
Z = (RELIES-ON-TRANSPORT FRED PUBLIC)

If the original compound proposition is now examined, with the new knowledge gained on the meaning of each atomic proposition, the simplification process is possible without recourse to predicate calculus and the repetitive use of simplification rules. This is, of course, because human inference is carried out, automatically with the aid of knowledge (and perhaps imagination). The example shows the problems faced by systems designers in the quest for true intelligent systems. However, an automation of the process of deduction outlined here would result in a useful level of deductive reasoning, and this approach has been adopted in the design of an artificial intelligence programming language called PROLOG.

There are certain problems associated with a strict, logical approach to inference. The first of these is concerned with the possible validity of a compound proposition given that one or more of the atomic propositions evaluate as false. In strict logic, all terms in the expression are required to be true. In the predicate calculus, there are structures available to do this, known as QUANTIFIERS. In actual fact, the quantifier is associated with variables within a proposition. For example, in a previous example, we saw that:

$$(\text{WORKS-IN X OFFICE})$$

Initial compound proposition:

$\neg\,(\,\neg\,X\,\&\,(\,Y\,\vee\,\neg\,Z\,))\,\&\,(\,X\,\vee\,\neg Y\,\vee\,Z\,)\,\&\,\neg\,(\,\neg\,X\,\&\,\neg\,Y\,\&\,\neg\,Z\,)$

using DeMorgan's theorem on : $\neg\,(\neg X\,\&\,(\,Y\,\vee\,\neg\,Z\,))$............................(a)

yields: $X\,\vee\,(\,\neg\,Y\,\&\,Z\,)$

Using the distributive laws on this yield: $(\,X\,\vee\,\neg\,Y\,)\,\&\,(\,X\,\vee\,Z\,)$

Taking : $(\,X\,\vee\,\neg\,Y\,\vee\,Z\,)\,\&\,\neg\,(\,\neg\,X\,\&\,\neg\,Y\,\&\,\neg\,Z\,)$............................(b)

and applying DeMorgan's theorem to : $\neg\,(\,\neg\,X\,\&\,\neg\,Y\,\&\,\neg\,Z\,)$

yields : $(\,X\,\vee\,Y\,\vee\,Z\,)$

Therefore, the two terms of (b) together are : $(\,X\,\vee\,\neg\,Y\,\vee\,Z\,)\,\&\,(\,X\,\vee\,Y\,\vee\,Z\,)$

Using the second distributive law of figure 1.4 on this yield $(\,X\,\vee\,Z\,)\,\vee\,(\,Y\,\vee\,\neg\,Y\,)$

But one of the basic Boolean manipulation rules says : $(\,Y\,\vee\,\neg\,Y\,)=1$

Therefore, placing the result of (a) with the result of (b) in order to complete the

expression yields : $(\,X\,\vee\,\neg\,Y\,)\,\&\,(\,X\,\vee\,Z\,)\,\&\,(\,X\,\vee\,Z\,)$

But another of the basic manipulation laws states that : $(\,X\,\&\,X\,)=X$

Therefore, the expression can be further simplified to :

$$(X\,\vee\,\neg Y\,)\,\&\,(\,X\,\vee\,Z\,)$$

Finally, using the distributive laws on this yields : $X\,\vee\,(\,\neg\,Y\,\&\,Z)$

Figure 1.5 Boolean simplification

---

where X is a variable within the proposition of class EMPLOYEE. It is possible to define the proposition for all employees by using the UNIVERSAL QUANTIFIER. For example :

$$(\forall \ (X) \ (\text{WORKS-IN X OFFICE}))$$

This has the meaning ALL EMPLOYEES work in an office. On the other hand, if the meaning should be SOME employees work in an office, another quantifier is available, the EXISTENTIAL QUANTIFIER. The proposition above would then appear as :

$$(\exists \ (X) \ (\text{WORKS-IN X OFFICE}))$$

Therefore, only SOME instantiations of the variable X would be true for the proposition to be valid. The flexibility afforded by these two quantifiers helps in the process of logical inference, especially in the case of long, complicated, compound expressions. The second problem associated with logical inference using the predicate calculus is directly related to the formality, or uniqueness limitation of each proposition or conclusion. For example :

IF (OWNS FRED CAR) THEN
(GOES-TO-WORK-IN FRED CAR)

is a reasonable conclusion, applicable to deduction, until perhaps Fred goes away on business, or his wife or children claim priority of use. In other words, the process of deduction does not completely emulate human reasoning (as we saw in Figure 1.5). Of course, it would be possible to selectively use quantifiers and apply more atomic propositions to the solution, but that leads to the third problem, the application of rules. In the simplification process of Figure 1.5, the logical manipulation rules were applied in a fairly STRICT ORDER to arrive at the desired result. Quite often, with the aid of EXPERIENCE, the order is obvious from the outset. On other occasions, simplification is not so easy and several attempts must be made in order to be conclusive, aided by further logical devices known as KARNAUGH MAPS. Couple this difficulty with the inability of the formal method to modify propositions or conclusions in the light of 'common sense', and the result is a highly complex deduction system, prone to inefficient and positively unreliable conclusions. The problem of CAUSALITY has been solved to a great extent in AI languages like Prolog, and advances have been made in the automation of the predicate calculus and deductive reasoning. Many workers in the early development of artificial intelligence, however, took an alternative approach to automated inference.

1.7 Abduction

As we saw in the previous section, deduction can be thought of as logically-correct inference, i.e. given a set of facts, or premises, a conclusion can be arrived at which can be relied on to be true. Deduction is fine when enough information is available to facilitate 'complete inference'. However, there are situations in which some of the vital information required for deduction is missing. Take, for example the following information :

(IS-RUSTY MOTOR-CAR)

We have no further information on MOTOR-CAR, but we could infer from the proposition, that the vehicle in question is old. This quite reasonable conclusion is arrived at by virtue of our experience, either directly or third party, of motor vehicles. We know that the car bodywork is probably made of steel. We know also that, no matter how that material has been treated, rust is always the eventual outcome (in time). The conclusion drawn is very similar to deduction, but is dissimilar in a quite subtle way. The conclusion may NOT be true. The car may have been left at the dockside, in a highly salty environment awaiting export, perhaps as a result of industrial action. In this case, the vehicle would, in all probability be new. Without the latter piece of information, i.e. with INEXACT or INCOMPLETE information, we have ABDUCED the conclusion that the motor car is old. Our abduction would take the form:

(MOTOR-CAR) (IF (IS-RUSTY MOTOR-CAR) (IS-OLD MOTOR-CAR))

If an automatic inference system were to be designed, able to deal with this sort of proposition, it should be sophisticated enough to look 'deeper' into the associated facts, i.e. to emulate human reasoning. For instance, given the motor car proposition, that the vehicle is rusty, a person would consider 'supporting evidence' to prove the theory that it is old. Such evidence might include :

1. Old cars tend to display other age-indicating features, such as evidence of damage, previous repairs, attempts at customisation by previous owners, cracked or faded paintwork, bald tyres, etc.

2. The registration/identification plates might indicate year of sale .

3. Verbal communication from a 'knowledgeable person' .

4. The vehicle documentation may be available for inspection.

Discounting (3) and (4), which would permit the use of deduction, human abductive processes would be aided tremendously by the supporting facts of (1) and (2). The actual sequence of events might be :

A - The conclusion IS-OLD may be abduced from the proposition (IS-RUSTY MOTOR-CAR)

B - The conclusion above is substantiated (although not proved) by (1) and (2)

C - Logically correct inference is made possible with the added information of (3).

Only when the documentation has been examined, can the deduction be made that the car is old.

Abduction is perhaps the most important human reasoning process in everyday life. In most realistic situations, a complete set of information is not available (at the most convenient time) to permit deduction, but this does not usually restrict or limit decision making. We may, for example, be interested in the age of a motor vehicle for reasons of pure curiosity. In such non-critical situations, the 'top level' abduction would probably suffice. As a matter of interest, we might make the effort to look at the vehicle and gain some satisfaction in the (near certain) knowledge that our abduction is true. However, we may be interested in purchasing the car, or hiring it, or even insuring it. Under these circumstances, the exact details would be required, and if they were not available, we would invoke procedures to acquire them. The evidence to support the abduced proposition that the car is old can be arranged graphically in several 'layers' as in Figure 1.6.

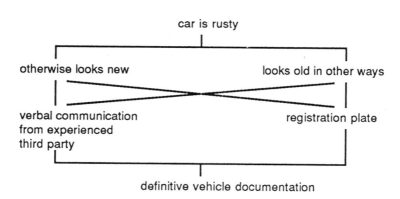

Fig. 1.6 A graphical representation of the abduction process

In computer terms, the process of substantiating an abduced proposition in this way involves an ORDERED data base search and may include data obtained from the invocation of a separate sub-program, or procedure designed to perform other forms of information search, acquisition or calculation. This strategy is well used in EXPERT SYSTEMS and is known as PROCEDURAL ATTACHMENT.

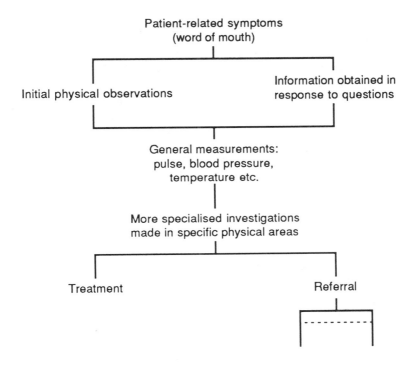

Fig. 1.7 A simplified medical diagnosis senario

One of the earliest and perhaps most suitable domains for this form of inference is that of medicine, or to be more precise, medical diagnosis. A medical diagnosis, in general practice, follows roughly the procedure shown diagrammatically in Figure 1.7. The patient presents at the surgery with symptoms which are initially communicated to the medical practitioner verbally. In some cases, a diagnosis could probably be made at this point in time, but would be supported in most cases by the 'second level' of Figure 1.7, that of two-way communication between the doctor and his patient. The medical practitioner's initial outline diagnostic 'hunch' would be either strengthened in this process or be made less plausible. In any case, more information is readily available at the third level of the diagram. The abduction process may terminate at this stage with a high probability of success, but in some cases, a particular biological system may require further, more detailed scrutiny before treatment. The final outcome may be referral to a medical specialist for reasons of intensive investigations or for more specialised treatment than that available at the general practice level. The whole process shown in Figure 1.7 is one of abduction up to the point (as yet largely unreached) of absolute certainty.

Some of the earliest, and still most established computer systems employing abduction were designed to aid clinical diagnosis. MYCIN for example, was developed at Stanford University to assist in the identification of bacteriological organisms causing specific diseases, and also to assist in treatment planning. CASNET was designed to assist in the diagnosis of specific eye disorders and INTERNIST is involved in the general clinical diagnostics area. These established and successful systems are, of course, more sophisticated in nature to that indicated in Figure 1.7, and employed some method of quantifying the degree of diagnostic certainty attached to each conclusion. These techniques are based on statistics, or other mathematical methods.

With the facilities of deduction and abduction, sophisticated automatic inference becomes a possibility, and computer systems able to incorporate these mechanisms in the solution to a predefined problem domain would indeed be able to emulate certain human reasoning processes. However, such a system could be relied on to produce the same result given a series of identical propositions. The system would not improve with experience. Humans have this latter ability, made possible by LEARNING.

1.8 Induction

Machine learning is one of the most intriguing concepts of today. A machine capable of continual, automatic knowledge building and concept modification, in the light of reasoning about its environment is a most attractive (and perhaps daunting) possibility. Simple induction can be demonstrated by this example :

(WORKS-IN FRED OFFICE)

AND

(WORKS-IN BILL OFFICE)

Therefore, induce that :

$$\forall \ (X) \ (\text{WORKS-IN X OFFICE})$$

This, of course, is a drastic conclusion, but is one arrived at through experience, or previous knowledge about instances of the class X. An analogous human reasoning process would be :

I have seen two employees working in an office

Therefore, my conclusion is :

All employees (of that company) are office workers

Quite often, a conclusion such as this would be made by human observation, but almost certainly not on such a small observation population. Humans would also, instinctively make supporting observations of the building itself and the surrounding grounds. The company name may supply some vital information.

Induction has proved to be the most difficult of all inference mechanisms to implement, but its potential is so great that research is certain to continue to eventual success.

1.9 Summary

The solution to many problems can be attempted with the aid of computer technology. In this chapter we have seen some extremely simple systems, deliberately chosen for their ease of understanding and the ease at which solutions can be achieved. However, even with simple, everyday problems encountered by us all, there always exists the possibility of extending the system boundary to include more information. As this process adds more complexity to the problem, so the need for assistance arises.

1.9.1 Choice of Problem

In some specialised areas, the requirement for automated assistance in day-to-day problem solving is increasing. The ultimate aim is for a computer system, able to handle extreme complexity with relative ease, and above all, consistency. If human reasoning can be emulated, and if the system is equipped with some form of human-like communications facility, then its reasoning process could be monitored and manipulated by the operator in order to optimise performance. However, the choice of problem, for which a knowledge-based problem-solving system is to be produced, is an important consideration to be made at the outset. The choice of problem is usually influenced by the following :

- *Solution possibility.* Can the problem be solved at all, with the current state of knowledge in that domain ?

- *Is the problem characterised by complexity* to such an extent that the existing human or machine is incapable of performing satisfactorily. That is, is the problem large and important enough to justify the financial and time costs involved in the development of a knowledge- based system ?

- *Are there enough domain experts* to permit the process of knowledge-acquisition in the building of a sufficiently powerful knowledge base ?

- *Is there sufficient in-house system building expertise* to permit the cost-effective creation of a knowledge-based system ?

All these considerations are, to some extent, obvious. The problem chosen for solution must be appropriate for this strategy, i.e. not amenable to solution by conventional means. The problem must also be an important one in the domain in question. This will ensure that time and effort will be spent on the solution, and the development will continue to eventual implementation.

As institutions interested in knowledge-based strategies begin to consider problem definition and eventual system development, there are certain steps in the development procedure which may help:

- The knowledge-based system approach should be applied to a problem of high financial value to the institution. The potential savings to the institution, as a result of its availability should be evaluated at the outset.

- The development time should be evaluated and costed. The requirements for special equipment and software should be researched in depth and costed. Generally, these costs are high, especially in the early stages.

- It may be necessary, or more cost-effective, to obtain expert consultancy advice in the formulation phase.

- The availability of domain experts is one of the most important considerations. It may be that relatively 'rare' expertise is currently available within the institution, but is fast approaching retirement. In actual fact, this is one of the most common situations, and it provides the most succesful means for knowledge acquisition. The expert at the end of his career will not feel threatened by the new system, and may even be complimented by the approach. It may also help in the knowledge acquisition process if the domain expert is provided with 'computational power' of his own. More than one expert should be consulted before the system is commissioned in order to clarify any anomalies.

All the above points help in making the decision, either to adopt a knowledge-based approach, with all its pitfalls, or retain the traditional (non-adventurous) stance. Equipment is a major problem. Dedicated hardware systems are available, and are discussed in Chapter Nine. However, most applications may be developed, at least to the concept-proving stage, on traditional computing hardware equipped with a suitable implementation language.

Chapter Two

Lisp

2.1 Introduction

It has been demonstrated in the previous chapter, that conventional implementation languages have certain limitations when applied to a problem solving approach which is dependent on reasoning and heuristics. Fortunately, there are readily-available programming languages ideally suited to this type of information processing. These languages are generally known as SYMBOLIC languages. New application areas result in the development of specialised methodologies, specific to a particular market. Some programming techniques are better suited to solving problems in certain domains than others. For example, pattern matching is well suited to searching loosely structured data or performing logical inference. Object-oriented programming techniques are often used for simulation.

In this book, LISP will be used throughout to demonstrate both the expressive power of symbolic computing, and the potential power and use of knowledge-based problem solving techniques. In the choice of LISP dialects, two versions were available. The first, iLISP (developed and marketed by Computing Insights, Wisconsin, USA) is based on the SCHEME dialect developed at the Massachusetts Institute of Technology. It is a relatively inexpensive LISP system which is capable of facilitating the development of useful knowledge-based systems within the relatively limited resources of the eight-bit CP/M operating system. Most of the small-scale program examples in this chapter are based on the SCHEME dialect, with the second system being introduced at the most appropriate time; the section on Lambda expressions. The second LISP system, chosen for its sheer power and extent, was IQLISP (developed and marketed by Integral Quality of Seattle, USA). IQLISP is designed to operate under the operating systems supported on the IBM range of personal computers, and by virtue of the storage (and speed) capabilities of those systems, applications are much less limited in their scope than with the first system. It incorporates facilities to permit the rapid development of large, complex systems, and provides an acceptable level of user-friendliness.

In the various discussions on LISP-like features commonly available, an emphasis is placed on generalities. From Chapter Three onwards, the discussion revolves around a specific implementation of LISP, which may not have the benefit of some of the (ideal) features outlined in this chapter.

2.2 The Requirements of an Ideal Implementation Language

For the purposes of this study, a computer programming language is required, capable of providing a means of solving highly complex problems, possibly characterised by inexact or incomplete information, thereby defying computational solution by traditional means. The requirements can be listed as below :

1. Convenient to use
2. Highly interactive
3. High performance
4. Good expressive power
5. Flexibility of data structure
6. An ability to modify functional aspects of programs at run-time
7. Automatic management of memory usage

These aspects can be considered in more detail. Each specific problem domain could be optimally associated with a particular programming language and development methodology. Numerical applications can be successfully managed using a statement-oriented language such as BASIC or a more structured language such as PASCAL. Of the two, BASIC could be considered the most convenient, and has traditionally lent itself to the expediency of INCREMENTAL PROGRAMMING, i.e. interactive program enhancement subsequent to the development of an initially simple system. Such a development approach is quite rightly criticised by software professionals in the 'numeric' domain, and the end result of such criticisms was the arrival of highly structured languages such as PASCAL. In PASCAL, data structures and types are explicitly declared and subsequent compliance is rigidly enforced. Development methodologies became characterised by modularity, with various levels of abstraction within the structure. The whole philosophy behind PASCAL is the need for detailed thought and planning prior to implementation, which is always the final step.

BASIC can be thought of as highly interactive, at least at interpreter level. At this level, interaction occurs within the programming 'environment', which incorporates some form of editor. The development environment isolates the user from the intricacies of the host computer operating system and presents a much simplified interface with a high degree of automation (and appropriate documentation). Programs may be rapidly developed, tried and easily modified/corrected in a highly interactive and user-friendly manner. This level of flexibility gives the programmer a large amount of responsibility in the quality of the resulting software. It is all too easy to lapse into bad habits in the process of haste, but a disciplined approach at the outset can minimise this danger. In response to these potential, but very real problems, PASCAL was developed. The programmer no longer had the comfort of an interpreter environment, and the responsibility for good programming practice was transferred, largely, from the programmer to the language itself. A great deal of care must be exercised in the development planning stage when using such a language. Indeed, a PASCAL compiler acts very much like a quality control supervisor.

As far as performance is concerned, BASIC and PASCAL are good in the strict numerical domain and could be considered as the languages of choice. Data structures are fixed and do not change in the computational process. A compiled language has the advantage (in the main) of speed, but if speed and compactness of code is a prerequisite, the programming language 'C' offers many benefits.

In the previous chapter, we saw that the human process of inference, if automated, would require that data structures and associations can be easily modified. The expression and representation of information and knowledge must therefore be flexible and under the control of the program during execution. This latter set of ideals implies a certain flexibility in the way memory is used dynamically, since we are concerned, not with the strict mathematical manipulation of data which can be expressed in numeric terms, but with the creation, deletion and manipulation of symbolic information, and its interactions within a 'volatile' information (or data) base. Memory management would have to be automated in a system capable of this sort of dynamic information handling. In the more traditional languages mentioned previously, usage of random access memory by the program is firmly the responsibility of the programmer and is governed by array, record or set boundaries. For inference purposes, this information is not too well defined.

In summary, for applications other than numerical problem solving, which are characterised by their highly complex nature, traditional computational approaches, using conventional languages may be used, but would ultimately prove to be inefficient. LISP provides all of the features listed at the beginning of this chapter, and provides all the benefits of an interpreter environment (for most implementations of the language), which affords a high level of development interaction. A fairly brief overview of the main features of LISP will be given here, with a strong emphasis on rule-based programming aspects. For a much more detailed treatment of the language, augmented by copious examples, reference should be made to one of the specialised, dedicated texts in the list of references included within the appendices of this book.

Unfortunately, unlike PASCAL, there are many dialects of LISP in existence, and standardisation is not a feature of the language. Perhaps, because of its range of diverse applications at the forefront of artificial intelligence research, the language is in the process of continual evolution. Certainly, the language itself is amenable to modification and expansion, and this facility in the hands of researchers enthusiastic about new avenues of computational sophistication, can hardly be left unused. The main disadvantage, as far as this text is concerned, is one of compatability. The programs included here have been designed to operate on a version (dialect ?) of LISP which operates under MSDOS, and cannot be guaranteed to run successfully when used with other versions. Every attempt has, however, been made to exclude definite 'non-standard' features which are found to have a high degree of variation from implementation to implementation (when included at all). Details of the programming language implementations used to develop and debug the examples given here can be found elsewhere in the text.

2.3 Information Representation in Lisp

In the context of the LISP programming language, information representation involves data to be manipulated and the program syntax and semantics. LISP (and its derivatives) is unique in that the program and the data with which it operates on is treated in the same way by the interpreter. This means that functions can be manipulated as data by other functions, and completely new 'program blocks' can be created at run time. The implications of this are significant in the design of knowledge-based systems, that may be required to emulate the human reasoning processes, which rely on concept modification (or learning).

The fundamental data structure in LISP is the LIST (LISP = list processing). A list is made up of SYMBOLS, which are strings of one or more characters called ATOMS. It is possible to create and use an empty list, but the list produced is more likely to contain one or more LITERAL ATOMS or NUMERIC ATOMS (numbers). The following is an example of a numeric list :

                    (3.14159 1.412 0.707)

The list of numeric atoms is delimited with outer parentheses and separated by one or more spaces. The following is an example of a list of literal atoms. Notice the identical structure of the data :

                        (FRED BILL JIM)

The next example is slightly more complex, but applying the same list structure, with the same delimiters and separator constructs, the meaning is clear :

                    ((FRED BILL) (TOM MIKE JOHN) X)

The overall list is composed of three EXPRESSIONS, collectively called SYMBOLIC EXPRESSIONS. One of these so-called 's-expressions', X, is an atom. The other two are lists in their own right. The parentheses, which can become overwhelming in some complex structures, help to identify lists within lists. As an example of a possible use of such structures applied to knowledge-based systems, examine the following construct :

```
(WORK_PLACE ((WORK_ROOMS OFFICE WORKSHOP STORES)
             (WORKFORCE LARGE)
             (BUSINESS ENGINEERING_MAINTENANCE)
             (ESTABLISHED 1986)))
```

Notice that this is just one more example of a list of symbolic expressions. The brackets and the indentations help to elucidate the meaning of the data structure. Using this notation, it can be seen that the list used to describe certain attributes of WORK_PLACE could be described as PROPERTIES of WORK_PLACE. A data structure such as this, where information associated with an object, or symbol, is part of a list which is not required to be dimensioned or 'typed' at the outset, and where new information may be added to the list or modifications made to it during program execution, is almost a 'gift' to our application.

The following list is somewhat different :

$$(SQRT \ (+ \ (* \ A \ A) \ (* \ B \ B)))$$

Certainly, the fundamental list structure is preserved, the overall symbolic expression being composed of literal atoms. A decomposition of the list above may help to identify the possible use of the structure :

$$(SQRT \ X)$$

$$\text{Where :} \quad X = (Y \text{ plus } Z)$$
$$Y = (A \text{ squared})$$
$$Z = (B \text{ squared})$$

The literal atoms SQRT, '*' and '+' are to be used to initiate mathematical operations on specific ELEMENTS or ARGUMENTS of the list, delimited by left and matching right brackets. For example, (* A A) should cause A to be multiplied by itself and (* B B) should result in B squared. The '+' symbol should cause the results of the two 'lowest level' operations to be summed, and SQRT, which is at the highest (outermost) level will result in the mathematical function of square root. In the light of this idea of a hierarchy, the above list decomposition can be represented in a more meaningful fashion :

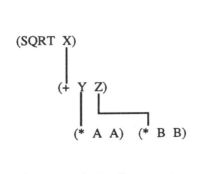

This example is similar to the previous ones in its list structure. However, the symbols (elements) SQRT, '*' and '+' are FUNCTION CALLS. The interpreter itself has the responsibility of deciding when and where a function is to be invoked. Internally, the symbolic mathematical operators (such as '+'), which result in function calls, are stored in an identical manner to the other elements in the list which make up the function parameters, or VARIABLES of the expression. In actual fact :

Variables Within Mathematical or Logical Expressions are Literal Atoms

AND

Mathematical and Logical Expressions Are Lists

This relatively simple data structure results in more flexibility, ease of use and applicability than other, more structured approaches.

2.3.1 Variables Scoping and Assignment

LISP, like all high-level computer programming languages, has the benefit of named variables. Memory locations linked to a literal string (literal atom) which can be manipulated symbolically by the programmer. In LISP, variable names can be long, but cannot include spaces within them, and should not be given the specific names reserved for special characters such as (,) and ';'. A variable can be introduced and assigned a value using the expression SETQ. For example :

$$(SETQ\ X\ 100)$$

will result in X being assigned the value 100. If the variable A and B had previously been assigned values, then the following expression :

$$(SETQ\ Y\ (SQRT\ (+\ (*\ A\ A)\ (*\ B\ B))))$$

will result in Y being assigned the final value of the overall expression. The execution of the hypotenuse expression above can be expanded to include the assignment operation and displayed as a hierarchy in such a way as to 'mimic' the internal execution flow in LISP. The structure below is identical to the hierarchy previously demonstrated, in all but the highest level operation, the assignment :

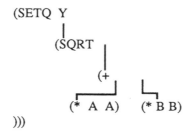

40

This implies a 'top level' operation of assignment, with the bottom level corresponding to the expressions constituting the lists within the innermost parentheses. Thus, the EVALUATION of the expression would begin at the lowest level list, (* A A) and (* B B), which happen to be multiplication function calls. These functions would return with the numerical value of the square of each variable (A and B). These values are then 'passed' to the next highest function call for evaluation. The result of the addition of the two squared values are passed to the summation function and the final operation is the square root function SQRT. The final outcome is an assignment of the numerical result of the mathematical expression to Y. This style of program flow is not unique. BASIC and PASCAL are able to perform predefined expressions in the same way. The difference with LISP programming is that program statements and data are stored in an identical fashion, in lists of two basic data types :

THE LITERAL ATOM

and

THE NUMERICAL ATOM

In order to provide the level of sophistication and flexibility required for systems capable of deleting data, adding new data and modifying existing structures on the basis of reasoning, the list itself is organised in a special way. All information is stored in the form of a LINKED LIST. That is, each element, or object in the list is made up of a pointer to the next logical (but not necessarily physical) element of the list. Figure 2.1 is a schematic diagram of the internal representation of the list :

(FRED BILL JACK JOHN MIKE DICK)

The list is shown in Figure 2.1(a) in tabular form, which includes, in the first column, each respective element in the list. This can be regarded as the physical order within the list, but is more properly described as the 'address' of that object in logical memory. Column two contains the list of literal atoms relating to the six persons mentioned, and column three represents the link to the next logical element in the list. This means that, for instance, JOHN precedes MIKE because the link within the row containing the literal atom JOHN is the number six, which corresponds to MIKE'S location in the list.

This structure may appear initially to be rather wasteful of memory space. Each element of the list contains two extra pieces of information which are redundant in the simple case of Figure 2.1(a). However, if JACK is to be deleted from the list for some reason, or the order in which the names appear is significant and must be changed, then manipulation of the list must be carried out. The situation may become worse if more names are to be added to the middle of the list. Figure 2.1(b) shows, in a very much simplified manner, a method of list manipulation by operating on the links only. JACK is effectively deleted from the list of (a) by simple modification to the link associated with BILL.

a) address	element	link		b) address	element	link
1	Fred	2		1	Fred	2
2	Bill	3		2	Bill	4
3	Jack	4		3	Jack	4
4	John	5		4	John	5
5	Mike	6		5	Mike	6
6	Dick	7		6	Dick	7
7	END			7	END	

c) address	element	link
1	Fred	2
2	BIll	7
3	Jack	4
4	John	5
5	Mike	6
6	Dick	10
7	Tony	8
8	Ted	9
9	Phil	4
10	END	

Fig. 2.1 A linked list

It can be seen from Figure 2.1 that, if this list were to be accessed sequentially, using the two sets of pointers and starting with FRED, the sequence would literally 'jump' over JACK. The now redundant row containing JACK and his two pointers is never accessed. They need not even be erased. Notice that the 'end' of the list is terminated with a special element shown in the diagram as END, but in reality is known as NIL. The last literal or numeric atom within each list always has a link to NIL. Figure 2.1(c) shows the more complex example of a list with JACK deleted, but with three more names added in his place. This diagram shows the methods used to create and modify lists with relative ease. Adding to the lists, in any specific place, can be facilitated merely by appending to the list and modifying the appropriate links.

One major problem with this technique is indicated in Figure 2.1(b): the accumulation of redundant data, made deliberately inaccessible in the process of deletion. In knowledge-based systems, such data can build up extremely quickly during program execution, and some means must be found to remove unwanted data regularly. Fortunately, this facility is available in LISP, called GARBAGE

COLLECTION, and is either invoked automatically (and regularly) or by program command. Thus, lists can be readily 'cleaned up' and memory usage optimised. A fuller treatment of this extremely important requirement in LISP is included in Chapter Nine, both from the software and the dedicated hardware points of view.

2.3.2 Function Definition

Almost all program execution in LISP is performed by functions. This approach is useful in the development of large programs since it forces modularisation and aids structure. The overall program is naturally segmented, or partitioned into sub-programs (functions) which are developed, tested and debugged independently. A program therefore can be properly described in LISP as a collection of previously-developed functions, which exist either as built-in 'primitives' or as functions written in LISP. Using the list structure of LISP, it is a reasonably straightforward exercise to construct functions of some complexity out of the available primitive (or non-primitive) functions.

In order to create a function in LISP, it must be defined using DEFUN (define function), or in the case of iLISP, DEFINE the formal definition of which is as below :

```
(DEFINE function_name (arguments)
        (function_body))
```

where 'function_name' is a variable which is BOUND to the function body and the list of arguments, or parameters. The function body contains the actual program execution definition. The function, when it is eventually 'called', provides a means of passing values from the calling program to the function body, manipulating variables within the function, in either its local environment or the global environment and returning a single value corresponding to the final result of function evaluation. The function, once defined, must be called with the correct number of arguments. Consider the following example :

```
(DEFINE DIFFERENCE (X Y)
   (ABS (- X Y)))
```

Difference is defined as the name of a function (a variable) which is bound to the arguments X and Y, i.e. memory space is allocated to them ready for values to be assigned. The function body is an expression which, when executed, calculates the absolute value of the numerical difference between X and Y. At the lowest level, or within the innermost brackets, the function (- X Y) is computed. This occurs as a result of a call to the subtract function '-' with the required arguments X and Y duly supplied. The function returns with a positive numerical value if X is larger than Y and a negative numerical value if the converse is true. In order to produce an overall positive value, a call is made to the (primitive) ABS function with a single parameter, i.e. the numerical result of the previous calculation. If the new function is now used, the following results should appear as below :

```
*    (DIFFERENCE 10 2)
  8

*    (DIFFERENCE 126 127)

  1
```

The function can be tested quite easily and simply by virtue of the simplicity of the function itself. The function is a self-contained program module with a well-defined input and output format. Since all variables manipulated in the body of the function have been 'itemised' in the argument list, they are bound to the function and are therefore local to it. This means, as far as the internal operation of LISP is concerned, memory space has been allocated for those variables used only by that function, and any values passed as arguments are copied into this dedicated space on entry to the function.

The modular approach to system development forced on the programmer by the environmental structure of LISP, assists in the production of good, maintainable software. Each self-contained module, once tested, can be saved in a LIBRARY for later integration into larger, more complete programs. To assist still further in the thrust for good software, a comment facility has been included in some (if not all) versions of LISP. The commonly-used formal definition is that any information included after a semi-colon is treated as pure documentational material and no attempt is made by the interpreter to evaluate it. For instance, the DIFFERENCE function could include comments :

```
(DEFINE DIFFERENCE (X Y)        ;the difference between X and Y
    (ABS (- X Y)))              ;calculate the absolute value
```

It is good programming practice to provide liberal quantities of relevant comments in the outline program. The function could include a title :

```
;DIFFERENCE            A function of two numerical arguments.
;                      The function calculates the absolute value
;                      of the difference and returns a positive number.
;
```

This practice does, however, result in physically larger source programs residing in memory during program execution.

2.3.3 LAMBDA

We have seen that functions can be defined in LISP in order to facilitate the execution of a particular expression. The effect is that a variable name is bound to an optional list of parameters and the body of the function itself. The newly created function therefore consists of the keyword DEFINE and the function name, in addition to the functional description, i.e. the function body, or the executable part. However, there are circumstances where, for one reason or another, a function description is all that is necessary. This could be desirable, for instance, in cases where a particular expression is only required once or is particularly simple. Other cases might arise where an unnamed function is required within the body of another function in order to synthesise one-input functions from related functions of two inputs.

Consider the following example:

```
(DEFINE F (Q)
        (MAP (LAMBDA (X) (* X X)) Q CONS ()))
```

Where Q may have previously been assigned as a list. e.g. :

```
(SETQ Q '(1 2 3 4))
```

The MAP function has the effect of mapping a function of a list, i.e. applies the FUNCTION DESCRIPTION (* X X) repeatedly over the list supplied in the argument, Q, resulting in the values being processed and stored by the function CONS (). The outcome of calling the newly defined function F to the list supplied will be a new list containing the original elements squared.

This example is a good one of the realistic use of the LAMBDA form. Another function could have been defined and called from within F, but this would have resulted in an unwanted level of complication. For example, the LAMBDA expression (* X X) could have been defined as :

```
(DEFINE SQR (X) (* X X))
```

and the function MAP would appear as :

```
(DEFINE F (Q)
        (MAP (SQR Q CONS ()))))
```

Whilst the SQR function in this example could be useful elsewhere, thereby justifying the creation of a named function, there may be many occasions where the function within the body of a function is not permanently required as a function definition, and can therefore be included as a LAMBDA expression.

In actual fact, in some versions of LISP, this is the internal method used in the definition of functions. For example :

```
(SETQ NAME (LAMBDA (ARGUMENTS) (FUNCTION_BODY)))
```

where the function name is bound to the function definition itself.
In IQLISP, all functions are defined using some form of LAMBDA explicitly. For example, the function DIFFERENCE would appear as below when coded in IQLISP:

```
(DEFUN DIFFERENCE (LAMBDA (X Y)
       (ABS (- X Y))))
```

The advantages of this approach can be appreciated by considering the behaviour of an IQLISP function in the relevant sequence :

1. *The function arguments are BOUND to the parameters.* The parameter to DIFFERENCE is a list containing two elements, X and Y. If the function is called as:

```
(DIFFERENCE 20 18)
```

then the number 20 will be bound to X and 18 will be bound to Y. On exit from the function, both X and Y will be restored to their original values existing before the function execution.

2. *The FUNCTION BODY* is evaluated. The function body is essentially a list of expressions to be evaluated. The expressions in the function body are all evaluated in turn, the value returned being the value of the last expression evaluation.

3. *The result of the function,* as specified in (2) above, is the result of evaluating the last expression in the list of expressions within the body of the function.

The actual binding process in IQLISP can be controlled by specifying the mechanisms required. Most functions would be defined as CALL BY VALUE. That is, the arguments in the function are evaluated before the process of binding. However, there are variations on this theme. Functions can be defined as CALL BY NAME, where the arguments are not evaluated before binding. It is also possible to define MACROs, which are special call by name functions, where the function is effectively evaluated twice. The overall effect of macro invocation is that the macro function is able to inspect and modify the calling function. This facility extends the power of the implementation language enormously. The 'binding control element' of IQLISP can be one of the following variations on LAMBDA :

1.   LAMBDA defines a call by value function ;

2.   NLAMBDA defines a call by name function ;

3.   MLAMBDA defines a macro.

Unfortunately, the internal mechanisms for LAMBDA are not at all standardised, but for most purposes, the internal operations invoked in the definition of new functions should be transparent to the user. The use of LAMBDA should result in the same 'top level behaviour' no matter which implementation is used.

2.3.4 Variable Scoping

In the previous section, variables have been assigned values using SETQ. Once an assignment such as this has been made, at the top of a program, that variable can be considered GLOBAL, i.e. it can be used (and changed) in other functions anywhere in the program using another SETQ. If, however, a variable is used as a parameter in a function definition, that parameter is said to be bound to the function name and is therefore LOCAL to that function. For instance, consider the following function :

```
(DEFINE SQR (X)
     (SETQ A (* X X)))
```

The variable X is bound to the function SQR and the value of X will be determined dynamically by the calling function in the DYNAMIC ENVIRONMENT. For example :

```
(SETQ A 10)

(+ A (SQR A))
```

This will result in A being bound with respect to SQR, i.e. A appears in the parameter list of SQR and is therefore local to it. Inside SQR, A is assigned the value A squared, but on entry, A becomes the value initiated globally. Consider the following example :

```
(DEFINE TRIVIAL (X)
        (SETQ N (+ X N))
        (SETQ X N))
```

X is bound with respect to TRIVIAL but N is not included in the function parameter list. N is said to be FREE. A free variable is capable of being modified globally. If N had been initiated (globally) using SETQ, then on exit from TRIVIAL, N would be permanently changed to the value (+ X N), whereas X would recover its 'external value', i.e. the value of X in existence before the function was executed. The original value of X would have been 'saved' before execution and subsequent local modification of the value of X. For a fuller treatment of the intricacies of the internal organisation of variables within LISP, reference should be made to one of the texts dedicated to LISP, referred to at the end of this book.

2.3.5 Information Structure Manipulation

Computer systems able to make reference to knowledge in the solution of problems, must have the ability to modify the information stored and to re-structure that information and its interrelationships. In LISP, this means that data stored in lists, in a significant order, and the lists themselves, must be accessible for such manipulation. A series of functions are available in most dialects of LISP to facilitate the necessary 'list surgery'. The basic (and most standard) of these are :

1. CAR   - *A function requiring one argument, a list.* It returns with the first element of that list.

2. CDR   - *A function of one argument, a list.* The function returns with a list containing all the original elements of the list supplied as the argument, except the first element of the list.

3. APPEND - *A function   with list arguments.* The function concatenates those lists to produce a single list containing all the elements of the lists supplied.

4. LIST   - *A function which builds up a list structure from arguments supplied.* Unlike APPEND, LIST does not create a single list, but rather a list of lists.

5. CONS   - *A function of two arguments, a list and an atom.* The function returns with the element supplied in the first position in the list supplied.

6. LENGTH   -*A function of one argument, a list.* The function returns with an integer corresponding to the number of elements in the list supplied.

7. REVERSE - *A function of one argument, a list.* The execution of this function results in the elements of the list supplied being reversed in order.

8. SUBST   - *A function of three arguments.* The function has the effect of substituting the first argument for the second argument in the list supplied as the third argument.

9. LAST   - *A function of one argument, a list.* It returns with a list containing only the last element in the list supplied.

The functions above can be regarded as a 'toolkit' available within the LISP environment for the purposes of list manipulation. Some are capable of taking lists apart (CAR, CDR), some are used to build new lists or to increase the size of existing ones (CONS, APPEND). LENGTH on the other hand provides essential information on specific lists.

Three lists to be used:

(SETQ ONE '(A B C D))
(SETQ TWO '(E F G H))
(SETQ THREE '(I J K))

Using 'basic' list manipulation functions :

1.	(CAR ONE)	A
2.	(CDR ONE)	(B C D)
3.	(APPEND ONE TWO)	(A B C D E F G H)
4.	(LIST ONE THREE)	((A B C D) (I J K))
5.	(CONS ONE THREE)	((A B C D) I J K)
6.	(LENGTH TWO)	4
7.	(REVERSE THREE)	(K J I)
8.	(SUBST 'X' 'B ONE)	(A X B C)
9.	(LAST ONE)	(D)

Fig. 2.2 Examples of manipulation

49

Examples of the use of these basic functions are given in Figure 2.2. With reference to these examples, the single quote character is used in an expression to deliberately prevent evaluation and is a shortened version of the prefix QUOTE. For example, the expression :

```
(SETQ Z '(SQRT 25))
```

results in Z having the value equal to a list of elements (SQRT 25) rather than the numerical result of the computation of the function SQRT. The prefix QUOTE has the effect of inhibiting evaluation of SQRT, and the value assigned to Z would be a list, which in its own right, if evaluated, would return the numerical square root of 25. The QUOTE prefix therefore permits the assignment and manipulation of lists which contain function calls, as if they were data. To invoke the procedure SQRT therefore, we have to force evaluation on the function call plus the argument that was assigned as a list to Z. We do this with the function EVAL, for example :

```
(SETQ Z '(SQRT 25))
```

results in Z being assigned (SQRT 25)

```
(SETQ Y Z)
```

results in Y being assigned (SQRT 25)

`(EVAL Y)` returns the number 5

`(EVAL Z)` returns the number 5

In other words, EVAL allows us to decide when to treat any list assigned to a variable as though it were an expression to be evaluated. Methods exist to manipulate programs as data in order to modify program flow, up to the point where evaluation of these program blocks becomes desirable.

With some knowledge of program execution flow as seen previously, it is fairly obvious that complex manipulation processes can be carried out on any list. For example, the results of evaluation the following complex list structure can be predicted by considering the expression as a list which is to be evaluated from the innermost brackets outward :

```
(REVERSE (APPEND '(HELLO) (SUBST '* 'k (APPEND ONE
       THREE))))
```

The order of computation (evaluation) would therefore be :

```
1)  (APPEND ONE THREE) ............  (A B C D I J K)

2)  (SUBST '* 'k .................  (A B C D I J *)

3)  (APPEND '(HELLO) .............  (HELLO A B C D I J *)

4)  (REVERSE ....................  (* J I D C B A HELLO)
```

hence the four closing brackets at the far right of the overall expression above. Other, non-standard enhancements are usually to be found in any implementation of LISP, but these may well be constructed from compound LISP functions.

2.3.6 Compound Functions

One of the most useful aspects of PASCAL is its ability to facilitate algorithmic structure implementation with the use of compound program blocks delimited by BEGIN and END. Between these two statements, program execution proceeds in a sequential fashion, and any modifications to the list of commands is easily accomplished. LISP also has this feature, made possible by PROGN, an iterative special form. In many ways, this keyword is largely redundant due to the list structure and built-in functions of modern LISP implementations. However, the ability to specify a group of separately identifiable expressions as a unified compound expression, permits us the luxury of recognisable structure. If nothing else, it aids documentation and therefore retains its place as an important facility (even a feature) of any version of LISP. For example :

```
(DEFINE PROMPT (MESSAGE)
        (PROGN
               (PRINT MESSAGE)
               (READ)))
```

This function could be used to prompt for, and return the answer to a question via the computer terminal. Each of the expressions within the PROGN argument list will be evaluated sequentially, and the value returned will be the value input by the user. Each of the two expressions READ and PROMPT are said to have a SIDE EFFECT, i.e. the value of a variable is altered, or input/output has occurred and the effect remains AFTER evaluation. This is one of the more valid uses of PROGN.

51

2.3.7 Conditional Branching and Predicate Functions

For any computer programming language to be useful at all, it must have some facility to permit conditional program execution branching, the ability to perform a variety of different functions on the basis of logical deduction. In LISP there are a number of functions which perform tests on data supplied and return either true (T) or false. They are called PREDICATE FUNCTIONS. Here is a short list of some of the more commonly used ones :

(= X Y) .... Returns T (for true) if X and Y are numbers and X=Y.

(< X Y) .... Returns T if X and Y are numbers and X is smaller than Y.

(NULL X) .... Returns T if X is an empty list ().

(ZEROP X) .... Returns T if X is equal to zero.

(NUMBERP N) ..... Returns N if N is a number.

(ATOM N) .... Returns N if N is an atom.

(LIST N) .... Returns N if N is a list.

There are predicate functions which can be used to test the nature of data. Some return with T, whilst others return a true result as the argument itself. They all facilitate selective program execution branching by providing definitive answers to specific inquiries on the nature of the function argument. In order to use those answers to direct program flow, there is a need for conditional special forms such as IF and COND. Here are some examples of conditional statements involving predicate functions :

```
(DEFINE BANK_STATUS (N)          ;bank balance function
    (IF (< N 0)                  ;..... IF ..........
        (PRINT 'Overdrawn)       ;.... THEN .....
        (PRINT 'IN_CREDIT)))     ;.... ELSE ......
```

This example demonstrates the use of IF in a fairly traditional IF-THEN- ELSE construct. It is possible to extend this to include ELSE_IF. For example :

```
(DEFINE BANK_STATUS (N)              ;an enhanced balance function
       (IF (< N 0)                   ;..... IF ......
           (PRINT 'Overdrawn)        ;.... THEN .....
       (IF (= N 0)                   ;... ELSE_IF....
           (PRINT 'Nothing left)     ;.... THEN .....
       (PRINT 'In_credit))))         ;.... ELSE .....
```

The COND form is also useful. It is roughly equivalent to the PASCAL CASE statement and has the format :

```
(COND
      ((TEST1) (ACTION1) (ACTION2) ........)
      ((TEST2) (ACTION1) (ACTION2) ........)
         :        :         :          :
         :        :         :          :
      ((TESTN) (ACTION1) (ACTION2) ........)
```

where each test is evaluated in sequence until a non-nil result occurs, at which time the actions within that row (clause) are evaluated in turn. The COND form returns with the value of the result of the last action in the non-nil clause. Generally, if the first non-nil clause has no actions, the result would be the value of the test itself.

The COND form, just like the CASE statement of other computer languages, allows program flow control by virtue of mutually exclusive tests within a list of possibilities. It serves to drastically reduce program structure complexity and legibility in cases where many possibilities exist, and nested IF-THEN-ELSE constructs would otherwise be required. Using the previous bank balance scenario, a comparison can be made :

```
(DEFINE BANK_STATUS (N)                    ;more obvious structure
       (COND                               ;the conditional statement
           ((< N 0) (PRINT 'OVERDRAWN))      ;condition (1)
           ((= N 0) (PRINT 'NOTHING LEFT))   ;condition (2)
           ((> N 0) (PRINT 'IN_CREDIT))      ;condition (3)
           ((> N 1E6) (PRINT 'WELL_OFF))))   ;condition (4)
```

It can be seen that this function has a more legible structure than the previous IF-THEN-ELSE example. New clauses could easily be added to the list if required without achieving overwhelming complexity.

2.3.8 Repetition - Iteration

At some stage, in any computer program, using any programming language, it becomes necessary to repeatedly execute a block of instructions many times over. The usual methods of choice are either repetition by iterative looping or recursion. In iterative algorithms, a block of program code is invoked repeatedly until a terminating test is satisfied. The format of such a loop can be idealised :

```
REPEAT THE FOLLOWING SEQUENCE UNTIL (TEST_A IS TRUE)
      EXPRESSION 1
      EXPRESSION 2
         :    :
      EXPRESSION N
```

In most LISPs, the syntactic form DO may be used to provide the control structure necessary to execute iterative loops. The format of the DO form involves a function call and a list of arguments which include an initial value, a terminating value or expression and a list of expressions which are to be executed in sequence (like PROGN). An example will serve to illustrate the point :

```
(DEFINE POWERS (X Y)                   ;X to the power Y
        (DO ((FINAL_VALUE 1)           ;initial value 1
          (EXPONENT N))                ;the power N
         ((ZEROP EXPONENT) FINAL_VALUE) ;return with final value
         (SETQ FINAL_VALUE (* X FINAL_VALUE))    body
                                              }  of
         (SETQ EXPONENT (- EXPONENT 1))))      loop
```

In this example, the argument list of the DO function includes variables which must be bound to values, or the values of expressions. For example :

```
(EXPONENT (* Y 10))                    ;Y times 10
```

The argument list is followed by a terminating list which corresponds to the algorithmic UNTIL (TEST=TRUE), i.e. the condition which, when satisfied, will terminate the loop and cause a return from that function. In the example above, this situation will occur when X has been multiplied by itself Y times, and Y has therefore become zero in the context of the DO loop. The rest of the argument list contains a sequence of executable expressions which, in this case, have the side effect of manipulating (re- assigning) the values of the variables FINAL_VALUE and EXPONENT. These side effects are essential, not only to provide a resultant value, but also to facilitate loop termination.

The format and execution of the loop is immediately apparent and easily understood. Data is successively manipulated in the body of the loop until the concluding specifications are met. Unfortunately, the syntax of LISP generally suffers from a lack of standardisation, and the format of special forms such as DO is subject to some considerable variation. It is wise to check the syntax (and semantics) of this special form in any version of LISP. The lack of standardisation is the result of a general lack of familiar iterative control structures in 'basic LISP'. Each version usually has extensions, but the form of these extra (but useful) functions is generally determined by the programming 'style' of the system developers. However, since they are usually supplied as LISP source programs, they can be modified to suit the particular needs of the system user.

A family of iterative control structures is available in LISP. One of these, MAP, has already been used in previous sections to carry out an iterative process on a list. REPEAT is another example of the sort of utility function which finds great use in iterative control structures. Often functions may be available which 'mimic' the conventional control structures found in PASCAL or 'C'.

2.3.9 Recursion

The main strength of LISP, as far as control structure is concerned, is its eminent suitability for RECURSION. Recursion ivolves two main steps:

1. Up to a predefined terminating condition, identical copies of the recursive function are called to solve 'simplified' problems.

2. The body of the function(s) is evaluated in a reverse process, which can be visualised as an 'unwinding' of the recursive operation of (1).

These processes infer the use of large amounts of memory, depending on the level, or number of invocations made, plus the size of the return address stack space required. In some LISPs this is true, whereas in others, recursion is implemented internally in a slightly different manner, designed to optimise memory useage. A simple illustrative example is a function which sums together all elements in a numeric list :

```
(DEFINE SUMIT (L)
    (IF (NULL L) 0)
    (+ (CAR L) (SUMIT (CDR L))))
```

This function has one argument, a list L. The function has an initial test for the invalid case of an empty, or null list, and if this is true, the value 0 is returned. If the argument L is a list, then the function SUMIT is called again with the simplified problem given by the function argument :

$$(+ \quad (CAR \quad L) \quad (SUMIT \quad (CDR \quad L)))$$

The operation of the recursive function which specifies the above format of its arguments can be visualised by considering the two 'main' steps :

1. The function arguments are evaluated and these values are bound to the appropriate variable in the function's formal parameter list. For instance, the list supplied in the first, and only, argument position is bound to L .

2. The body of the function is then evaluated with all values properly bound and assigned.

This means that (CAR L) will not operate on the (CDR L) which appears as the first argument passed recursively, since all arguments are evaluated first. An example will provide a fuller description. Assume that the list :

$$(1 \ 2 \ 3 \ 4 \ 5 \ 6 \ 7 \ 8)$$

is to be subjected to SUMIT. The process can be carried out by a function call, but first the list could be bound to an identifier, e.g. :

$$(SETQ \quad NUMS \quad '(1 \quad 2 \quad 3 \quad 4 \quad 5 \quad 6 \quad 7 \quad 8))$$

To accomplish the summing of all elements in NUMS, the following call is made :

$$(SUMIT \quad NUMS)$$

Taking care to provide the right number of arguments, the correct data types and in the (rather obvious) order required by the 'target' function. The operation of the function can be visualised by considering the application of identical copies of SUMIT to progressively simplified versions of the problem.

Figure 2.3 shows the 'progression' of the execution of the function, diagramatically from start to terminating condition (NULL L). The figure demonstrates the nature of general recursive functions, i.e. the successive simplification of a given problem by passing simplified versions of the problem to identical copies of the function. Each copy operates in sequence until the terminating condition is satisfied (NULL L in the example of Figure 2.3), in which case, the function is evaluated. In Figure 2.3 it can be seen that the body of the function :

$$(+ \ (CAR \ L) \ (SUMIT \ (CDR \ L)))$$

could not be computed until a value (ideally zero) is assigned to (CDR L). Once this has occurred, a numeric value could be passed 'backwards' to the preceding function in the recursive chain. For instance, at the terminating condition, (NULL L), the value returned is zero. Zero plus the (CAR L) is equal to 0+8, which becomes the value returned by that copy of SUMIT. The next function copy 'one up the sequence' has the (CAR L) equal to 7. 7+8 equals 15, which is the resultant value returned by that copy, and so the recursion 'unwinds' by returning definite numerical values to the function copy that was responsible for its creation, until the final result appears. The effect is that the first invocation of the recursive function is the last one to produce a value: the final value. Logistically, each function copy must have some knowledge of where to access the 'calling copy', and this is facilitated with the aid of a STACK of addresses, the size (or level) of which is determined by the number of simplifications, or calls to copies are required by the specific problem. In the example of figure 2.3, this is demonstrated by the number of values computed in arriving at the final result.

expressions		(CDR L)	(CAR L)
EVALUATE	(CDR L)	(2 3 4 5 6 7 8)	1
EVALUATE	(CDR L)	(3 4 5 6 7 8)	2
EVALUATE	(CDR L)	(4 5 6 7 8)	3
EVALUATE	(CDR L)	(5 6 7 8)	4
EVALUATE	(CDR L)	(6 7 8)	5
EVALUATE	(CDR L)	(7 8)	6
EVALUATE	(CDR L)	(8)	7
EVALUATE	(CDR L)	( )	8

The NULL list condition is now satisfied. The problem has been progressively simplified by executing repetitive calls to SUMIT. The recursion now 'unwinds', with each stored argument value assigned to the argument L :

VALUE	(SUM (L))						0
VALUE	(SUM (L))						8
VALUE	(SUM (L))					15	
VALUE	(SUM (L))				21		
VALUE	(SUM (L))			26			
VALUE	(SUM (L))		30				
VALUE	(SUM (L))	33					
VALUE	(SUM (L))	35					
VALUE	(SUM (L))	36					

Fig. 2.3 Diagramatic operation of SUMIT applied to NUMS

The usual example commonly given to typify the use of recursion is the 'classic' one of factorials. Its eminent suitability to recursion is almost obvious and for this reason, it is given here. Unlike the SUMIT example, this one is a natural recursive function (even though it may be expressed iteratively) which may be studied, along with the previous example to give a 'feel' for the admittedly difficult task of understanding, to the point of familiarisation. Factorial is a function defined as the product of all positive integers up to the argument supplied, which must be a non-negative integer. For example :

```
FACTORIAL 3 =  1 * 2 * 3 =  6
```

In order to implement this as a recursive function, it should have the following form :

```
IF THE ARGUMENT SUPPLIED IS 1 ..... THE RESULT IS 1

FOR N > 1 ..... FACTORIAL (N) =  N * FACTORIAL (N - 1)
```

The function can be implemented as follows :

```
(DEFINE  FAC (N)              ;recursive factorial function
        (IF  (= N 1)  1       ;for n=1 return 1
        (* N (FAC (- N 1))))))  ;function body
```

Again, the operation of this recursive function can be visualised by inspection of the modification, or simplification of the variables within the body of the function, up to the terminating condition (= N 1), which results in a definite numerical value being returned 'up the recursive chain'.

Variables	(FAC (- N 1))	(N)
EVALUATE	2	3
EVALUATE	1	2

At this point, the value of N = 1 and the terminating condition is true. The value 1 is returned by the function and the recursion starts to unwind:

VALUE (FAC (N))		1
VALUE (FAC (N))	2	
VALUE (FAC (N))	6	

Fig. 2.4 Diagrammatic operation of FAC (N), applied to factorial (3)

Figure 2.4 demonstrates the computations involved. It involves exactly the same kind of problem complexity reduction methods outlined in figure 2.3 and the format of the recursive function can be generalised to include :

1. The function name, with an argument list .

2. A terminating condition which signals the unwinding of the recursion .

3. The function body, which includes in the expression, a call to the same function.

The function, as it appears above and in 2.4 has one problem. If the function is called with an argument of value zero, the LISP interpreter would probably signal a STACK OVERFLOW error. This condition has not been included in the function FAC(N). A separate list for (ZEROP N) could be included with the use of PROG, but could easily be catered for as below :

```
(DEFINE FAC(N)
        (IF (ZEROP N) 1
        (* N (FAC (- N 1))))))
```

In IQLISP, this would be :

```
(DEFUN FAC (LAMBDA (N)
        (COND ((ZEROP N) 1)
        (T
            (* N (FAC (- N 1)))))))
```

Each of these examples demonstrates the power of recursion and shows its applicability to the LISP programming environment. There are two major disadvantages :

1. Algorithms, and the resulting functions may be difficult to visualise and implement. A full understanding, and more important, wide experience in the use of recursive algorithms is essential to their efficient use.

2. In the generalised form of the previous two examples, a stack space problem could ensue. The more simplifications of the supplied problem required, the larger the stack required and therefore the more random access memory space is allocated. This could be a real problem when implemented on small computer systems with relatively limited memory capacity.

Fortunately, there is a means of overcomming the second disadvantage associated with recursive functions, that of stack space. If a recursive function is written such that the last expression in the function body is the actual call to itself, rather than the recursive function call being made from within an expression, the stack is prevented from extending. The effect is that stack space is not needed. As an example of such a so-called TAIL RECURSION function, consider the function SUMIT, of Figure 2.3, written in a subtly different way :

```
(DEFINE SUMIT (L RESULT)                    ;recursive SUMIT
     (IF (NULL L) RESULT                     ;as before
     (SUMIT (CDR L) (+ RESULT (CAR L)))))    ;tail recursion
```

Notice the different format of this version of SUMIT to the previous one. The recursive call to itself is the last expression in the body of the function itself (in the 'tail'). Because the last expression in the function is the last operation of the function, it executes it without consuming stack space, to remember 'where' it has to return to. A comparative example would serve to demonstrate the operation differences of the two functionally similar SUMITs. Figure 2.5 shows the operations diagrammatically, to aid comparison. Tail recursive functions are preferred in most cases, but it may be quite difficult to modify a naturally non-recursive algorithm to provide this feature. Some problems may be more readily solved with the generalised recursive method, whilst others may be amenable to tail recursive implementation.

VARIABLES	(CDR L)	(+ RESULT (CAR L))	
EVALUATE	(2 3 4 5 6 7 8)	(+ 0 1)	= 1
EVALUATE	(3 4 5 6 7 8)	(+ 1 2)	= 3
EVALUATE	(4 5 6 7 8)	(+ 3 3)	= 6
EVALUATE	(5 6 7 8)	(+ 6 4)	= 10
EVALUATE	(6 7 8)	(+ 10 5)	= 15
EVALUATE	(7 8)	(+ 15 6)	= 21
EVALUATE	(8)	(+ 28 8)	= 36

The terminating condition (NULL L) has been satisfied. The recursive function has computed the desired expression and does not require an 'unwinding process'.

Figure. 2.5 Diagramatic operation of tail-recursive SUMIT applied to NUMBS

The approach to recursive function recognition and subsequent implementation is dependent, to a large extent, on experience, but rough guidelines may be helpful. The following design considerations should be borne in mind :

1. The repeated part of the algorithm should be isolated and designate the body of the recursive function ;

2. The terminating condition should be identified and implemented as the controlling test ;

3. Variables must be considered in terms of their data types, position in the function parameter list and methods of modification.

If the algorithm dictates an iterative function, it should be implemented as such. However, there are some, largely historically-based considerations :

1. Iterative control structures tend to be implemented as extensions, in LISP source format in libraries of utilities. Therefore, these functions generally run much slower than compiled primitive functions found in most LISPs.

2. Recursion, as permitted in LISP, has many versatile and powerful features. As such, it would be wise to study and experiment with recursion.

2.3.10 Property Lists

One of the most important and far-reaching features of LISP is its facility for maintaining attributes, values or related objects which are closely associated with an object. The very nature of LISP programs and data; the list structure, gives the language this inherent capability. As far as knowledge-based systems are concerned, the facility of associativity maintenance is crucial to the building and maintenance of information bases, which may be freely modified in every respect by rule-dependent procedures. Consider the following list :

```
((WORKS_IN OFFICE)  (OWNS_VEHICLE BICYCLE)  (HAS_HOBBY
                    SAILING))
```

This list of attributes may all be relevant to a particular person, say Fred. The above list can be bound to the variable FRED using SETQ, as below :

```
(SETQ FRED '((WORKS_IN OFFICE)            ;attribute 1 of FRED
            (OWNS_VEHICLE BICYCLE)        ;attribute 2
            (HAS_HOBBY SAILING)))         ;final attribute (3)
```

Now FRED has a list of attributes, or embedded 'sub-lists', which are associated with him. Each attribute is called a KEY and the list is said to be an ASSOCIATION LIST, which has special properties related to its internal representation.

The list of attributes associated with FRED can now be examined merely by typing FRED at the top level (within the 'read-eval' loop). The response to the evaluation of FRED will be the complete list of sub-lists bound to it. However, this would appear at the outset to be extremely limited. What the programmer really needs is a set of tools which can be used to carry out the following 'surgical' tasks on the association list :

1.   Search for, and return the value of a specified attribute in an   association list .

2.   Append an attribute and value to an association list .

3.   Delete an attribute and value .

4.   Modify the attribute and/or value within a specified association list.

A special tool is available for facility (1) above; the function ASSOC. This function is called with two arguments. The first is the attribute, or key required. The second is the list itself. An example will clarify :

```
(ASSOC OWNS_VEHICLE FRED)
```

The evaluation of this function will yield the result :

```
(OWNS_VEHICLE BICYCLE)
```

That is, the attribute plus the value is returned. If the specified attribute is not found in the attribute list, or it is found to be an atom, then a NIL list is returned. Thus we have a specific tool for accessing information within lists of related sub-lists bound to an object. If, in the above example, BICYCLE is the only value required, then the following could be used :

```
(CDR (ASSOC OWNS_VEHICLE FRED))
```

In other words, since a list is returned by ASSOC, all the standard list manipulation functions can be used. The same reasoning is applied to the outline specifications 2 to 4 of the association list manipulation rules given earlier. For instance, to modify the second element of a key-value list within the above association list, use could be made of the function SUBST. For example, to change the vehicle owned by FRED :

```
(SUBST MOTOR_CAR (CDR (ASSOC OWNS_VEHICLE FRED)) FRED)
```

will have the desired effect of list modification.

In order to append a complete sub-list, including the key to the association list, use would be made of CONS. For example, if a new attribute were to be needed, perhaps defining Fred's employment status within his company, the following expression would have the desired effect:

```
(CONS '(HAS_STATUS MANAGER) FRED)
```

The attribute that Fred is a manager would be placed as a sub-list within the association list bound to FRED.

The deletion of a sub-list can be accomplished by invoking destructive list manipulation functions such as REPLACA and REPLACD, but quite often, list element deletion utility functions are supplied, perhaps named DELETEL.

The association list is a powerful form of data representation and can be quite useful. However, there is a much more powerful and potentially vital construct, called the PROPERTY LIST. In LISP, any identifier, or symbol has an inherent property list which is initialised by the system to NIL. There are 'standard tools' for manipulating this very important list structure :

- PUT   Puts a 'property name' and a value on the property list of a named symbol. It can be used for replacing existing values

- GET   Retrieves a particular property of a symbol

- REMPROP   Removes a property entirely. Both the property name and its associated value.

Some implementations of LISP allow atoms to exist in property lists. On such occasions, these are termed FLAGS.

For example, the following list should be regarded as a property list in which (HAS_ STATUS MANAGER) and (WORKS_IN OFFICE) are PROPERTY-VALUE pairs and SUSPENDED is a FLAG :

```
(SUSPENDED (WORKS_IN OFFICE) (HAS_STATUS MANAGER))
```

2.4 Machine Code Interface

Most versions of LISP are supplied with a rich collection of PRIMITIVE functions. These are blocks of program coded in the machine code specific to the computer in use. Other program blocks, noticeably utilities, are supplied in a LIBRARY of such utility functions, coded in LISP themselves. Many libraries may exist in a particular supplied implementation, each particular to a certain application. For example, utilities may exist to provide a more powerful error-trapping or editing facility, and these may be supplied in libraries with meaningful names. Most LISPs allow some kind of library-building facility, which may be used to extend the power and 'specificity' of a particular LISP environment in a given application.

Although libraries of LISP utilities provide a useful means of extending the language, the interpretive nature of most implementations, when applied to those utilities, impose a significant time penalty. In effect, unlike primitive functions, the utility functions themselves are subject to the binding-evaluation cycle. Fortunately, there are techniques and facilities available to reduce the time overhead associated with the use of utilities. In IQLISP, a limited function compilation facility is provided, called INCREMENTAL COMPILATION. However, the most powerful method is the use of machine code to implement functions directly. If the appropriate ASSEMBLER is available, then low-level code can be generated in a very efficient manner, with relative ease. With this approach, it would be necessary to know the following :

1. How arguments and results are passed between functions .

2. How control is received from the LISP environment, and how control is passed to further ones .

3. How the assembled functions request basic services from LISP .

4. How, and possibly where in memory, to incorporate the new function in the LISP environment, either as a permanent feature, or as a utility which must be loaded when required .

5. How garbage collection will affect the operation of the new function.

The work involved in producing utilities as assembled functions may only be considered worthwhile in application domains in which speed is essential. As more knowledge-based systems are produced, especially for use in dedicated equipment as 'embedded' intelligence, this feature will inevitably become more important.

2.5 Summary

The existence, at the fundamental system level, of such a powerful data structure which can be accessed and manipulated freely, within a small but sophisticated number of software tools, plus the extreme flexibility of LISP itself, makes LISP the almost obvious choice for knowledge-based programming. Some fairly straightforward examples of property list construction and manipulation follow. Always be aware that data and programs are stored as elements of lists in LISP and (almost without exception), the standard list manipulation functions can usually be used alongside such specialised functions, to build powerful functions, the limits of which are largely left to the programmer's imagination.

Unfortunately, standardisation is not a positive feature of LISP, and the presence of a variety of different implementations, each with their own syntax peculiarities and extensions, adds an extra burden to the initial development stages. The symbolic language best suited to the application and the domain in question is not always easy to choose. For example, in applications where pure deductive inference is paramount, the implementation language PROLOG would be an obvious choice. New languages are available to fit the needs of existing and future applications, and these should all be considered in the early stages of knowledge-based system development. LISP has been chosen specifically for the examples incorporated in this text by virtue of its expressive power, improved over the relatively short number of years in which symbolic languages have been used seriously, to create useful systems. There is even a move to create and maintain a LISP standard in the form of COMMON LISP, and the advent of this, not inconsiderable software standard, will herald a new era of LISP-based expert system applications.

For programmers with experience in such computer languages as PASCAL, C or even FORTRAN, the move to symbolic computing with LISP will not be a simple one. Completely new philosophies will have to be learned and believed in. The only way to acquire a firm grasp of the subject and move forward to the position of software system development, is to attempt examples given in this and more specialised introductory texts. Once a reasonable understanding is gained, a particular project, requiring the unique style of LISP, should be identified and started, i.e. the concept of RAPID IMPLEMENTATION (or prototyping) so applicable to the knowledge-based system domain, can be initiated right at the implementation learning curve level. More information, understanding and language version familiarity can be gained from this exercise than any amount of literature-based research. Formal courses of instruction are, of course, useful. Indeed, many academic programming courses base their teaching philosophy on intensive 'hands-on' experience.

Chapter Three

An Information Base

3.1 Introduction

Functions will be required, most involving some form of controlled repetition. The subject matter included in this chapter involves the definition and development of functions which convey meaning, both in operation and in their syntax. Some functions discussed in the text may appear somewhat inelegant by virtue of the use of iteration rather than the more compact and efficient recursive techniques. The mixture of recursive and iterative functions within the systems described in this text is quite deliberate, and hopefully, appreciated. All too often, in powerful computer languages such as LISP, the fairly simple semantics of a compact function can be lost to the reader in the drive for efficient structure.

Almost all the iterative functions included in this text can be redefined recursively, thereby reducing program size. However, care must be taken to ensure that the usually severely limited stack space of microcomputer implementations is not violated in the process.

3.2 A Suitable Problem

It is sometimes quite difficult to establish whether a particular problem is suitable for a knowledge-based approach to solution. The problems included in this text are good candidates for these reasons :

1. They have relatively complex data structures with much related information .

2. Associations between data structures exist and are significant to the problem .

3. Data structures are amenable to modification and expansion in all respects .

4. Domain-specific specialist information on objects within the information base may be incorporated, for use by the 'expert' inference mechanism .

5. Due to points 1 to 4 above, the problem is capable of modelling and the solution is able to be refined in a 'step-wise' fashion.

The problem, if it can be called such, is one of family relationships: the family tree. For most of us, a personal family tree could easily be constructed to include all relatives up to at least the grandparent level, and this is eminently suitable for a hierarchical data tree representation, of the form:

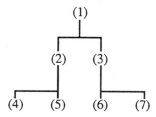

where (1) would be the 'original' grandparent (say), and (4) to (7) are the present younger generation. (2) and (3) are the children of (1) and the respective fathers or mothers of the youngest generation. A more detailed family tree is shown in Figure 3.1, with four levels of hierarchy and includes a total of 29 people. Figure 3.1 is not intended to represent any existing family. It is the result of pure imagination.

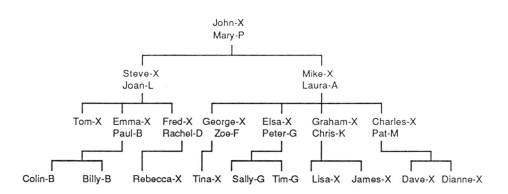

Figure 3.1 An example family tree (fictitious).
For married couples, the direct descendant is shown uppermost and the married partner is shown immediately below.

3.3 Information Representation

To represent a formal model of a family tree structure as might be created and used by genealogists, a great deal of care must be exercised in the representation of all relevant data. In this text, a much simplified scenario will be adopted, with enough detail to permit a realistic visual representation of the required interrelationships. Indeed, one of the great advantages of the knowledge-based approach is the ease by which data structures may be modified, both from 'top-level' or at run-time.

In LISP, it is quite easy to initiate a data structure which includes all the objects (people) in a named list of named relatives, as below:

```
(SETQ RELATIVES '(JOHN-X MARY-P
                  STEVE-X JOAN-X
                  MIKE-X LAURA-A
                  TOM-X
                  EMMA-X PAUL-B
                  FRED-X RACHEL-D
                  GEORGE-X ZOE-F
                  ELSA-X PETER-G
                  GRAHAM-X CHRIS-K
                  CHARLES-X PAT-M
                  COLIN-B BILLY-B REBECCA-X
                  TINA-X SALLY-G TIM-G
                  LISA-X JAMES-X DAVE-X DIANNE-X))
```

Thereafter, each person may be accessed by referring to RELATIVES. The required objects comprising the family exist in the list as a starting point for further structuring and expansion. The direct relationships, which would permit the reconstruction of the tree structure diagram are not present. We need to know which groups of people to place at which level, i.e. which position each object should occupy. The minimum extra information is:

1. The sex of the object. Input as eithei MALE or FEMALE .

2. The names of the parents .

3. The married partner (if any) .

4. The names of any chidren.

This would permit the correct associations to be made in order to construct a family tree diagram. Additional information would be of some academic interest. For example:

5. Occupation .

6. Birth date (and death date) .

7. Place of birth (or place of residence).

Specialist information relating, say, to an individual's medical history can also exist on the data base and could find much use as flexible medical records. In certain cases, for instance where genetically related or inheritable disease is recorded somewhere in the data base, the structure could be of some use, in a knowledge-based system, to assist in genetic counselling.

As we discovered earlier in the text, the property list facilities of LISP are extremely powerful and are convenient for associating relevant information on an object with that object. Most knowledge-based systems implemented in LISP use property lists in some way. Some use association lists bound to property list variables, with the information included in the association list structured in some rigid way. In the system to be described in subsequent chapters, lists will be bound to specific property list variables, but the structure of those lists will not be rigid. They may contain any number of objects.

At the LISP command level, the following instruction could be used to include the information that JOHN-X married MARY-P, on the property list of JOHN-X :

```
(PUT 'JOHN-X '(MARY-P) 'MARRIED)
```

Which initiates a list as the property list variable/value pair. The information can subsequently be retrieved by :

```
(GET 'JOHN-X 'MARRIED)
```

which returns (MARY-P). Further information can be placed on the property list of JOHN-X in the same way, by repeated use of PUT. The property list, when completed to our satisfaction at present, should be of the form :

```
(SEX MALE)
(FATHER  NIL)   ............................. not known, therefore NIL
(MOTHER  NIL)   ............................. not known, therefore NIL
(CHILDREN STEVE-X MIKE-X)
(BIRTH-DATE  1960) ....................... say
(OCCUPATION  PROFESSOR) ............. say
```

With plenty of practice, this form of information could be placed on the property list of each person in the list of RELATIVES, but this would be inappropriate for the reasons listed below :

1. Repetition exists in the application of PUT to each and every object, and also in the type of information relating to each object. In other words, the information must be identical in type and index. It would not be appropriate to have property list variables of, say, BIRTH-DATE on the property list of JOHN-X and an equivalent variable BORN-WHEN on the property list of some other person.

2. As interest increases and personal research into 'ROOTS' advances, more relatives may be discovered, and the facility should exist to add them to the existing store of information with the minimum of effort. The possibility of error should also be minimised.

3.4 An Information Base Toolkit

In view of the points raised in Section 3.3, a function is required to assist in the repetitive process of creating the information base and controlling its structure. However, there are many more tasks that may become necessary in the maintenance of the information base. For example, objects may need to be added or removed. Details existing in the information base may be incorrect and therefore require modification. In short, a complete 'toolkit' should be available for the efficient modification of any part of the information base, both from the LISP command level, and from within a function during execution time. The ability of LISP functions to dynamically modify existing data structures is one of the strong points of the language. It is convenient to list the functions which will eventually be part of the maintenance toolkit and list some of their required attributes :

1. CREATE -

Create a new information base on the basis of a previously-stored list of property list variables. All specified property list variable/value pairs to be 'filled in' via user-responses to output prompts.

2.   ADD-OBJECT -

Add an object to the association list of an existing information base CREATEd previously. All property list variable/value pairs to be completed for the new object.

3.   ADD-VARIABLE -

Add a property list variable to the property list of all objects. The function to control the inclusion of the associated value for each object.

4.   MODIFY-VALUE -

Modify any specified property list value. The actual object which 'owns' the property list value/variable must be specified.

5.   MODIFY-OBJECT -

Rename an incorrectly named object.

6.   REMOVE-VARIABLE -

Delete a property list variable/value. The function required would remove this information from the property lists of ALL the objects.

7.   REMOVE-OBJECT -

Delete an object (into the void). In actual fact, a number of variations of this function are required. For instance, it may be necessary to use a function to remove the first occurrence of a specified object in a specified list, or it may be necessary to remove all occurrences. It may be necessary to remove objects found in one list from another list.

Different levels of abstraction may be required to utilise specific functions in a particular order from a 'higher-level' function. For example, it may be desirable to modify some, if not all, the properties of a particular object. This higher level function could make use of MODIFY- OBJECT, ADD-VARIABLE and possibly REMOVE-VARIABLE.

The first task to undertake is the CREATE process, and an algorithm for this is shown below :

Problem:

To create an information base with information associated with each individual, on a list of individuals, recorded as property list data. The information relating to each individual should be input from the computer keyboard in response to prompts and should terminate when all objects have been dealt with.

Solution:

A list exists, called RELATIVES, which includes all persons in the family of interest corresponding to our current state of knowledge on the size and constituency of the family. A further list is required which includes all the property list variables to be on the property list of each individual in RELATIVES. The function will access each individual in turn and thereafter loop through the list of property list variables, prompting for the relevant property list values. Two loop structures are inferred in the solution.

INPUT :   KEYBOARD -
The identifier of the list of RELATIVES and the list of property list variables.

ENVIRONMENT -
The lists specified by the identifiers input via the keyboard.

OUTPUT :   DISPLAY -
Questions, in the form of prompts, on specified property list values. A title would be useful, and would include the name of the individual in question.

ENVIRONMENT -
A 'completed' information base.

BEGIN
    Check on the current status of the lists supplied. If properties do not already exist, then do the following :
        Repeat the following until all objects in the list of relatives have been dealt with
            Print the name of the individual
            Ask all the questions specified in the list of property list variables, and input the corresponding values. A check must be made on the previous existence of that information
            Put the information on the property list of the individual
    Otherwise abort the process
END

If a function called CREATE is defined, it would require, as arguments, the list of objects in RELATIVES which constitutes the application, and a list of property list variable names which may be used in the interactive process of computer-prompt/user -input required to build the information base. If the CREATE function is designed to repeatedly prompt for property list values via access to a list of property list variables, then the way is open to manipulate, not only the variables appearing in the information base, but also the number and type of variables used to create and modify properties on a permanent basis.

Perhaps the first task required of create, is a check on the current status of the supplied lists. If the list (RELATIVES) already exists as a viable information base, with non -NIL properties associated with the objects in the list, then a warning should be given, or alternatively, the process should be immediately aborted.

Bearing in mind the program design methodology outlined in this text, let us begin by considering the first problem which has been identified as a module capable of independent development and test: the initial status check function. The 'ideas' stage involves a consideration of the problem and requirements. It should be pointed out before the following suite of programs is defined, that all information such as the list of relatives, the property list variables and specific objects will be supplied as arguments to the function, and therefore will be LOCAL to them. This results in a test situation protected from global, permanent effects on free variables. Some functions in the system will obviously be required to permanently modify lists, and modifications to those functions, or extra higher-level functions will be required later. The algorithm for the initial status test is shown below.

Problem :

The system user may invoke the CREATE function using an incorrectly- supplied list of family relations, which has already been subjected to the information base creation process, and therefore should be protected from accidental corruption. By its very nature, the CREATE function will cause dramatic changes to be made to the information existing in the data structures which form the information base.

Solution :

An initial check must be incorporated into CREATE, which looks for property list information existing on the property lists of any object within the supplied association list. If any information of this nature is found, the process should be aborted.

INPUT :   KEYBOARD -
            An association list name

            ENVIRONMENT -
            A list to be checked

OUTPUT :   DISPLAY -
            possibly a warning. Most probably none required

            ENVIRONMENT - None

BEGIN
    Repeat the following until the properties of all objects in the supplied list have
    been checked
            Check for the existence of any property list variable/value information
            associated with the individual.
            If any such information is detected THEN
                    Immediately abort the process
END

The algorithm is a simple one and is iterative. It represents a very general case which
should be expanded to include as much detail as is necessary. For example, in the
algorithm above, even at this simple stage, it can be seen that two conditions arise :

1.   The iteration proceeds until all objects are considered, with the test for property
      list information failed .

2.   The property list information test has succeeded.

The details on the actual test strategy are largely related to the specific LISP
implementation in use. It is essentially a coding problem, but abstract definitions can
be considered. Actions on the information- presence test results are not included but
are quite easy to generalise. They will, almost by examination be :

1.   If the test is true (information exists), abort the operation.

2.   If the test is false (bare list), transfer control and list to the CREATE function.

Of course, the test function could exist in a more elegant form, in which specific
information is given at each stage in the operation, but as this is primarily intended
to be one small (but important) part of a larger function, prompts are not essential.

In Chapter 2, a methodology was discussed for the recognition and design of functions
suitable for recursion. It would be instructive at this point to use those rules to assist

in designing the basic test function in a recursive manner. We will consider the points mentioned in 2.3.9, but not necessarily in the order given previously :

1. The terminating condition should be isolated and implemented as the controlling test .

2. The repeated part of the algorithm should be isolated and designated the body of the recursive function .

3. Variables must be considered, etc.

In the general algorithm for the initial information base test process, which we will call PROP-CHECK, there are two identifiable terminating conditions :

1. The property lists of all objects in the list (RELATIVES) have been examined, and no information has been found - return NIL .

2. Property list information has been found (return T).

These conditions can conveniently be implemented as clauses within a COND expression. The first of these is simple; a call to NULL with the list in question sent as an argument will provide the appropriate test for an empty list. That is, all objects considered in a function which examines repeatedly, the CDR of the remaining objects. With such a scheme in mind, the second test can be considered. In many ways, the second test is the most important part of the function. It involves the actual test for property list information.

In the second part of the test, if any non-NIL information is found on any object, the function should return T for true. Therefore, the function is required to test for a non -NIL list within the property list of the CAR of the remaining objects in the association list, which may have undergone 'surgery' in the recursive process. Fortunately, there is a property list function which returns the complete property list of an object. The function name is PROPS, and its format is :

```
(PROPS 'OBJECT)
```

The function NULL, with the above supplied as its argument, will return T if the property list is empty. Therefore, in order to return T if the converse is true, a function call to NOT will invert the meaning in the required fashion. Therefore the format of test 2 will be :

```
(NOT (NULL (PROPS 'OBJECT)))
```

However, the test above is destined to become part of a clause within a COND expression and is to operate on the CAR of a list which will become progressively shorter as recursion proceeds, up to the point at which no more objects exist within the local list. At this stage, the function returns NIL. Therefore, the object, which is the single argument of PROPS, will be derived as the CAR of the local list :

```
((NOT (NULL (PROPS (CAR local-list)))) T)
```

where the final atom in the above list is the action part of a COND clause, i.e. returns T.

The rest of the recursive function is simple to design. We merely need to complete the recursion by supplying simplified versions of the problem - the list, to copies of itself if neither of the two terminating conditions are satisfied :

```
(PROP-CHECK (CDR local-list))
```

Therefore, test 2 will operate on the next (new) CDR of the list which is local to PROP-CHECK. The complete function can therefore be 'assembled' :

```
(DEFUN PROP-CHECK (LAMBDA (RELATE)
     (COND ((NULL RELATE) NIL)
           ((NOT (NULL (PROPS (CAR RELATE)))) T)
           (T
              (PROP-CHECK (CDR RELATE))))))
```

In actual fact, the use of recursion to carry out operations on lists which may be thousands, or perhaps many thousands of objects in length may well be inappropriate (as mentioned before) due to stack space limitations. PROP-CHECK, and some other functions appearing in this, and subsequent chapters have been defined recursively when deemed to be the most appropriate strategy. PROP-CHECK has also been instrumental in demonstrating the design methodology outlined in these pages. In future function developments, iteration and recursion will be mixed with little or no explanation.

The next, and arguably most important of the information base manipulation processes, is the function required to carry out the building of the data structures comprising the family. This function will be called BUILD. The general algorithm can be constructed :

Problem:

A list exists, which contains all the names of persons known to occupy a place in the family tree bound to the identifier RELATIVES. A data structure has been chosen as an appropriate representation of relevant information on each of these objects, i.e. property list variables/values. Each property could be placed via the LISP primitive command PUT, but this would be time consuming and prone to error. A function is required capable of automation in the process of property list manipulation.

Solution:

Assuming that a check has already been made on whether the association list has been initialised, via PROP-CHECK, the required function should be invoked, with the association list and a list of property list variables as arguments. The function should step through the association list, dealing with each person in turn, and for each person, should prompt for, and place the consequent property list variable/value information. This involves more repetition, in that the list of property list variables must be stepped through for each person.

INPUT :   KEYBOARD -
            Property list values in response to prompts.

            ENVIRONMENT -
            Association list, property list.

OUTPUT :   DISPLAY -
            Information sufficient to accomplish error-free user-input of property values. Also, the name of the current list object and property variable.

            ENVIRONMENT -
            A 'completed' information base.

BEGIN
    Clear screen.
    Repeat the following until all objects in the list supplied have been dealt with.
        Output object name (person's name).
        Repeat the following until all properties have been placed.
            Output property variable.
            Input property value corresponding to the property variable.
            Place on the property list of the current list object.
END

In this algorithm, the process of modularisation is fairly straight- forward. Two iterative functions can be identified from it. The outermost loop involves a certain amount of 'housekeeping' with its clear screen and output object information. This is crucial to the efficacy of the process, which may eventually involve many objects. In other words, all information of this sort must be unambiguous.

The outermost loop, once it has supplied information, then proceeds by calling an inner loop with the association list and current object supplied as arguments. The inner loop, which will be called PLACE is shown below :

```
(DEFUN PLACE (LAMBDA (PROPS NAME)
    (COND ((NULL PROPS) NIL)
        (T
            (PROG ()
                (PUT NAME
                    (PROG ()
                        (PRINC (CAR PROPS))
                        (SPACES (- 30 (LENGTH (EXPLODE
                        (CAR PROPS)))))
                            (RETURN (LIST (READ))))
                    (CAR PROPS))
                (PLACE (CDR PROPS) NAME))))))
```

This function uses two levels of iteration within an outermost recursive process. The advantages of this approach are that iterative control variables are not required, thereby simplifying the programming, and GOs are not required. It must be stressed however, that this technique is likely to be slow and, internally quite cumbersome. A TRACE of this function will display a double assignment process which has the ultimate effect of reversing the contents of the list. The recursion terminating condition is a NULL association list. The body of the outermost PROG structure includes two functions. The first is the LISP property list construction function PUT. The first argument to PUT is the current object given by the BUILD function (yet to be developed). The second argument is the actual property value obtained via the function READ. Because we may require that the property list variable/value information exist in our information base as lists, the information input is converted into a list via LIST. The other functions within that PROG loop are necessary to output appropriate prompts and position the screen cursor suitably. For example, a command of the form :

```
*       (PLACE PROPVAR 'JOHN-X)
```

will respond with :

```
FATHER              _
```

where '_' denotes the cursor position ready for READ. The following sequence of events may occur :

```
FATHER              CLIVE-X
MOTHER              SARAH-H
BIRTH-DATE          1990
MARRIED             PETER-Y
OCCUPATION          TEACHER
CHILDREN            HERBERT-Y
```

where PROPVAR would exist as a result of :

```
(SETQ  PROPVAR  '(FATHER  MOTHER  BIRTH-DATE  MARRIED
OCCUPATION CHILDREN))
```

The sequence of events above continues until all property list variables in the list of property list variables (PROPVAR) have been prompted, and corresponding values (including NIL if appropriate) have been input. The returned value of PLACE is NIL. Notice the effect of :

```
(SPACES (- 30 (LENGTH (EXPLODE (CAR PROPS))))))
```

There is, however, one minor problem with the function as it stands at present. The 'bug' can easily be traced by using the actual family tree data as it exists in Figure 3.1. JOHN-X has two chidren; STEVE-X and MIKE- X. In response to the CHILDREN prompt, we would input two names. This would result in an error caused by the argument requirements of READ. The simple solution to the problem is the use of a similar function READLINE, which reads in a complete line of data up to some terminating condition (usually carriage return/line feed). The details of this function make the call to LIST redundant. The new line of input in the function PLACE will therefore become :

```
(RETURN (READLINE))
```

One more complication exists with the use of READLINE and its inherent behaviour. The effect is a return of NIL on first invocation, whilst subsequent calls to the function result in correct and predictable behaviour. The solution to this problem is a 'dummy' call to READLINE from a higher level calling function (see later, in the function BUILD).

The outermost loop of the information base build algorithm has an iterative structure. The iterative structure macro available in some LISP implementations could have been used for this, and subsequent iteratively- defined functions. However,it is considered more suitable, for reasons of clarity, to structure the loop in the most primitive way. The function used to build the information base, which represents a higher level control to PLACE, is shown below :

```
(DEFUN BUILD (LAMBDA (PROPLIST RELATE)
   (COND ((NULL RELATE) NIL)
         (T
           (PROG (I)
             (SETQ I (LENGTH RELATE))
           LOOP
             (COND ((GT I 0)
                     (WINCLR)
                     (SPACES (- 40
                        (ABS (/ (LENGTH (EXPLODE (CAR
                        RELATE)))
                             2))))
                     (PRINC (CAR RELATE))
                     (TERPRI (TERPRI))
                     (PLACE PROPLIST (CAR RELATE))
                     (SETQ I (- I 1))
                     (GO LOOP))
                   (T
                     (RETURN NIL))))))))
```

This function has been defined as purely iterative. The loop control variable is the length of the list RELATE, and a local variable with a value equal to the length of this list is initialised in the PROG body. Within the loop, there are several functions. WINCLR effects a clear window operation (supplied with no arguments to effect a global clear). The SPACES.... and PRINC.... functions produce a title at the top of the screen and centred. Then, after two blank screen lines, the call is made to PLACE, sending with it, the list of property variables and the current object name.

During the test phase of this function, rather than using BUILD on the existing, fairly large list of relatives in the tree of Figure 3.1, a dummy list can be used, as follows :

```
(SETQ DUMMY-LIST '(ONE TWO THREE))
```

and a simple controlling function can be defined, capable of accepting as an argument, the list of dummy objects :

```
(DEFUN TEST1 (LAMBDA (PERSONS)
   (PROG ()
     (READLINE)
     (BUILD PROPVAR PERSONS))))
```

which allows the building of a 'test' information base involving a small number of related objects. Once verified, it may be used to build the information base that will

be the basis of the rule-based system of later chapters.
The other information base manipulation functions that may be required are :

```
ADD-OBJECT              ADD-VARIABLE
REMOVE-OBJECT           REMOVE-VARIABLE
MODIFY-OBJECT           MODIFY VALUE
REMOVE-LIST
```

It is instructive at this stage, to produce outline algorithms for each of these proposed functions. The information available would then permit comparisons and subsequent identification of sub-tasks which are common to each individual function (or at least more than one), and therefore should be designed as functions in their own right. Beginning with the ADD-OBJECT function :

Problem:

An association list exists with the names of all persons currently believed to be family-related. It is almost inevitable that new names will be added to the information base in the light of fervent research. A facility must exist to add new individuals into the structure. In addition to the new object being placed on the association list, the property list of that new object must be 'filled in' to the same level as its relatives on the information base.

Solution :

A check must be made to ensure that the new name does not already exist on the specified association list. If the name is not already there, a function is required to place it there and make a subsequent call to PLACE, in order to complete the property list.

INPUT :   KEYBOARD -
            An individual's name and a list of relatives to include it on

            ENVIRONMENT -
            The list specified and a list of property list variables

OUTPUT :   DISPLAY -
            Messages to the user - prompts

            ENVIRONMENT -
            An updated information base if the name was not already on the list
            supplied

BEGIN
    Clear the display screen.
    Print the appropriate message as a title.
    Prompt for NAME to be added to a specified list.
    If the NAME does not already exist
        append name to the list supplied.
        Complete the property list information on NAME.
    Otherwise
        return without doing anything to the information base.
END

Already, from this algorithm, it can be seen that the clear screen, print message and prompt processes are common to PLACE. The printing of a message at the top of the screen will include the clear screen entry and the implementation is straightforward without recourse to the involved process of problem definition and algorithm design. The separate implementation of simple functions such as this provides a good degree of FUNCTION ABSTRACTION and aids structure. A function to clear the screen and print a title, centred at the top of the display screen is shown below :

```
(DEFUN TITLE (LAMBDA (TTL)
    (COND ((NULL TTL) NIL)
          (T
           (PROG ()
              (WINCLR)
              (SPACES (- 40 (ABS (/ (LENGTH
               (EXPLODE TTL)) 2))))
              (PRINC TTL)
              (TERPRI)
              (TERPRI))))))
```

The argument to SPACES is the calculation of exactly half the character width of an eighty column display screen minus half the length of the title as supplied. The absolute value is used to remove the possibility of error caused by a title with an odd number of characters.

A similar function to TITLE can be defined to effect a 'pretty prompt' and this is shown below :

```
(DEFUN PROMPT (LAMBDA (MESSAGE)
   (COND ((NULL MESSAGE) NIL)
         (T
            (PROG ()
               (PRINC MESSAGE)
               (SPACES (- 30 (LENGTH (EXPLODE
               MESSAGE))))
               (RETURN READLINE))))))))
```

Both BUILD and PLACE become considerably more compact and legible by virtue of the abstraction afforded by these two latter functions. Abstraction also permits the straightforward editing of functions, which eventually form part of an integrated system under program control, thereby minimising user-interaction.

Referring back to the algorithm ADD-OBJECT, it would seem sensible to concentrate on a sub-task identifiable within it, i.e. the actual function required to add a specified name to a specified list. However, this process involves a check on the existence of the specified name on the list supplied, and that would appear to be a good function to begin with. It is quite possible that some later functions will have use of it. The following function requires an object and an association list and operates well in the area specified in the ADD-OBJECT algorithm :

```
(DEFUN EXISTS (LAMBDA (A-LIST NAME)
   (COND ((NULL A-LIST) NIL)
         ((EQ NAME (CAR A-LIST)) T)
         (T
            (EXISTS (CDR A-LIST) NAME)))))
```

This recursive function returns NIL if the object name does not appear in the list supplied and T if that object is found. The next process in the approach to abstraction is the definition of a function having the simple task of adding the new object to the list :

```
(DEFUN ADD-NAME (LAMBDA (A-LIST NAME)
   (COND ((NULL A-LIST) NIL)
         (T
            (CONS NAME A-LIST)))))
```

The function tests for a NULL list and then goes on to add the new object via CONS. The function adds the name to the head of the list, but since, in the present application, interrelationships may not be known at this stage, this would appear to be satisfactory. In any case, it would be easy to define the function in such a way that the new object is added to the tail of the list. The actual position of each of these objects in the family tree is of the utmost importance and is determined by information in the property list of each individual.

Having accomplished the addition of the new name, the property list must be initialised. Fortunately, this function has already been defined and tested. A call to PLACE, with the appropriate list of property list variables and the relevant name supplied as arguments will complete the desired task.

The next list manipulation function required concerns the removal of a specified object from a list supplied. The following function provides the facility to delete the first (and, in the present application, the only) occurrence of the specified object :

```
(DEFUN REM-OBJ1 (LAMBDA (A-LIST NAME)
    (COND ((NULL A-LIST) NIL)
          ((EQUAL (CAR A-LIST) NAME) (CDR A-LIST))
          (T
              (CONS (CAR A-LIST) (REM-OBJ1 (CDR A-LIST)
              NAME))))))
```

This makes a removal possible, but only on a list local to the function. On leaving the function, the arguments are re-assigned their original values on entry to the function. In order to make global changes to the list, a SETQ would be required in the higher level calling function.

If it is desired to remove more than one occurrence of a specified object in a specified list, the function REM-OBJ1 can be suitably modified. It can be extended to form an outer recursive process to continue the deletion operation until the complete list is examined. The function is not of any real value in the present application, since by its very nature a family tree cannot include more than one person with the same name, i.e. the same position in the hierarchy. It is included below to demonstrate the power of recursion, and indicate an alternative to some of the doubly iterative structures found at various places in this text :

```
(DEFUN REM-ALL (LAMBDA (A-LIST NAME)
    (COND ((NULL A-LIST) NIL)
          ((EQUAL (CAR A-LIST) NAME)
                    (REM-ALL (CDR A-LIST) NAME))
          (T
              (CONS (CAR A-LIST)
                    (REM-ALL (CDR A-LIST) NAME))))))
```

It can be seen, by inspection, that the outermost loop, which is invoked on condition of equality, will ensure that all occurrences of the object of interest will be removed by forcing the process to continue after each successful match. This function is doubly recursive. It would be illuminating to compare this function to a similar one defined iteratively. As with ADD-OBJ, the modification is made to a list which is local to REM- ALL.

To complete the set of removal functions, a further task has been identified, that of removing objects appearing in one list from another list. This can quite easily be implemented by making as many calls to REM- OBJ1 or REM-ALL as there are objects in list1 (say). A higher level controlling function is required, capable of invoking one of the single object removal functions, with the correct arguments supplied on each iteration. The function below has been defined iteratively :

```
(DEFUN REMOVE (LAMBDA (LIST1 LIST2)
    (COND ((NULL LIST1) NIL)
          ((NULL LIST2) NIL)
          (T
              (PROG (I X Y)
                  (SETQ I (LENGTH LIST1))
                  (SETQ X LIST2)
                  (SETQ Y LIST1)
              LOOP
                  (COND ((GT I 0)
                  (SETQ X (REM-OBJ1 X (CAR X)))
                  (SETQ I (- I 1))
                  (SETQ Y (CDR Y))
                  (GO LOOP))
              (T
                  (RETURN NIL))))))))))
```

Next in the sequence of list manipulation functions is one to alter the name of a list object, effectively renaming it. It is a simple matter to alter the name of an object in this situation by utilising REM-OBJ1 to first delete the old name, and then using CONS to replace it with the new name at the head of the CDR of the list. For example :

```
(DEFUN ALT-OBJ (LAMBDA (A-LIST OLD-NAME ALT-NAME)
    (COND ((NULL A-LIST) NIL)
          ((EQUAL (CAR A-LIST) OLD-NAME)
              (CONS ALT-NAME (CDR A-LIST)))
          (T
```

```
(CONS (CAR A-LIST)
        (ALT-OBJ (CDR A-LIST) OLD-NAME ALT-
NAME))))))
```

The limitations of this function become obvious when considering the data structures in use by the information base. Information is stored on the property lists of individuals. This function alone does nothing to transfer the properties of the old object to the new. This can be achieved within the recursive loop of ALT-OBJ by making a call to the LISP primitive RPLACP before the final CONS. RPLACP has the effect of replacing the property list of a specified object with a list supplied as an argument. It also operates and modifies globally. The function becomes :

```
(DEFUN ALT-OBJ (LAMBDA (A-LIST OLD-NAME ALT-NAME)
    (COND ((NULL A-LIST) NIL)
          ((EQUAL (CAR A-LIST) OLD-NAME)
              (PROG ()
                (RPLACP ALT-NAME (PROPS OLD-NAME))
                (RETURN (CONS ALT-NAME (CDR A-LIST)))))
          (T
    (CONS (CAR A-LIST)
          (ALT-OBJ (CDR A-LIST) OLD-NAME ALT-NAME))))))
```

Great care must be exercised in the use of this function. RPLACP modifies globally, but the object modification occurs locally. The responsibility for correct global changes rests firmly with the calling function. In order to verify correct operation of ALT-OBJ therefore, a higher level test function will be defined to operate on the previously defined list of RELATIVES. This function merely calls ALT-OBJ with a pre-determined set of arguments. The function below alters one of the objects deep within the list called RELATIVES and the resultant modified list is bound to a global variable with the use of SETQ :

```
(DEFUN CHANGE-ONE (LAMBDA ()
    (SETQ MYLOT
            (ALT-OBJ RELATIVES
                    'DAVE-X
                    'HUGO-X))))
```

If some variable/value information is PLACEd on the property list of DAVE- X, the invocation of CHANGE-ONE should result in the modification of the object's name, without loss or corruption to the all-important attributes on the property list. It will be seen that, by examination of the property list of HUGO-X via PROPS, on the first version of ALT-OBJ, that property list is NIL, whereas with the latter version, it is the required copy of DAVE-X's property list.

ADD-VAR will be required inevitably, in a system capable of expansion by step-wise refinement. In the course of development, more properties will become necessary to the ever-improving inference mechanisms, and a specialised function is required to carry out that operation on ALL the objects in the list of family members. The function must first check that the new property list variable does not already exist, and on assurance that this is not the case, it will perform the necessary addition. Several functions can be identified in the modularisation process. Working from the lowest level upwards, these are :

1. A function to add the new property list variable name to the list of property list variables. PROPVAR in the present application.

2. A function to actually prompt for and place the variable/value information on the property list of each individual in the list supplied.

3. A function to check for the existence of the new variable supplied.

4. An overall controlling function, which invokes the check function, initialises the display and finally causes (or permits) the additional information to be included in the information base.

A function which performs the first operation above is :

```
(DEFUN NEWPROP (LAMBDA (A-LIST PROPLIST NEW-VAR)
   (COND ((NULL A-LIST) NIL)
         ((EXISTS PROPLIST NEWVAR) NIL)
         (T
           (PROG (I)
              (SETQ I (LENGTH A-LIST))
           LOOP
              (COND ((GT I 0)
                      (TERPRI (TERPRI (PRINT (CAR A-
                      LIST))))
                      (PUT (CAR A-LIST) (PROMPT NEW-VAR)
                      NEW-VAR)
                      (SETQ I (- I 1))
                      (SETQ A-LIST (CDR A-LIST))
                      (GO LOOP))
                 (T
                      (RETURN NIL))))))))
```

Notice the embedded use of EXISTS. This function could be further subdivided to provide a further level of abstraction, but as it stands, over-complexity is not a problem. In addition to the use of EXISTS, PROMPT has also been incorporated and their meaning is quite clear in NEWPROP.

A refinement can be included, to be consistent with the solutions to the current problem so far, for a function which performs the inclusion of the new variable on the property list variable list (PROPVAR). In the function below, a check is again made on the existence of the new variable on the specified list. This has been included, even though the identical operation is performed in NEWPROP, for reasons of generality, i.e. the function may be useful in some other context elsewhere :

```
(DEFUN ADD1VAR (LAMBDA (PROPLIST NEW-VAR)
    (COND ((NULL PROPLIST) NIL)
          ((EXISTS PROPLIST NEW-VAR) NIL)
          (T
          (REVERSE (CONS NEW-VAR (REVERSE PROPLIST)))))))
```

The expression which performs the actual variable inclusion involves CONS, which places the new variable at the head of the reversed PROPLIST, and REVERSE, which places each list element in its original position. This has been implemented in ADD1VAR to retain the order of property list variables as it would appear in BUILD. The order in this case is significant. The modifications to the list of property list values are local to the function ADD1VAR. A test function, capable of error checking, sequential invocation of NEWPROP and ADD1VAR, and of globally re-defining the list of property list variables is shown below.

```
(DEFUN TEST2 (LAMBDA (NEWVAR)
    (COND ((EXISTS DUMMY-LIST NEWVAR) NIL)
          (T
            (PROG ()
               (READLINE)
               (NEWPROP  DUMMY-LIST  PROPVAR  NEWVAR)
               (SETQ PROPVAR
                        (ADD1VAR  PROPVAR  NEWVAR))))))
```

This function assumes that the dummy-list of variables is in existence within the current LISP environment. It was initialised when testing the BUILD function and was used by the function TEST1. Care must be exercised with TEST2 and its in-built SETQ function call. Permanent additions will be made to PROPVAR. Of course, any unwanted additions can now be easily removed with our previously-defined REM-OBJ1 as below :

```
(REM-OBJ1 PROPVAR 'unwanted-variable)
```

In order to remove a property list variable, use must be made of REMPROPS, a LISP primitive function, which carries out the deletion, in a global sense, on a property list variable/value pair. From our point of view, if a property list variable has been chosen for some reason, for deletion, then we can safely say that all objects in our list of relatives should be subject to the same 'surgery'. The function below deletes one supplied property list variable from a list of objects. PROPLIST is supplied in order to check for the existence of the variable in the list of property list variables :

```
(DEFUN REMVAR (LAMBDA (A-LIST PROPLIST VAR)
   (COND ((NULL A-LIST) NIL)
         ((NULL PROPLIST) NIL)
         ((NOT (EXISTS PROPLIST VAR)) NIL)
         (T
          (PROG (I)
             (SETQ I (LENGTH A-LIST))
           LOOP
             (COND ((GT I 0)
                    (REMPROP (CAR A-LIST) VAR)
                    (SETQ A-LIST (CDR A-LIST))
                    (SETQ I (- I 1))
                    (GO LOOP))
                   (T
                    (RETURN NIL)))))))))
```

The function required to modify a property list value has two possible modes :

1. Most property list information exists in pairs, i.e. the CAR is the variable and the CDR is the value .

2. Some value information exists as lists containing more than one element.

In any case, all the property list information is stored in the information base in the form of lists rather than DOTTED PAIRS. The function below caters for the more simple case of (1) above, i.e. lists of two elements. This can be easily arranged by the LISP primitive function PUT. The second case mentioned requires the invocation of another function, which manipulates the value information as a list, and then uses

PUT to place the updated information on the relevant property list. Close inspection of the second function will reveal its similarity to ALT-OBJ developed earlier :

```
(DEFUN ALT-VAL (LAMBDA (NAME VAR OLD-NAME NEW-NAME)
    (COND ((GT (LENGTH (GET NAME VAR)) 1)
             (PUT NAME (ALT-ELEMENT (GET NAME VAR)
             OLD-NAME NEW-NAME) VAR))
           (T
             (PUT NAME (LIST NEW-NAME) VAR)))))
```

And the function ALT-ELEMENT, which is called when the specified variable has more than one associated value :

```
(DEFUN ALT-ELEMENT (LAMBDA (LIST OLD-NAME NEW-NAME)
    (COND ((NULL LIST) NIL)
           ((EQUAL (CAR LIST) OLD-NAME)
             (CONS NEW-NAME (CDR LIST)))
           (T
             (CONS (CAR LIST) (ALT-ELEMENT (CDR LIST)
                                   OLD-NAME NEW-NAME)))))))
```

It may also be necessary to add a new value to the list of values associated with an individual. This would be a property list variable, and the necessary manipulation can be achieved with the following function, called ADD-VAL :

```
(DEFUN ADD-VAL (LAMBDA (NAME VAR NEW-ELEMENT)
    (COND ((NULL (GET NAME VAR)) NIL)
           (T
             (PUT NAME (REVERSE (CONS NEW-ELEMENT
                           (REVERSE (GET NAME VAR)))) VAR)))))
```

Again, we see an initial test for valid data with the NULL function, and an ordering sequence resulting from the use of REVERSE and CONS. As before, with TEST1 and TEST2, this suite of functions should be tested on the DUMMY-LIST initiated previously. In fact, these functions should be brought together under the 'umbrella' of a top-level controlling program able to invoke the correct function on the basis of user-interaction facilitated by some form of menu feature. All the tools specified in this chapter would then be available at command level, to create a new information base or maintain an existing information base. This has the 'civilising' effect of removing the possibility of error caused by inappropriate usage of function arguments. The function would have the task of prompting for the arguments specified in each 'tool' function and would also be responsible for error checking. Much user-interaction is required of this sort of 'supervisory function'.

Summary

At this stage, we have a complete, albeit fairly basic, set of information base manipulation functions. This set of functions is now available in the LISP environment for use, either from the command level of LISP, or by an intelligent system designed to provide conclusions of some kind on the basis of inference. The functions presented early in this chapter have been included with all algorithmic development steps (apart, perhaps, from all the rather intangible thoughts involved). In fact, the philosophy behind the chapter, and text, is the elucidation of viable development methodologies, and not necessarily the presentation of maximally-efficient list processing utility functions.

The functions developed so far, have been presented with a discussion of advantages, disadvantages and special LISP features. Some of the more high-level functions are refined during the development process and these refinement steps have also been discussed in the test. A good practice, at this stage, is to make a list of all the functions developed so far under the following headings :

1.   Function name and arguments .

2.   The task of the function .

3.   The side effects - local or global changes.

The specifications for each of these functions has been drawn up in this format, and is included in APPENDIX 1. The specifications within Appendix 1 provide a useful and convenient reference and index to the fuller discussions and definitions in this chapter.

Chapter Four

A Rule-Based Problem Solving Approach

4.1 Introduction

The data structures chosen for the family tree information base provide a simple means for the storage of information associated with each individual in the list of individuals thought to be family-related, and any interrelated information required of an eventual system capable of building a family tree. It does not appear as the classical frame structure, but it does provide similar capabilities. The requirements of any system using inference are fairly easy to define. They include a good, well-structured data base which is easy to access and to manipulate, as a result of new information pertinent to the current knowledge, represented within that data base.

There are many tasks that we may expect a knowledge-based system to successfully undertake. The first of these is perhaps the most obvious; to take the information within the information base, which has been input via our BUILD function, and produce an actual tree structure in the form of some kind of meaningful output. The output of such a system would ideally be in the form of a graphical representation of a family tree, but initially, a good deal of information can be gained from a sequence of textual messages. The procedure may involve :

1.   Search.

2.   Information modification.

3.   Access to, and use of knowledge in the form of RULES .

4.   Meaningful input and output.

4.2 Tree Root Search

The first problem to be tackled is the determination of the 'root' of the family tree. The solution to this problem can be viewed as a separate, identifiable task capable of existing as the one and only goal in a knowledge-based system. However, in this text, we will assume that the root finding process is a sub-task of a larger system, with the overall resonsibility of building a family tree. The information base toolkit developed in the previous chapter does nothing to force any kind of family related information structure on the incomming data. This means that individuals may exist within the information base, having absolutely no family relationships with the family of interest, or any other individual for that matter. Therefore, any system capable of finding the ROOT of a family tree within a possibly large information base, may find many others too. There may, in effect be several family trees in existence. In the first part of the problem, we will assume that only one 'original' married couple exist and they represent the root of the family tree as it will be traced and displayed. The second part will be capable of tracing the rest of the family tree, on the basis of the root couple determined in the first.

In the initial ideas stage of system design, several considerations should be made. The problem is basically one of user-understandable structure representation and structure ordering. The knowledge-based system will be required to produce a hierarchical representation of the information base in existence, and finally to display the result in the manner proposed.

It is beneficial to construct a very general algorithm for the solution to the problem. At this stage, the overall problem should be considered in order to maintain consistency of approach in the solution of each sub-task. The overall problem includes the actual tree building process, and the root finding system will merely be the starting point of the complete, integrated knowledge-based system. In the design of the information base toolkit and after the preliminary process of 'thought', a deeper understanding of the problem has been gained. In order to document this, the algorithm is required :

Problem :

To build a family tree structure using the information retained in the property lists of individuals within a list of such individuals. To help and guide the process, a list of rules is to be used.

Solution :

The solution is to begin by searching for the root of the tree. The root is defined as the 'original' member, who is characterised in the information base as having no parents (not known, i.e. as far as back as we can go), is married and whose married partner also has no recorded parents. Children must, of course, be recorded. This may be regarded as an extreme simplification, but it does provide a reasonably realistic scenario. Once the root has been found, a search can be made for the children of that family. The search algorithm could find the generation after the 'root couple', then the generation (if any) following each child of the root, and so it goes on until no more children are to be found. This latter solution arises when an 'end of branch' is detected.

INPUT :   KEYBOARD -
            The list of objects (persons) representing the information base and a list
            of rules.

            ENVIRONMENT -
            The complete information base, rule lists and temporary 'working lists'.

OUTPUT :   DISPLAY -
            Output of all required information - the ROOT object and the family
            tree.

            ENVIRONMENT -
            Temporary list information, useful for later introspection and, possibly,
            an altered information base.

BEGIN
    Repeat the following until all the objects in the information base have been
    inspected :
        Find the married couple, neither of which has any recorded parents.
        Find and record the male partner as ROOT (or female partner, whichever is
        selected at run-time.
    Repeat the following until all the (relevant) objects in the information base have
    been inspected and classified :
        Classify each family member in the hierarchy represented by the family tree.
END

This represents the general algorithm stage of the development process. The two
important stages in the solution to the problem in hand have been articulated. That is,
the problem has already been roughly partitioned from the more general definition,
'produce family tree'. We have isolated two steps in the process. The first is to find
the original parents, i.e. those individuals who represent the oldest generation in our
information base and therefore the ROOT of the family tree. Once that has been
achieved, it would appear to be fairly straightforward to repeatedly search for the next
generation until no new generations are recorded. An alternative algorithm could, of
course, be constructed for the alternative process, which would involve a search for
the 'end branches', i.e. the youngest generation, and work up to the top (ROOT). This
would appear to have two disadvantages :

1. The algorithm would be more difficult to construct. The initial search would be
    directed to find an unknown number of individuals. This may result in an over-
    complicated programming task. In this text, the overall philosophy is the
    reduction in complexity.

2. The information base may be 'less than perfect'. It may include individuals who
    are not related to the family in question. The eventual system should be capable
    of accessing information, and including or excluding individuals on the basis of

strict family relationship rules. A search and tree building exercise which is based on contradictory information may result in disaster, if the system does not incorporate mechanisms to deal with this sort of potential catastrophe. The consequent increase in system complexity has already been discussed.

Having satisfied ourselves on the validity of the general algorithm, it is necessary to take each statement and refine it. Starting with the first part, that of searching for the root of the tree, and bearing in mind the knowledge-based approach which will be made, we can consider certain rules to help identify the 'first couple'. Age could be the basis of approach. The information base contains data on the birth date of each individual (if known). Problems could arise with this approach, if for instance, one of the younger generation happened to marry a very much older person. A much more reliable test would involve the parents of individuals. If an individual's parents are not known, it could mean that one of two possibilities exist :

1. The individual married one of the persons already included in the family tree, and whose parents are obviously known

or

2. The individual is one of the original parents.

This may be an extreme simplification of potentially complex human-inspired relationships, but it does contain enough realism to make it recognisable. In this overview of family relationships, it would appear reasonable to assume (infer) that, if two individuals are married to each other AND each member of those couples have no recorded parents, THEN that couple are very good candidates for our original parents classification. Put another, more formal way, in the form of a rule therefore :

```
IF    FATHER AND MOTHER OF THE INDIVIDUAL IS NOT RECORDED
   AND
      THE INDIVIDUAL IS MARRIED
   AND
      CHILDREN ARE CREDITED TO THE INDIVIDUAL
   THEN
      THE INDIVIDUAL IS A DEFINITE  POSSIBILITY FOR ROOT
```

This is sufficient to find all those persons who could possibly be one of the people we are searching for. It will include all those persons who are on the periphery of the tree and whose parents may not be of much interest in the present application. It could also include those persons who :

1.   Are not in any family tree ;

2.   Are original parents of some other family tree existing in the information base.

As far as the second of these points is concerned, we can easily arrange for the system to consider only the first couple (initially).

In order to find the original couple, another rule could be incorporated, namely :

```
IF
    ONE OF THE POSSIBILITIES IS MARRIED TO ONE OF THE
    OTHER POSSIBILITIES

THEN
    THAT COUPLE REPRESENTS THE ORIGINAL COUPLE
```

This would appear to be fool-proof, on the understanding that the information base is not contradictory at this level, e.g. only one wife per husband and one husband per wife. Results could also be unpredictable if mistakes are made, such as a person being recorded as being married to himself or herself.

Up to this point, the original couple is identified. The process could be expanded to find the original person, either the male or female partner in the couple. For this example, we will choose the male partner. A further rule would therefore follow the previous one :

```
IF
    THE INDIVIDUAL'S SEX IS MALE

THEN
    THAT INDIVIDUAL IS THE ORIGINAL PERSON (ROOT)
```

Notice that these rules are, effectively parts of an algorithm. All major steps articulated in these rules, represent conventional conditional statements in an algorithm. They have merely been represented in another, more abstract way. One obvious omission from the conventional algorithm implementation is the CONTROL STRUCTURE of the sequential process. Obviously, the first rule mentioned must come first, followed by the second, then the third, and so-on. In the traditional approach, we may see the phrases :

```
        REPEAT -- UNTIL, WHILE -- DO, etc.
```

which defines a control structure. In the system which follows, the control mechanisms will be crucial to the design and implementation of a successful, versatile system. Knowledge is represented, both in the rules and how those rules are implemented. A versatile rule-based system would be one in which the behaviour of the system is seen to be controlled by the rules, and therefore, changes in the rules should cause predictable changes in system behaviour.

One other, very important feature of the system as it is already becoming developed, is that each rule will fire only when appropriate data is available. The system is already recognisable as one being DATA DRIVEN. The type of rule-based approach outlined here is termed FORWARD CHAINING, i.e. it looks for rules that depend on previously defined assertions. After the first rule has fired, a list may (or may not) be available for use by subsequent rules. The second rule requires a list of possibilities before it can reach a conclusion. The assertion here is that individuals A,B,C ...N are possibilities, and they can be used by the rest. The next part of the system, i.e. the part which builds the tree will perhaps be more identifiable as a forward chaining system, in that it tests available rules over and over, until no rule applies. This set of rules would be applied in turn only once, for the first original couple.

The necessary control structure can be easily abstracted at the algorithmic level as :

APPLY ALL THE RULES ON EACH INDIVIDUAL ON THE INFORMATION
BASE

This tells us only that each individual is initially a possibility, and must be narrowed down by application of the rules. It is not too helpful. The next stage is to refine the control system to a level at which coding can begin. Unfortunately, the other part of the system must also be considered prior to this, since it will eventually be controlled by the same control structure.

The second part of the general algorithm involves search. The root finding section implies search, but at only one level, i.e. the complete information base is searched from start to finish until the desired person is found. When he is found, the goal is reached. With the second part, repetition is implied by virtue of the hierarchical tree structure itself. We can proceed by finding all the immediate descendants of ROOT, then finding all their immediate descendants, and so-on until the youngest generation is reached. This would be termed BREADTH FIRST search and is shown diagrammatically in Figure 4.1. Alternatively, we could search from root, down one path, until a limited group of the youngest generation are identified, thereafter moving back to ROOT (or near), and proceeding down the next path. This is termed DEPTH FIRST search and is shown diagramatically in Figure 4.2.

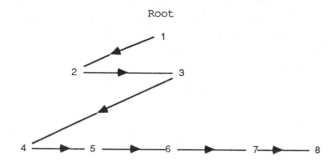

Figure 4.1

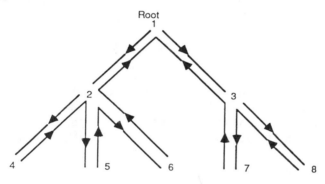

Figure 4.2

Search routines may be implemented to carry out these functions, and indeed, such routines will be used in this text. However, the search process for the ROOT object will again be implemented as a rule-base system, but will be seen to be essentially depth first in nature. Again, rules will be abstracted to deal with the problem. If it assumed that ROOT has been identified previously :

IF
    FATHER OR MOTHER IS ONE OF THE LISTED OLDER GENERATION

THEN
    THAT INDIVIDUAL IS ONE OF THE NEW (OR NEXT) GENERATION

This rule has one difference from the earlier ones: it incorporates an OR. The rules identified previously were made up of ANDs. The structures can be readily standardised by splitting the above rule into two rules :


```
RULE-1 :

IF
    FATHER IS ONE OF THE LISTED OLDER GENERATION

THEN
    THAT INDIVIDUAL IS ONE OF THE NEW (OR NEXT) GENERATION

RULE-2 :

IF
    MOTHER IS ONE OF THE LISTED OLDER GENERATION

THEN
    THAT INDIVIDUAL IS ONE OF THE NEW (OR NEXT) GENERATION
```


It can be seen that these two rules are all that is required in the solution to the problem of building a family tree. Obviously, these rules must be applied over and over to a continually updated information base until neither of these two rules above fire. It represents a true DATA DRIVEN, FORWARD CHAINING approach.

All the rules so far have been expressed in the same format. There is, however, one difference in the implementation details of the two system 'parts'. In the first part, a conclusion exists after one pass of the rule list. In the second, possibly many passes are required before a complete solution exists. It would be possible to arrange for the first three rules to be incorporated into one global control system by careful choice of list processing techniques, but that would increase complexity in the name of versatility. It is much easier, at this stage, to visualise two distinct lists of rules, implemented in two different ways: one list applied to the information base once, and one list applied as many times as necessary. The control system can now be visualised as below :

1.   Apply rules 1 to 3 (find root) on all data .

2.   Apply rules 4 to 5 (build tree) on all data not already identified and classified, UNTIL
            no more classifications can be made.

100

The entire system will comprise :

1. *An information base,* consisting of objects, each with its own properties related to the current problem .

2. *A set of rules* which are able to utilise the information base, and produce conclusions, or partial conclusions (assertions), which may be used by other rules .

3. *A control system*, which determines which rules to apply and the application details .

4. *A rule interpreter*. In advanced systems, this may incorporate a natural language interface, which may itself be an expert system of some sort. The main task is the interpretation of a rule, expressed in the most human-legible and meaningful fashion.

By careful study of this list, it is apparent that the rule interpreter is a vital constituent of the control system and deserves some initial consideration. The rules, as expressed earlier, can be abstracted :

```
IF          (TEST-1
             TEST-2
             TEST-3
              .  .  .
              .  .  .
             TEST-N)
THEN
            (ACTION)
```

So, assuming that IF and THEN always exist, the rule consists of only two parts; the TEST and the ACTION. The same format applies to all the other rules. In addition to this, it can be seen that the action part is always something like :

```
IS ONE OF  ..........
IS THE  .............
...
...
etc.
```

That is, the action part always appears as INCLUDE the individual(s) in some kind of list. A common and viable structure is appearing. Using the list structure of LISP, a convenient structure, based on the above discussion, is :

```
(IF LIST ((TEST1) (TEST2) (TEST3) ...... (TEST-N))
         (THEN (ACTION)))
```

where LIST is the list of relatives in the present problem domain.

Using this structure, the test list can be accessed via (CADDR RULE) and the action can be accessed for evaluation by :

```
(CAR (CDAR (CDDDR RULE)))
```

Within the test list, each test, which will be implemented as a specific antecedent of the rule, can be accessed in a similar way. For example, for TEST1 in any rule, the following could be used :

```
(CAR (CADDR RULE))
```

Another similarity in the almost algorithmic representation of rules to this point, is the subject of each test, which appears either at the head of the list comprising the antecedent, or very close to the front. Consider the comparison of antecedents from some of the rules so far :

```
FATHER IS NOT RECORDED
MOTHER IS RECORDED
CHILDREN ARE CREDITED TO THE INDIVIDUAL
MARRIED TO ONE OF THE OTHER POSSIBILITIES
FATHER IS ONE OF THE LISTED OLDER GENERATION
MOTHER IS ONE OF THE LISTED OLDER GENERATION
```

The other antecedents could be expressed in this form to standardise antecedent format. For instance :

```
IF ...... THE INDIVIDUAL IS MARRIED
```

could be re-arranged as MARRIED PARTNER EXISTS,

```
IF ...... ONE OF THE POSSIBILITIES IS MARRIED TO ONE OF
          THE OTHER POSSIBILITIES
```

could be re-arranged as MARRIED TO ONE OF THE OTHER POSSIBILITIES,

and, finally,

```
IF ...... THE INDIVIDUAL'S SEX IS MALE
```

could be re-arranged as SEX IS MALE

All of these cosmetic rearrangements have little effect on the meaning of the statement, but they do have the very real advantage of standardising the format of the rules.

The very first object in the list (antecedent) is a property variable bound to every person in the list of relatives. One essential part of the test has been selected and corresponds very well indeed to the data structures which have been chosen. This degree of standardisation will also have a profound effect on the nature of the rule interpreter, and overall control structure.

To implement a rule-based system, each antecedent in the list attached to each rule must be matched to a specific situation within the data base, and by their very nature, the match must return either true or false. Up to this point, we have had a method of accessing an individual's specific property value as the first object in the antecedent. The second part has yet to be identified. Again, consider antecedents with common characteristics. In particular :

```
RULE1     FATHER .......  NOT RECORDED      (NIL)
          MOTHER ......   NOT RECORDED      (NIL)
          CHILDREN ....   EXIST             (NON-NIL)
          SEX .........   MALE (OR FEMALE)  (SPECIFIC)
          FATHER .......  OLDER-GENERATION  (SPECIFIC)
          MOTHER .......  OLDER GENERATION  (SPECIFIC)
```

For the first two abstracted antecedents, it would be quite simple to match a specific individual's FATHER or MOTHER property list value with NIL. The test would be quite simple and would return either T or not. The required function would be based on something like :

```
(EQUAL (LIST (GET INDIVIDUAL (CAR ANTECEDENT)))
       (LIST (EVAL (CAR (LAST ANTECEDENT))))))
```

a fairly simple match of the individual's property list value specified by (CAR ANTECEDENT) with the last object in the antecedent, which would be NIL. This would also work quite well, in essence for the antecedent SEX .... MALE. Unfortunately, due to the differences in the form of value returned when the test is for NIL or some specific value. A modification of this is required :

```
(EQUAL (GET INDIVIDUAL (CAR ANTECEDENT))
       (LIST (EVAL (CAR (LAST ANTECEDENT)))))
```

The two cases could easily be supplied as arguments to the OR function. For example :

```
(OR (EQUAL (LIST (GET INDIVIDUAL (CAR ANTECEDENT)))
           (LIST (EVAL (CAR (LAST ANTECEDENT)))))
    (EQUAL (GET INDIVIDUAL (CAR ANTECEDENT))
           (LIST (EVAL (CAR (LAST ANTECEDENT))))))
```

This forms the basis of a crucial function - the test of the actual antecedent. It must obviously return either true or false, and as it stands above, provides a suitable test for three of the cases documented. There are, however, some antecedents which require more processing than a simple match. The two obvious and very general ones remaining are :

1. Find a NON-NIL match .

2. Find the existence of an object on a specified list.

The first of these would be easy to implement as a function, using something of the order (NOT (NULL X)), and the second of these could be catered for by a function which checks for the existence of an object on a list. Both cases would appear to require the invocation of a separate function. Fortunately, this can also be catered for with a little care in the design of the rules. For example, the antecedent :

```
(CHILDREN  . . . . . . . . .  EXIST)
```

could be re-arranged in a meaningful manner, to become :

```
(CHILDREN ARE RECORDED AS (NON-NIL))
```

A slight departure perhaps from 'perfect syntax', but the semantics remain intact. With this latter format, the object within the last parentheses (NON-NIL) could easily be a function identifier. For example :

```
(DEFUN NON-NIL (LAMBDA ()
   (NOT (NULL (GET INDIVIDUAL (CAR ANTECEDENT)))))))
```

The function tests for the existence of a property list value assigned to the specified property list variable. If, for instance, the property list variable CHILDREN had not been assigned during the information base building process, the function would return NIL via the NOT function. Therefore, this would result in a T or NIL returned value if the last object in the antecedent was processed as a function invocation. This is fine as far as the overall philosophy of the test is concerned, but it is a departure from the standard arrived at earlier, i.e. the perfect match. Fortunately, if this is adopted as the third (and final) possible case, it too can be incorporated in the OR clauses. The 'body', or active part of the final function, which will be called TEST-ANTECEDENT becomes :

```
(OR (EQUAL (LIST (GET INDIVIDUAL (CAR ANTECEDENT)))
           (LIST (EVAL (CAR (LAST ANTECEDENT)))))
    (EQUAL (GET INDIVIDUAL (CAR ANTECEDENT))
           (LIST (EVAL (CAR (LAST ANTECEDENT)))))
    (EQUAL (EVAL (CAR (LAST ANTECEDENT))) T))
```

where the final clause actually tests for a T result.

The final case: that of finding the existence of an object on a specified list is, perhaps, more difficult to realise, in particular, the antecedent :

```
MARRIED TO ONE OF THE OTHER POSSIBILITIES
```

It would be possible, as before, to build a function POSSIBILITIES, but it would seem more sensible, and meaningful, to arrange for POSSIBILITIES to be a list (of possibilities). Even so, a separate function is definitely required. The function should ideally be general, and require arguments in the form of a list (of possibilities) and an object to find on that list. Therefore, a function will be defined, called RECORDED, which takes two such arguments, a property value and a list. The function is required to find if ANY of the persons on the supplied list are married to ANY other person on the supplied list. The function should operate along the lines outlined in the following algorithm :

Problem :

To take a list and find one couple who are married to each other. The problem is characterised by a match of a property list value and an object in the list supplied.

Solution :

An elegant solution to this problem would proceed by initially finding a list object which corresponds to an individual's property list value. It would then make a cross check on the equivalence of that person's property list value. The solution could be made to report on the condition of more than one couple. In the solution defined here, no cross check will be made, and the first occurrence of a candidate couple will be tested.

```
INPUT :    KEYBOARD - None

           ENVIRONMENT -
           A property variable name and list, supplied as
           arguments

OUTPUT :   DISPLAY - None
           ENVIRONMENT -
           NIL if an empty list is supplied
           NIL if the test fails
           T if a married couple are found
```

105

```
BEGIN
   Repeat the following until all the objects  in the
   list have been checked :
      Check the value of the property variable (MARRIED)
      Return T if the value corresponding to that
      variable is the name of an individual on the
         supplied list
END
```

If no cross check is required, the function can be expressed either recursively or iteratively, operating with a succession of list 'heads' on the rest of the list. On each loop, the head is replaced by the CADR of the list.

The complications arising from the two distinct parts of the outline function, RECORDED can be approached via the technique of ABSTRACTION. The required function has two identifiable parts :

1. A loop structure which operates on the list and invokes .

2. A function which carries out the actual test on specific individuals and their existence on the list.

It is beneficial to begin at the lowest level, i.e. part 2. The actual task to be carried out is incorporated in the algorithm, and can be stated as the matching of a given name (MARRIED TO ...) to a name existing in the list supplied. This assumes that the name has been 'extracted' from the property list of an individual. The function is completely general and will take two arguments; a list and an object. The function name will be EXISTS :

```
(DEFUN EXISTS (LAMBDA (A-LIST NAME)
   (COND ((NULL A-LIST) NIL)
         ((EQ NAME (CAR A-LIST)) T)
         (T
           (EXISTS (CDR A-LIST) NAME)))))
```

The function makes an initial test for an empty supplied list, and returns T if a successful match (excuse the pun) is made. The function is recursive and the recursion terminates on a NULL list. The meaning of the function is clear.

The first identifiable part of the problem can be considered an outer loop, continually invoking EXISTS and supplying the correctly updated arguments, until all persons have been checked. The next function will be required to extract the specified property list value from the current head of the list of individuals, and supply a continually 'shortened' list to EXISTS. The function has been defined iteratively, and again without the use of iteration MACROs to maintain clarity :

```
(DEFUN RECORDED (LAMBDA (PROP A-LIST)
   (COND ((NULL A-LIST) NIL)
         (T
            (PROG (I X)
               (SETQ X A-LIST)
               (SETQ I (LENGTH A-LIST)))
            LOOP
               (COND ((EXISTS X (CAR (GET (CAR X) PROP)))
                        (RETURN
                           (FIND X (CAR (GET (CAR X)
                              PROP)))))
                     ((GT I 1)
                        (SETQ X (CDR X))
                        (SETQ I (- I 1))
                        (GO LOOP))
                     (T
                        (RETURN NIL)))))))
```

Prog has two arguments which are used as local variables. X is assigned the value A-LIST and I to the length of the list supplied (the number of objects in the list). The loop terminates, either as soon as a successful match is made, with the name of the married partner returned, or when all the individuals in the list have been checked, i.e. I goes to zero. In this latter case, the function returns NIL. The function FIND is required to satisfy the needs of TEST-ANTECEDENT, and is basically a variation on EXISTS. The full iterative definition of FIND is :

```
(DEFUN FIND (LAMBDA (A-LIST NAME)
   (COND ((NULL A-LIST) NIL)
         (T
            (PROG (I V)
               (SETQ I (LENGTH A-LIST))
               (SETQ V A-LIST)
            LOOP
               (COND ((EQUAL NAME (CAR V)) (RETURN (CAR
                        V)))
                     ((GT I 1)
                        (SETQ V (CDR V))
                        (SETQ I (- I 1))
                        (GO LOOP))
                     (T
                        (RETURN NIL)))))))
```

By virtue of FUNCTION ABSTRACTION, the task has been accomplished efficiently and with maximal clarity of meaning. RECORDED may be specialised, even dedicated, but at the heart of the process, there is a general function.

As far as the FIND ROOT preliminary stage is concerned, the TEST-ANTECEDENT facility exists and can be shown to work well with antecedents supplied in the strict format specified. However, the rule base consists, at present of five rules, all operating on the list of relatives and a specific group of persons within that list. TEST-ANTECEDENT and all its required abstractions has been defined. The control structure has yet to be developed.

4.3 Control Structure

The control structure development has already begun with perhaps the most important facility of all - the actual antecedent test. In many ways, the rest of the control structure is determined, largely by the way the 'lowest' level function operates. However, the rest of the control structure can be designed with respect to the algorithm discussed at the beginning of this section, i.e. the two identifiable parts of the problem. In this chapter, we have already considered in great detail, the implications of our chosen rule structure as it applies to our selected information base structure and general algorithm. A common, reasonably standard rule format has been refined for use in the problem domain of interest, and by this process, the way ahead is clear to design an overall control mechanism.

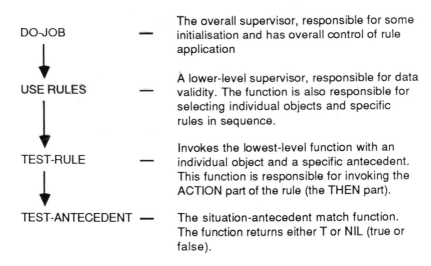

Figure 4.3 A suggested control structure able to operate on one pass of a list of rules applied to an information base comprising a list of objects

The overall control structure may be partitioned into levels of responsibility. A convenient modular structure would be as shown in Figure 4.3 for one pass of the rule list. The distinction between DO-JOB and USE- RULES may be difficult to establish on first view. They both appear to require the same arguments, and in actual fact, could both be incorporated into one larger function which employs double recursion or iteration. Again, for reasons of clarity, function abstraction has been used to separate multiple loops into separately identifiable sub-tasks in some form of responsibility hierarchy.

The control structure, as depicted in Figure 4.3 may be seen to be incomplete. This structure may be used to obtain some form of conclusion after one pass of the rule list. There is a distinct lack of a further loop structure which causes a repeated invocation of this mechanism until a definite goal is achieved. Fortunately, as far as the ROOT finding part of the problem is concerned, one pass of the selected rules represents the correct means of solution. Therefore, the structure of Figure 4.3 can be used to solve the initial part of the problem directly, and used as the body of some kind of controlling loop structure for the final part.

4.3.1 Test-Antecedent

Having established the 'active' part of a function to test each antecedent - TEST-ANTECEDENT, the rest of the function should be defined. In fact, the only remaining task to be built into TEST-ANTECEDENT to complete the function definition is the data validity error checking. Therefore, the final definition is as below :

```
(DEFUN TEST-ANTECEDENT (LAMBDA (ANTECEDENT INDIVIDUAL)
   (COND ((NULL (PROPS INDIVIDUAL)) NIL)
         ((NULL ANTECEDENT) NIL)
         (T
           (OR (EQUAL (LIST (GET INDIVIDUAL (CAR
                   ANTECEDENT)))
                      (LIST (EVAL (CAR (LAST
                      ANTECEDENT)))))
               (EQUAL (GET INDIVIDUAL (CAR ANTECEDENT))
                      (LIST (EVAL (CAR (LAST
                      ANTECEDENT)))))
               (EQUAL (EVAL (CAR (LAST ANTECEDENT))) T
           ))))))
```

where initial tests are made on the property list of the individual of interest and the antecedent supplied.

4.3.2 Test-Rule

The next part of the control structure will be defined from the next highest level, i.e. TEST-RULE. A suitable algorithm is shown below :

Problem:

TEST-ANTECEDENT requires a specific antecedent, from an unspecified number of antecedents within a rule. An outer loop is required to control the supply of antecedents to TEST-ANTECEDENT, and cause the invocation of the rule's THEN clause, i.e. the action part. Each rule conforms to a strict format, and this permits the use of LISP's powerful list 'surgery' primitives.

Solution:

A function is required to take, as arguments, a specific rule and an individual. Each antecedent should then be applied to that individual. Recursion will be used to control the loop, and on a 'true' result of ALL the tests involved, the action part of the rule will be invoked. This will be abstracted with a function call to ACTION, which will have, as an argument, the expression following the THEN clause. To do this, the technique below will be used :

```
(ACTION (CAR (CDAR (CDDDR RULE))))
```

INPUT :   KEYBOARD - None

            ENVIRONMENT -
            A rule supplied from a list of rules
            A list object (person's name)

OUTPUT :   DISPLAY - None

            ENVIRONMENT -
            NIL on the condition of ANY failed tests
            Invocation of ACTION on condition of ALL tests being successful (T returned)

BEGIN
    Repeat the following until all the rule's antecedents have been matched
        Test each antecedent for a true match.
      If any tests fail THEN
        Return NIL
    Return true (T)
END

A suitable function, based on this algorithm is :

```
(DEFUN TEST-RULE (LAMBDA (RULE INDIVIDUAL)
    (COND ((NULL (CADDR RULE))
               (ACTION (CAR (CDAR (CDDDR RULE))))))
          ((NOT (TEST-ANTECEDENT
              (CAR (CADDR RULE)) INDIVIDUAL)) NIL)
          (T
              (TEST-RULE (LIST (CAR RULE)
                               (CADR RULE)
                               (CDAR (CDDR RULE))
                               (CADR (CDDR RULE)))
                         INDIVIDUAL))))))
```

The function returns NIL immediately a result of TEST-ANTECEDENT returns NIL. If the recursion reaches the terminating condition, then all the antecedents must have matched, and the rule's THEN clause is the next logical step in the run-time sequence of events.

4.3.3 Use-Rules

The previous function (TEST-RULE) requires a specific rule format, consisting of :

```
(IF LIST ((ANTECEDENT-1)
          (ANTECEDENT-2)

               .     .     .
               .     .     .

          (ANTECEDENT-N))
    (THEN
          (ACTION)))
```

The function performs its task on the basis of the property list of a specified individual and returns a Boolean value as a result of a test of all the antecedents in the rule. However, a list of rules exists, which define the overall task. At present, in order to find the root of the family tree, we have three of them. Some form of outer loop structure is required to select specific rules in sequence, and request that the tests defined in that rule be carried out on the property list (list of attributes) of a given individual within the list of relatives. The algorithm then is :

Problem :

To take a list of relatives and a specified rule list, and control the application of a rule to each individual in the list. The function should perform a check on the status of the supplied list, i.e. that the list contains information, and whether any of the rules are not bound to a list which constitutes the rule (IF .. THEN).

Solution :

A function is required to repeatedly invoke TEST-RULE on one individual and one rule. The function will be required to loop continually, supplying as arguments to TEST-RULE, consecutive individuals and one rule. In this way, each rule is applied to each individual in turn, until all the antecedents of that rule have been matched to the specific property list values of each individual. In effect, we merely require an 'outer loop' to TEST-RULE.

INPUT :   KEYBOARD - None

              ENVIRONMENT -
              A list of objects bound to an identifier
              A list which incorporates one rule

OUTPUT :   DISPLAY - None

              ENVIRONMENT -
              NIL returned on completion of the function execution
              The function causes indirect changes to occur due to its function
              invocations

BEGIN
    Repeat the following until all individuals have been checked
        Apply one rule to each individual via TEST-RULE
END

The required function with the usual error checking built in to maintain generality is as below :

```
(DEFUN USE-RULES (LAMBDA (RULE-LIST A-LIST)
   (COND ((NULL A-LIST) NIL)
         ((NULL RULE-LIST) NIL)
         ((NOT (BOUNDP (CAR RULE-LIST))) NIL)
         (T
           (PROG (I)
                 (SETQ I (LENGTH A-LIST))
             LOOP
                 (COND ((GT I 0)
                           (TEST-RULE (EVAL (CAR RULE-LIST))
                                             (CAR A-LIST))
                           (SETQ A-LIST (CDR A-LIST))
                           (SETQ I (- I 1))
                           (GO LOOP))

                       (T
                           (RETURN NIL)))))))))
```

The function has been defined iteratively and can be seen to operate on successive objects in the list of relatives, until all of those objects have been applied to TEST-RULE with one rule (CAR RULE-LIST). The function terminates when all objects have been so tested, i.e. when the loop control variable I has been reduced to zero. The function used BOUNDP to ensure that the rule identifier has been previously bound to a value, i.e the actual rule.

Yet another outer loop is required to control the selection of the rule to be used by USE-RULES. This could, of course, be incorporated directly in USE-RULES, by an outer iterative loop, or as higher level recursion. Again, however, for reasons of overall clarity, this outer loop will be abstracted and treated as a separate function.

4.3.4 Do-Job

This is the extreme outermost loop as depicted in Figure 4.3. It represents the highest level of responsibility in the 'responsibility hierarchy' implied in that diagram. Its function has been deliberately rendered simple by the expediency of function abstraction. A very simple algorithm is all that is required.

Problem :

To control the application of rules within a specified rule list to successive objects and their property list values, within a list of objects. Each rule must be applied to ALL objects in the list until ALL rules have been applied. The sequence must then terminate.

Solution :

The function will require, as arguments, a rule list and a list of objects. Assuming the existence of all lower-level functions, the task is fairly simple. A loop must be set up with the length of the rule list as the loop control variable (for iteration). USE-RULES must be repeatedly invoked with the list of objects and a continually modified rule list (via (CDR RULE- LIST)), until all rules have been applied. This function may well be invoked directly from the keyboard.

INPUT :   KEYBOARD -
             The function name plus arguments :
             1. The rule list identifier
             2. The list of relatives

             ENVIRONMENT -
             As above, if used from a higher level function

113

OUTPUT :   DISPLAY - None (possibly)

ENVIRONMENT -
Whatever modifications to the existing environment are defined in
ACTION

BEGIN
    Repeat the following until all the rules have been applied :
        Invoke USE-RULES, sending to it the list of rules and the list of relatives
        Modify the rule list by removing the CAR of the list of rules
END

An iterative function has been defined to accomplish this sequence :

```
(DEFUN DO-JOB (LAMBDA (RULE-LIST A-LIST)
   (COND ((NULL RULE-LIST) NIL)
         ((NULL A-LIST) NIL)
         (T
           (PROG (I)
              (SETQ I (LENGTH RULE-LIST))
           LOOP
              (COND ((GT I 0)
                      (USE-RULES RULE-LIST A-LIST)
                      (SETQ RULE-LIST (CDR RULE-LIST))
                      (SETQ I (- I 1))
                      (GO LOOP))
                    (T
                      (RETURN NIL)))))))))
```

The function has the benefit of the usual error checking facilities. Iteration begins by
setting the control variable I, to the length of the rule list. The body of the loop
repeatedly invokes USE-RULES on the list of relatives and the current CDR of the
rule list.

At this stage, we have a simple control structure, dedicated to the problem of finding
the root of the family tree. By virtue of early and detailed thought on the rest of the
problem in hand, we can be reasonably sure that this painstakingly developed
structure will be applicable to the next part of the problem - that of actually building
the family tree. A structured development process has been rigidly adhered to.

4.3.5 Action

Before considering the second, and perhaps more interesting part of the problem, we
have yet to decide on, and define the function ACTION, which will be used to carry
out the tasks defined in each of the rule's THEN clause. The necessity for ACTION

has been identified, and fairly detailed considerations have already been made in this text. It has been decided to incorporate the function ACTION within the function TEST-RULE. The function is to be called from TEST-RULES with the following single argument :

```
(CAR (CDAR (CDDDR RULE)))
```

where the rule in question must conform to the very strict rule format as described in this chapter.

Let us examine the THEN clauses of the rules identified so far in the search for the root of the family tree :

```
RULE-1   IF ..........
              THEN
                    THE INDIVIDUAL IS A DEFINITE POSSIBILITY

RULE-2   IF ..........
              THEN
                    THAT COUPLE IS THE ORIGINAL (couple)

RULE-3   IF ..........
              THEN
                    THAT INDIVIDUAL IS THE ROOT
```

and expanding this analysis to the two further rules :

```
RULE-4   IF ..........
(and 5)       THEN
                    INDIVIDUAL IS ONE OF THE NEW-GENERATION
```

The action, or THEN clause is identical in format in all cases. The action can be conveniently re-phrased as :

```
INCLUDE INDIVIDUAL(S) IN SPECIFIED LIST
```

where the specified list could be the list of initial possibilities as specified in rule one, or a list of one object, the goal object (ROOT) as specified in rule three. In actual fact, this provides an excellent means of FORWARD CHAINING, where each newly-created/modified list becomes the next assertion for the subsequent rule to use. An evaluation of the LISP expression comprising the THEN clause should be carried out therefore, on a function which could conveniently be called INCLUDE. This function should be capable of appending a specified individual to a specified list. Therefore, the arguments are likely to be those items. An algorithm will serve to clarify :

Problem :

To include an individual, which has 'passed the test' (or tests) specified in a given rule, on a list of objects which have similarly behaved.

Solution :

A function is required to include, on a specified list, the specified individual. Simply use CONS.

INPUT :   KEYBOARD - None

ENVIRONMENT
A list and an object

OUTPUT :   DISPLAY - None

ENVIRONMENT -
the list with the supplied object added to it (the head)

BEGIN
    Use the LISP primitive function CONS to place the object supplied onto the front or head of the supplied list
END

The extreme simplicity of the algorithm is reflected in the function. The function should, perhaps, have the benefit of some error checking, but this has not been built into INCLUDE :

```
(DEFUN INCLUDE (LAMBDA (INDIVIDUAL TEMP-LIST)
    (CONS (INDIVIDUAL TEMP-LIST))))
```

One slight variation of the above function is required however, due to our simplified determination of the original couple from the list of originals. The relevant rule does not involve cross checking. Therefore, a function is required, which embodies INCLUDE, but includes two persons. These persons are, of course, a married couple. The function for this task is easy to define from the previous algorithm and the requirements of the system :

```
(DEFUN COLLATE-COUPLES (LAMBDA (INDIVIDUAL TEMP-LIST)
    (PROG (I)
        (SETQ I (GET INDIVIDUAL 'MARRIED))
```

```
(RETURN (CONS INDIVIDUAL (CAR (CONS I TEMP-
LIST))))))))
```

A very small modification to INCLUDE.

4.3.6 Final Rule Structure

In the forward chaining system, new assertions are produced in the form of lists, as the outcome of each rule 'firing'. It would be straightforward, and perhaps reasonable to define a list, called say, ASSERTIONS, which would be seen to expand or contract as each rule is applied. However in the interests of system verification and evaluation, it would also be possible to arrange for a separate list to be maintained for each rule. This approach is, perhaps, wasteful in memory space and may even appear inelegant, but it does provide a means of incremental verification, i.e. each list is available for inspection after the suite of functions are executed. Of course, to provide this level of 'permanence', each list would have to be defined as global free variables. Not good practice generally, but in this case, highly useful.

The means for the rule interpreter to recognise a rule's 'source list' already exists in the rule format chosen :

```
(IF LIST ((ANTECEDENT-1) ( .......
```

The CADR of the rule gives us a list identifier - the SOURCE list. The destination list can be easily catered for by specifying it as one of the arguments supplied when invoking INCLUDE. For example :

```
(INCLUDE INDIVIDUAL POSSIBILITIES)
```

The CADDR of this ACTION expression yields the desired destination list. The whole expression takes on a clear meaning. It says quite simply :

```
INCLUDE THE INDIVIDUAL ON THE LIST CALLED POSSIBILITIES
```

For test purposes therefore, we can define three lists, which may be inspected later to verify correct system behaviour. The list below details the rules defined in the root finding system, and alongside each rule is shown the list defined as the destination list :

```
RULE-1 ......... POSSIBILITIES
RULE-2 ......... ORIGINALS
RULE-3 ......... ROOT
```

The rule format, in its completed form, is as shown in Figure 4.4 and represents the definitive set of rules 1 to 3. The THEN clauses of the rules of Figure 4.4 are catered for by the ACTION function, and all necessary functions have been defined at this point.

Rule-1 :
```
(IF POSSIBILITIES
    ((FATHER IS RECORDED AS 'NIL)
     (MOTHER IS RECORDED AS 'NIL)
     (MARRIED PARTNER IS RECORDED AS (NON-NIL))
     (CHILDREN ARE RECORDED AS (NON-NIL))
  (THEN
     (INCLUDE INDIVIDUAL POSSIBILITIES)))
```

Rule-2 :
```
(IF POSSIBILITIES
    ((MARRIED TO ONE OF THE OTHER
                (RECORDED 'MARRIED POSSIBILITIES)))
  (THEN
     (COLLATE-COUPLES INDIVIDUAL ORIGINALS)))
```

Rule-3 :
```
(IF ORIGINALS
    ((SEX IS MALE))
  (THEN
     (INCLUDE INDIVIDUAL ROOT)))
```

Figure 4.4 Rules are one to three in rule base ROOTS

At this stage, it is instructive to test the efficacy of the rule- based system by adding another rule to the list of rules (RULE-4). Let us find and list the first generation after the root object. The rule is very simple :

IF - THE FATHER OF THE INDIVIDUAL IS THE ROOT OF THE FAMILY TREE
THEN - THAT INDIVIDUAL IS ONE OF THE NEXT GENERATION

and in the strict rule format articulated here :

RULE-4

```
(IF FULL-COPY ((FATHER IS RECORDED AS THE ROOT))
    (THEN
            (INCLUDE INDIVIDUAL FIRST-ONES)))
```

The CADR of rule four must be a full copy of all the relatives, and FIRST- ONES will be the list of all the children of the original person in the information base defined by rules 1 to 3 (ROOT).

The list of rules has yet to be created. It will incorporate rules 1 to 3 to enable the system to find the root object, and it will include this new rule (rule 4). The rules must, obviously, be arranged in strict order :

```
(SETQ ROOTS '(RULE1 RULE2 RULE3 RULE4))
```

In view of these enhancements to the rule format, an enhancement can be made to the outermost (or uppermost) function DO-JOB. These modifications are,specifically :

```
    :     :
    :     :
    :     :
(PROG (I V)
    :     :
    (SETQ V A-LIST)
    (SETQ FULL-COPY (APPEND V (SETQ FULL-COPY
    NIL)))
LOOP
    :     :
    (SETQ V
        (EVAL (CADR (EVAL (CAR RULE-LIST)))))) 
    :     :
```

Within the PROG sequence, one of the local variables, V is assigned the value A-LIST. From here, a completely new copy is made via APPEND. the second enhancement appears within the LOOP. For each iteration, the local variable V is assigned the source list as defined in each rule. By this means, only those individuals required to have consecutive rules applied to them are 'dispatched' to USE-RULES.

Intermediate lists are modified in the course of the search for the root of the tree. The contents of these lists represents the current understanding of the relationships within the information base and may be visualised as intermediate conclusions. These lists are, currently :

POSSIBILITIES - Those persons who 'might' be the root of the tree .

ORIGINALS - The married couple who represent the 'first couple' .

ROOT - The MALE partner of ORIGINALS (say) .

FIRST-ONES - The immediate next generation after ROOT.

It would be possible to ensure that new lists for each of the intermediate steps are automatically created during execution of the relevant function in the hierarchy of Figure 4.3. In this way, the list identifier, which appears as the CADR of each rule, automatically becomes initiated when required and made available for processing thereafter. It would also be possible for the system to use one list only. However, it is much easier, for our purposes, to initialise all result lists at the outermost level. The easiest method for this would be with the use of a dedicated initialisation function, which will be called INIT-LIST. If a known set of lists were required, a very simple function could be defined. For example :

```
(DEFUN INIT-LIST (LAMBDA ()
    (SETQ FIRST-ONES
        (SETQ ROOT
            (SETQ ORIGINALS
                (SETQ POSSIBILITIES NIL))))))
```

However, this is far too limited to be of any value whatsoever. What, for instance would occur, if a new rule were to be included in the system at some later stage? With the rule format chosen and adhered to in this chapter, the source and destination lists are included in the rule. This is a powerful technique and provides a versatile facility for rule-base expansion. Of course, a knowledge of the temporary lists in use would be an advantage, but this could easily be provided to the user via some sort of rule explanation function.

In order to retain flexibility, ease of use, and most importantly, ease of maintenance, the information coded into the rule base will be utilised to the full. The important points to recognise are :

1. Each rule is a member of a list of rules bound to an identifier .

2. Each rule has, incorporated into it, the source and destination temporary lists which it operates on. The identifiers of those temporary lists are in a standard position within the list which makes up the rule.

Therefore, it is possible for a function to be defined, capable of inspecting the two positions representing source and destination lists of each rule, and performing the initialisation of each list in turn. Using iteration, the function which may be used for this purpose is as below :

```
(DEFUN INIT-LIST (LAMBDA (RULE-LIST)
    (COND ((NULL RULE-LIST) NIL)
          (T
              (PROG (I)
                  (SETQ I (LENGTH RULE-LIST)))
              LOOP
                  (COND ((GT I 0)
```

```
(SET (CADR (EVAL (CAR RULE-LIST))) NIL)
(SET (CAR (LAST (CADAR
(CDDDR (EVAL (CAR RULE-LIST))))))) NIL)
(SETQ RULE-LIST (CDR RULE-LIST))
(SETQ I (- I 1))
(GO LOOP))
(T
(RETURN NIL)))))))))
```

where, in the body of the iterative loop, the two lists mentioned in each rule are initialised to NIL. The necessary 'surgical tools' are :

```
- (SET (CADR (EVAL (CAR RULE-LIST))) NIL)

- (SET (CAR (LAST (CADAR (CDDDR (EVAL (CAR RULE-
                   LIST)))))) NIL)
```

These two nested expressions may appear to be rather 'heavy-weight', but if the strict rule format is adhered to, they can be used without worry. One possible cause for concern is related to the powerful means of data modification used. The use of SET will initialise, or change the value of a global free variable. The side effects are dramatic. Care must be taken to ensure that original and valuable lists within the information base are NOT INCLUDED in any rule. It was partially for this reason that the following modification was made to DO-JOB :

```
(SETQ FULL-COPY (APPEND V (SETQ FULL-COPY NIL)))
```

Where V is a local variable within the iterative loop bound to the list RELATIVES (if RELATIVES is an argument sent to DO-JOB). The nested expression above merely creates a copy of the list, which is not therefore EQUAL to the original. INIT-LIST will find use in the overall controlling function which will be used to invoke, first the root-finding sequence, and then the tree building mechanism.

4.4 Summary

The system developed in this chapter is capable of performing the tasks required in the solution to the problem as specified in the algorithms outlined. The emphasis has been on the logical development methodologies, which are considered to be essential to the successful design and implementation of a knowledge-based system. The system described here is dedicated to a problem which may appear to be 'beneath' a strategy optimised for highly complex and unstructured problem domains. Indeed, it would probably be far easier to implement such a system with traditional implementation languages, but the overwhelming advantage of the rule-based approach is its flexibility. The versatility of this approach was highlighted by the ease with which a new rule could be added to the rule base to carry out the classification of another group of people. The actual rule base, and the order in which they are presented to the control structure represent true knowledge of the task represented in the various algorithms. Finally, the system can be seen to be DATA DRIVEN in that each rule requires partial conclusion data from its immediate predecessor. If any rule is prevented from 'firing' then the system is rendered incapable of reaching a final conclusion, even though intermediate conclusions are available by virtue of a deliberate attempt to provide some future means of introspection.

Chapter Five

A Forward Chaining System

5.1 Introduction

An intelligent problem solving system is said to be functioning as a FORWARD
CHAINING system if it starts with a structured set of information, in the form of
assertions, and tries all available rules within a rule base, adding or modifying
assertions as it goes, until no rule applies. At this stage, a conclusion of some kind
exists. By its very definition, when no rule is applicable, then no more new
assertions can be made to aid the solution process. In the rule-based system of the
previous chapter, the rules were used in turn until the last rule had been applied. This
type of system, although data driven, cannot really be classified as a true forward
chaining process according to the definition above. It could be treated as some kind of
search process with an 'all or nothing' task. However, as we saw in the later parts of
that chapter, the use of a rule base and a controlling structure endowed the system
with capabilities, perhaps more conceptual than proven. It was amenable to
modification, both in its rule expression and in its overall outcome. In effect, the
actual meaningful part of the solution was seen to be totally reflected in the rules.
The control system eventually became 'transparent' to us as problem solvers, once the
structure of the complete, integrated system had been developed, tested and trusted. In
other words, we were able to express the solution totally by the rules, articulated in
the most human-legible form and in a meaningful order. In this chapter, a true forward
chaining system will be developed, based on a separate rule base.

5.2 The Family Tree

The next part of the overall system, which has been specified to produce a family tree,
will require the assignation of the ROOT object. The problem could be tackled with
the aid of a conventional search algorithm, defined either as a depth first or breadth
first process, as described in the previous chapter. The technique of expedition will be
accomplished in this chapter with the aid of a rule base and using the control structure
designed primarily for the root finding system.

In the early stages of system design, the requirements for this second part were
considered in some detail. An adherence to these principles has resulted in a
standardisation which will increase overall utility and ease future maintenance.

At this stage, a general algorithm is required in order to provide an indication of the optimal sequence of events and to guide the refinement process.

Problem :

To search through the information base, identifying relationships and providing an output (to the display) sufficiently detailed to indicate the tree structure. The root of this tree structure has already been determined in the previous part of the system. The process should terminate when all relatives have been categorised and output.

Solution :

An essentially depth first search from the root object down to the last (youngest) generation will be used. A search and display will be made down each branch of the tree until the youngest generation is identified, i.e. no children. These objects will be output along with their parents and then removed from the 'local information base'. The control structure will operate iteratively on a decreasing information base until either no rules apply, or all the objects in the information base have been removed. This latter condition also results in inapplicable rules.

INPUT :   KEYBOARD -
             The function name plus arguments :
             1. The rule list identifier ;
             2. The list of relatives.

             ENVIRONMENT -
             Possibly all the information above plus :
             The ROOT object.

OUTPUT :   DISPLAY -
             Family relationship information in the form of hierarchically-
             structured data.

             ENVIRONMENT - None

BEGIN
     Repeat the following for all persons in the information base, who belong to the
     family of the person recorded as ROOT :
     Repeat the following for each 'branch' of the family tree :
          Find and display the next generation down, plus their parents.
          Remove those persons from the list of persons to be identified.
END

Since the end of any branch represents a terminating condition in a depth first search, it should be possible to modify the information base in such a way that, once those individuals have been identified and displayed, further searches do not go that far, or even in that direction. With such a philosophy, the way is open to apply a forward chaining system which relies on each pass of the rules, on a modified information base. The modified (reduced) information base presents a new set of facts (assertions) to the rules, thereby providing a data driven sequence. The system will have reached a conclusion when no rules have fired on a complete pass of the rule list. The terminating condition may, or may not correspond to the situation where each person in the information base has been categorised. It may well be the case that not all those objects belong to the family of ROOT.

The rules required to expedite the task have already been discussed in the previous chapter and are quite simple. They require, on the first pass, a complete list of individuals, but on subsequent passes that list will be modified. Therefore a FULL-COPY will be provided in the first instance. FULL-COPY has been defined and catered for in DO-JOB. Therefore, we can use this list in the rules for tree building. The rules required to carry out this task are :

```
RULE-5    (IF  FULL-COPY
              ((FATHER  IS  ONE  OF  THE  OLDER-GENERATION))
              (THEN  (INCLUDE  INDIVIDUAL  NEXT-GENERATION)))
```

The same rule applies to RULE-6, with the one exception of MOTHER being one of the current older generation. If DO-JOB is used for each pass of the rule list, then some points are worthy of consideration :

1.   FULL-COPY is the source list .

2.   NEXT-GEN will be the destination list .

3.   The last object in the FATHER IS .... antecedent must be either a valid property list value or a function invocation (enclosed in brackets).

The FULL-COPY list has already been catered for in DO-JOB and NEXT-GEN will be automatically initialised by INIT-LIST. However, those persons rightly belonging in the categories OLD-GEN and NEXT-GEN are very much dependent on the hierarchy level reached at any one time. The contents of those categories are dynamic. In fact, the algorithm shows that it is this very dynamism which is the basis for our forward chaining system. If OLD-GEN and NEXT-GEN are assigned as lists and used in the obvious context, the sequence of events, as the system 'ripples down' a relationship branch can be expressed in algorithmic form. For each generation, or hierarchy level down :

1. The current NEXT-GEN becomes the new OLD-GEN .

2. The new NEXT-GEN has not yet been determined. Therefore, initialise it to NIL.

3. Find the children of the new OLD-GEN and include them in the initialised NEXT-GEN.

The sequence of events 1 to 3 requires an outer controlling loop to invoke them either iteratively or recursively until the tree is determined.

5.3 The Control Structure

The control structure defined for the root finding system provides an efficient single pass facility and will form the basis of the control structure of this part of the problem. It was deliberately designed with this purpose in mind right from the start.

DO-JOB requires arguments in the form of a rule list and a list which comprises the complete information base. Function abstraction will be used to optimise clarity as in the previous chapter, and it is instructive to consider and construct a model of the overall system as performed with the root finding system. In fact, the model depicted in that section will be used over and over with each pass of the rule list, and provides yet another level of abstraction. These details will appear, in the system, to be totally transparent. That is, DO-JOB and all its consequent function calls will form one (major) abstract function, with well-documented specifications, to perform a specific task on a particular structured information base.

5.4 The Model

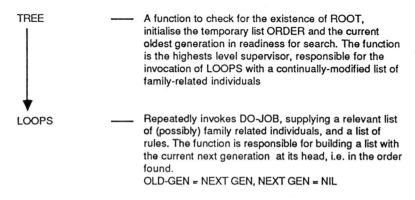

TREE —— A function to check for the existence of ROOT, initialise the temporary list ORDER and the current oldest generation in readiness for search. The function is the highests level supervisor, responsible for the invocation of LOOPS with a continually-modified list of family-related individuals

LOOPS —— Repeatedly invokes DO-JOB, supplying a relevant list of (possibly) family related individuals, and a list of rules. The function is responsible for building a list with the current next generation at its head, i.e. in the order found.
OLD-GEN = NEXT GEN, NEXT GEN = NIL

Figure 5.1 A suggested control structure for the family tree search system

The model is shown in outline in Figure 5.1. It incorporates at the lowest level, a loop which causes invocation of DO-JOB on a list of relatives, until the end of one branch of the tree is found. The terminating condition is clearly shown. This provides a consistent algorithmic model and illustrates each level of higher control. The model identifies five lists which are used by the system :

1.	ROOT	(from part 1)
2.	FIRST-ONES	(from part 1)
3.	ORDER	(used to provide a record of search path)
4.	OLD-GEN	(initially set to ROOT, but then modified dynamically)
5.	NEXT-GEN	(the next generation - initially NIL)

The first list above is available from the root finding process. NEXT-GEN is automatically initialise by INIT-LIST, but the other two are not specifically catered for in any of the other parts of the system as it exists at present. Both OLD-GEN and ORDER are initialised in the hierarchy level shown as TREE. This is a convenient place to carry out these initialisations - immediately prior to the function responsible for the repeated invocation of DO-JOB, and the inclusion of each new identified generation in the ORDER in which they are found (hence the identifier name). The intermediate step in the hierarchy (TREE) has the main task of information base modification after each invocation of LOOPS. By this means, the family will become ever-smaller, until no new relationships can be found. Notice that this stage is the ideal one for the provision of display output.

The objects to be removed are, effectively, the next generation and their parents. A simple PRINT function will suffice at this stage.

The highest level step (MAKE) has overall control over branch direction search.

5.5 Loops

Beginning at the bottom level, i.e. with the stage identified as LOOPS, the algorithm is :

Problem :

To invoke DO-JOB on the list of relatives, applying a list of rules developed specifically to facilitate traversal down the family tree. DO-JOB operates on temporary lists, and the lists incorporated into rules five and six use the lists FULL-COPY and NEXT-GEN. LOOPS will therefore be required to supply a relevant list of objects and a list of rules to DO-JOB. The dynamic contents of lists OLD-GEN and NEXT-GEN must be swapped in order to update the current state of knowledge, and the function will repeat until the youngest generation in that branch has been found, i.e. their CHILDREN property list value is NIL.

Solution :

Use an iterative control structure with the terminating condition of an empty OLD-GEN list. On first invocation, OLD-GEN will contain the ROOT object and will therefore only become NIL when the transferral of NEXT-GEN to OLD-GEN produces such a result. For each iteration, NEXT-GEN should be initialised to NIL prior to the invocation of DO-JOB.

A temporary list will be maintained throughout the traversal from one of the FIRST-ONES to the end branches (ORDER). The order in which the contents of ORDER are stored will be important in the next hierarchical step.

INPUT :   KEYBOARD - None

               ENVIRONMENT -
               A list of relatives
               A rule list

OUTPUT :   DISPLAY - None

               ENVIRONMENT -
               The lists OLD-GEN, NEXT-GEN and ORDER are modified

BEGIN
    Repeat the following until all generations are dealt with :
        Invoke DO-JOB to test the rules in the relevant rule list.
        Modify list NEXT-GEN.
        Include the individual selected by the rules and returned by DO-JOB in the list
          ORDER.
        Transfer the contents of NEXT-GEN to OLD-GEN.
        Set the contents of NEXT-GEN to NIL.
END

A suitable function designed to carry out the tasks outlined in this algorithm is :

```
(DEFUN LOOPS (LAMBDA (A-LIST RULE-LIST)
    (COND ((NULL A-LIST) NIL)
          ((NULL RULE-LIST) NIL)
          (T
              (PROG ()
              LOOP
                  (COND ((NOT (NULL OLD-GEN))
                          (DO-JOB RULE-LIST A-LIST)
                          (SETQ ORDER (CONS NEXT-GEN
                          ORDER))
```

```
                                (SETQ OLD-GEN NEXT-GEN)
                                (SETQ NEXT-GEN NIL)
                                (GO LOOP))
                 (T
                                (RETURN NIL))))))))
```

This function will provide, as side effects, suitably modified lists OLD- GEN, NEXT-GEN and ORDER. ORDER would appear, after the first invocation of LOOPS something like :

```
        (NIL (TOM-X EMMA-X FRED-X) (STEVE-X MIKE-X))
```

With reference to the family tree as illustrated in Figure 3.1, the structure of this list includes two lists representing two generations in the order in which they appear in that diagram.

5.6 Tree

The intermediate stage of the system hierarchy involves the system in the initialisation of ORDER for each new generation found in LOOPS. It will perform, essentially a depth first search via a parallel or 'level- shifting' process. The aim is to continually reduce the number of persons in the information base as each individual is detected as the current next generation. An application of the two rules (5 and 6) to this simple control structure will ensure that these basic operations will be carried out successfully :

1. All the individuals in the information base will be checked for belonging to the family of the individual stored as ROOT .

2. A family tree will be searched and categorised, no matter how many individuals are contained in the information base, and in what order.

The algorithm for TREE therefore is :

_____

Problem :

To perform the initialisation of the temporary list ORDER and the list OLD- GEN. To repeatedly invoke LOOPS with a modified information base which has the last detected new generation plus the parent removed. To incorporate a suitable loop control to facilitate termination at the correct time, and possibly to incorporate the output of interesting information.

Solution :

The function will take three arguments :

1. A list of relatives .
2. An initial object for OLD-GEN (usually ROOT).

Within the loop, the value of OLD-GEN will be re-initialised to the specified original value, and the temporary list ORDER will be re- initialised to NIL prior to re-setting during execution of LOOPS. The youngest generation and their parent will be removed, using REMOVE as defined earlier.

INPUT :   KEYBOARD -
               A list of relatives
               A list of rules
               A ROOT object

               ENVIRONMENT -
               A modified list as returned by REMOVE

OUTPUT :   DISPLAY -
               Whatever informative output is required to verify system operation

               ENVIRONMENT - None

BEGIN
       Initialise lists. ORDER = NIL, OLD-GEN = ROOT
       Repeat the following until all the objects in ORDER have been removed :
            Invoke LOOPS to traverse the next branch of the tree
            Print the objects in a meaningful order
            Remove the youngest generation and parent for the next iteration
END

A suitable function, iterative in nature is :

```
(DEFUN TREE (LAMBDA (A-LIST RULE-LIST START-POINT)
   (COND ((NULL A-LIST) NIL)
         ((NULL START-POINT) (PRINT "NO ROOT FOUND"))
         (T
            (PROG ()
            LOOP
               (SETQ OLD-GEN START-POINT)
               (SETQ ORDER NIL)
               (LOOPS A-LIST RULE-LIST)
```

```
(COND ((CADDR ORDER)
            (LOOPS A-LIST RULE-LIST)
            (PRINT (CONS (CAR (CADDR ORDER))
                  (CADR ORDER)))
            (SETQ A-LIST (REMOVE
                  (CONS (CAR (CADDR ORDER))
                  (CADR ORDER)))
            (GO LOOP))
        (T
            (RETURN NIL)))))))))
```

In the function TREE above, one invocation is made before the loop control COND function, to prevent the function terminating immediately on a NULL CADDR order, as it would if it were immediately preceded by :

```
(SETQ ORDER NIL)
```

Remove is called to remove the persons required for the next loop, and before that occurs, those persons are output to the display. This very simple output serves to demonstrate the progress made by the system in its 'travels' around the family tree structure coded into the information base, and also gives information to the user which is highly relevant to the solution sought after.

5.6.1 Progress

If the function TREE is invoked with the following arguments :

1.   The list of relatives corresponding to the family tree defined earlier .

2.   A rule list containing the previously-defined rules 5 and 6 (GENS) .

3.   The ROOT object list provided from the first part (ROOT).

    then, the following output will be seen on the display screen :

```
((MIKE-X STEVE-X))
((CHARLES-X GRAHAM-X ELSA-X GEORGE-X) (MIKE-X STEVE-X))
((DIANNE-X DAVE-X) (CHARLES-X GRAHAM-X ELSA-X GEORGE-X)
      (MIKE-X STEVE-X))

((MIKE-X STEVE-X))
((GRAHAM-X ELSA-X GEORGE-X) (MIKE-X STEVE-X))
((JAMES-X LISA-X) (GRAHAM-X ELSA-X GEORGE-X) (MIKE-X
      STEVE-X))

((MIKE-X STEVE-X))
```

```
((ELSA-X GEORGE-X) (MIKE-X STEVE-X))
((TIM-G SALLY-G) (ELSA-X GEORGE-X) (MIKE-X STEVE-X))

((MIKE-X STEVE-X))
((GEORGE-X) (MIKE-X STEVE-X))
((TINA-X) (GEORGE-X) (STEVE-X))

((MIKE-X STEVE-X))
```

The function invoked from the keyboard has traversed the branch whose root is MIKE-X. The upper level control structure MAKE, makes sure that all branches are covered.

5.7 Make

This function provides the higher level of Figure 5.1. It is responsible for the utilisation of the list FIRST-ONES, which has been discussed in the previous chapter. It merely invokes TREE with each member of FIRST-ONES until all the further generations of FIRST-ONES have been categorised. The algorithm for this level is very simple indeed :

Problem :

To invoke TREE on successive members of the immediate next generation after ROOT. Each of these individuals in turn, effectively becomes the new root of identical branch searching sequences.

Solution :

With an iterative control loop, a local variable will be initialised as a list containing the individuals previously identified in the root finding system. After each iteration of the loop, the head of the list is removed with the utility REM-OBJ1 before invoking TREE. The family tree is complete when FIRST-ONES is emptied. In addition to the required list of relatives and rules, the function will take, as an argument, the starting point in the process, which may not be ROOT. By this means, it will be possible to use MAKE to determine and display a selected subset of the family tree.

INPUT :   KEYBOARD -
            A list of relatives
            A list of rules
            A list of one object which is to be used as ROOT

            ENVIRONMENT -
            Possibly the above values if used from a higher level function
            Otherwise none

132

OUTPUT :   DISPLAY - None directly

ENVIRONMENT - None directly

BEGIN
    Repeat the following for all members of the immediate next generation after
    ROOT
        Invoke the sequence beginning with TREE
        Remove the root of that branch
END

With the expediency of removing the current start object within the list created by
TREE, i.e. the root of each specific branch of the tree, the control structure and rule
list can be invoked repeatedly. The function developed for this algorithm is defined
iteratively and is shown below :

```
(DEFUN MAKE (LAMBDA (RELATIONS RULE-LIST GEN)
   (COND ((NULL RELATIONS) NIL)
         ((NULL RULE-LIST) NIL)
         (T
           (PROG (X)
             (SETQ X FIRST-ONES)
           LOOP
             (COND ((NOT (NULL X))
                     (TREE RELATIONS RULE-LIST GEN)
                     (SETQ RELATIONS
                         (REM-OBJ1 FULL-COPY (CAR X)))
                     (SETQ X (CDR X))
                     (GO LOOP))
                   (T
                     (RETURN NIL))))))))
```

5.8 A Top Level Control

A suitable function, capable of completing the task of family tree determination,
which involves the suite of functions designed to find the root, and those to complete
the categorisation, albeit via the display, is very easy to define without the aid of a
separate algorithm. The general algorithm which appears at the beginning of the
previous chapter will suffice. A function could be defined, which supplies the correct
lists to each of the highest level functions in both sections. For example :

```
(DEFUN TRIBES (LAMBDA ()
   (PROG ()
      (INIT-LIST ROOTS)
      (DO-JOB ROOTS RELATIVES)
```

```
(MAKE RELATIVES GENS ROOT)
(RETURN 'DONE))))
```

The function calls beneath PROG ensure a correct sequence of events, starting with the initialisation of the lists as defined in all the rules within the rule base ROOTS. The second part of the system, controlled by MAKE does not, as it happens, require initialisation. It could, of course, be catered for with no harmful effects with the additional line :

```
(INIT-LIST GENS)
```

With the use of TRIBES, the family tree may be re-determined at any time without corruption of the information base or the original lists. After the system has been executed, the lists :

POSSIBILITIES
ORIGINALS
ROOT
FIRST-ONES

remain with their values intact, as assigned by the system in the course of operation. It may be noticed that the output lists contain the direct relations of our root object. It would be simple to access the MARRIED property in order to print the name of each partner (if they exist).

5.9 Application

It would be quite possible to design another part to the system, capable of determining the precise relationships between two persons in the information base. For example, given two names, it could be required to return the following type of information :

```
INDIVIDUAL X IS THE GRANDFATHER OF INDIVIDUAL Y

                    OR

INDIVIDUAL X IS THE FIRST COUSIN OF INDIVIDUAL Y
```

It could even be directed to find a person who corresponds to a relationship value associated with a given individual. For example :

```
FIND THE PERSON WHO IS THE GRANDMOTHER OF INDIVIDUAL Z
```

The control structure would have to be modified to accomplish this, but enough standardisation has been built into the system to facilitate it with the minimum of effort.

Another possibility, not required in the simple problem addressed here is the dynamic use of the list manipulation functions developed to create and modify the information base. If the system were to be given the facility of ABDUCTION or INDUCTION, then it may have at its disposal, enough 'surgical tools' to enable it to dynamically expand, contract or modify the information base. The system is capable of incorporating all these facilities at some later time. This feature of rule-based systems is very important in the long-term utility of the system in a problem domain which is usually only partially understood at the implementation time. This capability of INCREMENTAL DEVELOPMENT is one of the most important advantages of this approach to the solution of 'complex' problems and will ensure its use in the future.

Heuristics are not recognisable in the system. This is because all the rules are based on antecedents which we, as experts, know to be true. We have, in effect, incorporated our own expertise into the rules, and perhaps more importantly, into the way those rules are applied. We have produced a knowledge-based system which uses a particular strategy to arrive at the specified conclusion, with the aid of PRODUCTION RULES. The system can be described as an EXPERT SYSTEM, even though the knowledge can be seen to be generally owned. Further rules may, of course be defined, on the basis of pure heuristics. For example, the rules below, which are not presented in the strict format required of the system developed here, could be used to find various classes of persons within the information base :

```
IF -- THE INDIVIDUAL IS CREDITED WITH MORE THAN TWO
       CHILDREN
THEN -- THAT INDIVIDUAL LIKES LARGE FAMILIES
IF -- THE INDIVIDUAL'S OCCUPATION IS PROPERTY
       -DEVELOPER
THEN -- THAT INDIVIDUAL IS RICH
```

These two outline rules are, of course, based purely on heuristics, but they do appear reasonable. Consider the following rule :

```
IF -- THE INDIVIDUAL'S BIRTH-DATE IS LESS THAN 19xx
THEN -- THAT INDIVIDUAL IS PROBABLY NO LONGER ALIVE
```

Notice the keyword PROBABLY. One could arrive at a conclusion with a
CERTAINTY factor, based perhaps on some knowledge of the average life span of
individuals. It could include more facts pertinent to a more thorough life span
calculation, for example, SEX and OCCUPATION. Even more intriguing would be
the inclusion of the previous family history. In fact, this particular system could be
developed into an expert system able to assist in GENETIC COUNSELLING. That
is, it could trace back (or forward) into the family tree and search for individuals
showing a specific familial trait. The rules of (genetic) inheritance for some human
characteristics are quite complex, but others are not so difficult to understand. It
should be possible, with a suitably complete information base, to apply quantitative
rules to determine the likelihood of a particular trait or syndrome appearing in the
next generation. The application of specific rules may involve a high degree of
specialised knowledge in the form of detailed analytical techniques. Such a system
would be said to use DEEP KNOWLEDGE, i.e. would be able to determine
conclusions from 'first- principles', on the basis of specialised knowledge and
experience. Simple rules and heuristics are grouped as SHALLOW KNOWLEDGE.

The second part of the system: the part which traces the tree and produces an output
giving some indication of the tree structure, has been developed, deliberately, as a rule-
based system. In effect, we have implemented a search problem in a knowledge-based
manner. Most problems can be expressed as some form of hierarchy or tree
(sometimes called a GOAL TREE). The diagnosis of a medical problem starts with
the obvious, presenting symptoms, and by a process of question/answer, and/or the
results of specific clinical tests, a specific cause is identified. Indeed some of the
earliest expert systems were concerned with this type of problem. However, the
problem addressed in this chapter could have been successfully solved with a non-rule-
based approach. Search algorithms have been developed, capable of tracing from a
specified root object in such a tree, down to a specified 'target', which in this case,
would be the youngest generation. For example, the function below takes, as
arguments, the root object and the target object. It searches through the information
base until it arrives at the target person. It does this by invoking a function called
OBTAIN, which merely GETs the listed children of the current individual in the
search path :

```
(DEFUN BY-DEPTH (LAMBDA (BRANCH TARGET)
    (COND ((NULL BRANCH) NIL)
          ((EQUAL TARGET (CAR BRANCH)) T)
          (T
             (BY-DEPTH (APPEND (OBTAIN (CAR BRANCH))
                               (CDR BRANCH)) TARGET)))))
```

The required function OBTAIN is very simple. It is required to obtain the children of the individual specified as the calling argument :

```
(DEFUN OBTAIN (LAMBDA (INDIVIDUAL)
   (GET INDIVIDUAL 'CHILDREN)))
```

and a suitable outer controlling (or invoking) function may be used to instantiate a list for BRANCH.

```
(DEFUN SEARCH (LAMBDA (ROOT END)
   (BY-DEPTH (LIST ROOT) END)))
```

By virtue of the use of GET, which has a global effect, the actual list of objects need not be supplied as an argument.

This set of functions would represent a starting point for a system required to determine precise relationships, as discussed earlier. It requires some kind of reporting facility, an output of the dynamic list BRANCH. Such output could be directed to a controlling system capable of applying rules to the list at each level to determine relationships, and could be responsible for re-direction of the search path. The COUSINS problem would be typical of a search which would not be totally top-down, but would have to be capable of bottom-up search. The control structure would direct this operation.

5.9.1 Procedural Attachment

In the system developed in this chapter, functions are invoked by the control structure to carry out such tasks as DO-JOB and USE-RULES, etc. They are required to perform certain essential tasks required of the particular solution. Function invocation is also carried out via the rules. The rules themselves cause function calls to be made in order to perform list manipulation and search processes. For example, in RULE1 :

```
(IF ...... (MARRIED PARTNER IS RECORDED AS (NON-NIL))
```

The last word in that statement, NON-NIL is a function call. The control structure has been designed to recognise this fact and to act upon it. The relevant controlling function in this case is TEST-ANTECEDENT, and control is passed to the relevant function (NON-NIL in this example) by virtue of the following OR clause

```
(EQUAL (EVAL (CAR (LAST ANTECEDENT))) T)
```

Other examples of function calls being implicit in rules can be found in all the rules outlined in this text. Not only do function calls appear in the IF... clauses of the production rules, but they also appear in the action clauses. For example :

```
(INCLUDE INDIVIDUAL POSSIBILITIES)
(COLLATE-COUPLES INDIVIDUAL ORIGINALS)
(DISPLAY INDIVIDUAL NEXT-GEN)
```

It would appear to be quite difficult in fact, to design the system in such a way that calls to previously-developed functions need not be made. It is this facility which gives direction advice to the control structure.

The family tree system, at its current state of development, has been shown to have 'potential'. Any new facility not already catered for in the present environment can quite easily be added by virtue of our 'standardisation' philosophy. However, the potential of the system could be extended still further by incorporating function call directives in the information base itself. There are two major considerations to be made at this stage. These are : INHERITANCE and PROCEDURAL ATTACHMENT.

5.9.2 Inheritance

Inheritance, as applied to knowledge-based systems, can be visualised with the aid of an ASSOCIATIVE NETWORK. A very small part of the information base used in this chapter is shown in the form of an associative network in Figure 5.2. It is plain to see why this type of diagram is so called. It represents an excellent way of visually identifying associations. However, in addition to this, it also highlights the possibility of inheritance. In the diagram, LISA-X is shown as an INST of (RELATIVE OF JOHN-X), who, it may be recalled, is the ROOT of our family tree.

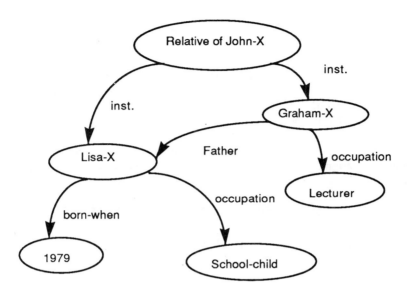

Figure 5.2

Let us consider the question which may be asked of an intelligent system :

```
IS -- LISA-X FINANCIALLY RICH ?

OR

DOES -- LISA-X HAVE MORE THAN 4 WEEKS HOLIDAY PER YEAR ?
```

The information required to reach a satisfactory conclusion is not present, directly, in the information base. However, with reference to the associative network, the reader would be in no doubt that, since LISA-X is a school child, she is bound to have more than four weeks' holiday per year, because we have some knowledge about the class of person SCHOOL- CHILD. We can infer, with (almost) certainty, that LISA-X's periods of academic inactivity extend far beyond four weeks. Those attributes are said to be INHERITED by LISA-X by virtue of the 'class' to which she belongs. Similarly, if we had information relating to JOHN-X such as :

```
            JOHN-X IS A WEALTHY PROPERTY TYCOON
```

then, we can infer that all of his direct offspring share, to some extent, in his fortune. That is, if the family is rich, then all those persons belonging to the class (RELATIVE OF JOHN-X) are also rich. That attribute is perhaps more easy to recognise as an inherited one.

In knowledge-based systems, the concept of inheritance is extremely important. It serves both to rationalise the information base and also to ease maintenance through the facility of standardisation. Many relevant facts can be associated with a class.

5.9.3 Implications of Procedural Attachment

With reference to the associative network of Figure 5.2, we can see one other striking possibility. If the question is asked :

```
                    HOW OLD IS LISA-X ?
```

again, the answer is not directly available in the information base. We do however, have access to the birth date of LISA-X, and from this we can arrive at an approximate solution :

```
         AGE = (CURRENT YEAR) - (BIRTH YEAR)
```

Using this approximation, the maximum error would be almost one year. The key word that springs to mind in this application is CALCULATE. The calculation required could be invoked directly by the control system, but could also be facilitated, perhaps more appropriately, with an IF-NEEDED property list value bound to each object. The control system, on accessing an IF-NEEDED property list value, would look for more information within that list of property list values, such as CALCULATE. Once calculated, the choice, as far as the system designer is concerned, is whether to merely use the results of that calculation or use the list manipulation toolkit to modify the information base. In effect, this would involve the use of the specialised list modification utilities to replace the IF-NEEDED value with the numerical value resulting from the calculation of age. If the first of these alternatives is used, the relative advantages and disadvantages are :

1. The system always calculates results from first principles, i.e. from the minimum data representation. If the value input to the information base is later found to be incorrect, then the new value can be placed without the extra stage of calculation.

2. The age value will change from year to year. This is usually not a problem for genealogists. They tend to be more interested in longevity (death-year - birth - year). But even so, it is applicable to the youngest generation who may be surviving.

The disadvantages are quite significant :

1. Calculations invoked by procedural attachment slow the system down quite considerably.

2. More complexity is required of the system at the design stage.

These points should not deter the eager knowledge-based system designer from exploring all possibilities.

5.10 Summary

The system developed and described in this chapter has been defined as a forward chaining rule-based system, which depends on new information being presented for each rule in the sequence to operate on. If this information is interpreted loosely as being in the form of assertions, then the system is also recognisable as data driven.

The rule base has been implemented in the strict format laid down in the previous chapter, and the order in which those rules are listed is important. However, this does not pose any problems, at least not in the domain as specified here. Indeed, the very ordering of the rules gives a meaning to the solution strategy.

There are several deficiencies in the system as it appears up to this point :

1. There is no overall control mechanism which can be used to easily produce a new information base or modify an existing one. The tools required to accomplish this are present however, and they have been used on a 'stand-alone' basis for the creation of RELATIVES. The system developed for this function has been omitted in this chapter and directed to a specialised chapter dealing with suitable user- interfaces.

2. The output of the system so far is anything but exciting. The display is used to output lists at various stages in the tree search process, and this gives an adequate indication of system progress. For example, each list, output via the function TREE, will include, as lists of lists, all those persons found to be related down

one particular branch of the family tree. The order in which they are printed on the display is significant. The head of the list represents the current youngest generation, whilst the last of the list represents the current root. Although this information is sufficient, it is not ideal. We would expect a system of this type to be able to demonstrate its power by producing a graphical representation of the familiar family tree structure on the display (or the hard copy peripheral). This subject is discussed more fully in Chapter Six.

The system to this point is identifiable as an 'intelligent' problem solver. It uses data contained in a store of facts, and uses as many of those facts as required to solve the two problems defined in this and the previous chapter. It is relatively complete. However, there are many problems that may be addressed by this type of system. By its very nature, new assertions can be made and new conclusions drawn, merely by implementing carefully designed rules.

The system developed here should be seen as very much a starting point for the implementation of a particular class of expert system. The potential power of this strategy has been demonstrated, as is the almost unlimited refinement potential. With fairly minor modifications to the structure of the control section and the rule base, it is possible to dedicate the system to a particular problem domain. Unfortunately, it appears that each problem domain has its own peculiarities which call for such minor changes to be made to any expert system shell, even the commercially-available ones. Generally, it is the case that 'off the shelf' expert system shells, i.e. systems incorporating a well documented control structure and rule base format, ready to be 'filled' by the user, very soon become inadequate as the system develops.

Chapter Six

User Interfaces

6.1 Introduction

The fairly simple rule-based system developed in the early chapters of this book, and the set of functions which make up the system, are characterised by complexity. Some twenty or more separate functions, each with their own (well-documented) specifications, may be present. In addition to these, there are other utility functions which are developed to assist in the creation of a well-structured information base. Function (or procedure) abstraction has been used to partition the problem and provide an orderly, meaningful path to progress with the minimum possibility of error. Whilst this approach is an extremely powerful one for producing good software, it results in a varied 'kit of tools' which must be integrated in the correct manner by a 'supervisory' function capable of applying the correct tool to the relevant data at the correct time. In essence, this is exactly the process carried out by rule-based systems, with the added versatility afforded by the 'directional' information incorporated into the rules. It does however, pose a real problem, both to the system designer and to the eventual user, or domain expert. We require a USER-INTERFACE to the many and varied features of any knowledge-based system.

User interfaces take many forms. They include the following :

6.1.1 Textual Interface

This is perhaps the most usual form of computer-user interface. It is ideal for input/output during any question/answer scenario, typical of knowledge-based system operation. It may also be used in an explanation facility. Such a facility may use a textual output to provide the following explanatory information :

RULE3   tells us that the individual is MALE
Therefore .. that individual must be the required ROOT object

In other words, the textual interface system has extracted key words from the rule structure and its conclusions, and phrased an explanation of its findings in the most meaningful way. Explanation facilities are beccoming more and more important in knowledge-based systems, as complexity grows and conclusions are relied on. For example, a KBS used to assist in the diagnosis of malignant tumours would almost certainly be required to justify its conclusions to a medical specialist. Unfortunately, these facilities have, in the main, been restricted to an output list of all the rules used in the process, with brief details of data used and data modified. Although this may appear to be a perfectly satisfactory situation to a system designer, who is conversant with the rule base and information base structure, it may seem quite unintelligible to a user with little experience in the KBS or general computer fields. One of the earliest knowledge-based systems accepted by the medical profession was concerned with the diagnosis of bacteriological infection (MYCIN). The work was carried out at Stanford University and incorporated a facility to question the system on the reasoning behind its conclusions. Two questioning strategies were employed, WHY and HOW. The user is able, with these systems, to probe deep into the system by repeatedly posing either of these two questions. Why questions result in the system basing its explanations on the next rules(s) in the current rule base, whilst HOW questions cause the system to look 'back' into the rules used to that point in arriving at its deliberations. However, even with such extended explanation features, the communication is based on a rehash of the the rules as they exist in the rule base.

Much work is currently being undertaken in the AI area, on natural language interfaces. That is, essentially textual interfaces capable of 'understanding' textual input in the form used in everyday life by human beings. Textual input to the system in this form is subject to much variability and this must be catered for in the parsing process.

The ultimate aim is to provide an interface ideally suited to the human user, i.e. a speech interface. With such a facility, communication would be possible between the computer system and any user, independent of their level of computer science competence. Their only qualification would be an understanding of the domain in question.

6.1.2 Graphical Interface

Computer operators and general users alike have a great affinity for 'pictures'. Most of us resort to some form of pictorial representation of problems in the process of solution. Even in mathematics, graphs and waveform diagrams are constantly used to help in understanding complexity. In knowledge-based program design, this approach is particularly relevant. In such systems, complexity is deeply rooted in associations present within a typically large information base, and we have seen some attempts to illustrate those interrelationships in this text.

Graphics interfaces are usually limited in their implementation and usefulness, by the size and power of the computer in use, and also by the speed at which graphics can be produced in response to specific requests. As far as the 'target' computer is concerned, we would be interested in the following :

1. *Graphics resolution.* The number of individually addressible picture elements (PIXELS) in the vertical and horizontal direction. This set of figures is a measure of the type and density of information displayed in graphical form. There is, of course, a decision to be made on the amount and density of such information capable of being readily understood by the user. The object of the exercise may be contradicted if too much data is presented on one display screen.

2. *Speed of plot.* Knowledge-based systems are not generally well known for their execution speed when implemented on conventional computer hardware. They would be even less attractive if all output was directed to devices similarly limited. In most cases where a graphical interface has been implemented, the overriding philosophy is that 'the end justifies the means'. That is, the benefits gained by the graphics approach outweigh the many problems associated with it. Nevertheless, the relevant considerations must be made before departing from the traditional textual interface and 'rushing headlong' into the more visually attractive graphics approach. Speed of plot is obviously an important consideration and the problem is under constant reappraisal by the specialist hardware designers.

3. *Provision of peripheral hardware.* Graphics can be used to provide output in the most human-meaningful way. The output of a family tree in the usual form is a good example for the purposes of this text. However, although output can easily be catered for with the aid of in- built display hardware, input poses its own set of problems. The utility of a system designed to input data from a computer non-expert may be greatly improved with the addition of a dedicated graphics input facility. To assist in 'civilising' the necessary communication, special hardware devices may be incorporated into the system. Devices such as digitising tablets, mouse and light pens. With the use of these pieces of equipment, special driving software is necessary.

4. *Number and power of available graphics utility functions.* If graphics are to be used in an eventual knowledge-based system, the implementation language itself must be the subject of special scrutiny. The functions available, both as primitives and utilities, must be examined in any computer programming language evaluation. For eventual graphics output, all the graphics functions should be appraised after the outline decisions on the type of display required are made. In the LISP system used in the bulk of this text, there are only two primitives, LINE and POINT. Whilst they are available for use in user-defined functions, they do not represent a facility of any real power. Some versions of LISP have the benefit of facilities which may be used to scale and to skew graphical data. They may even incorporate some form of cursor position monitoring functions.

With a satisfactory reply to the above questions, it should be possible to represent most aspects of knowledge-based systems, from the information base structure to the final output. Some kind of animation is always helpful in providing a visual check on progress. It can be used to great effect in advanced teaching systems and games.

6.2 Knowledge Elicitation

In the case of the rule-based system developed in the previous chapters, the system was built up to a viable state with the aid of specially designed and suitably abstracted functions, applied to an information base and rule base which had been decided upon through a process of detailed discussion and algorithmic construction. The rule-base structure was designed and implemented for use in a very narrow, specialised area, even though it was demonstrated that, with the addition of one more rule to the relevant rule base, new information could be 'gleaned'. In most realistic situations which are appropriate for a knowledge-based approach, both the information base and the rule bases cannot be definitively implemented. As an example, consider the problem of diagnosing the cause of a failure symptom displayed by a diesel locomotive. The system required must be capable of accessing a relatively huge information base, which contains information on the design and construction of the engine, and also on related matters such as environmental tolerances, wear characteristics of materials used and performance as a function of time. The necessity of a computer-based assistant may well be increased by virtue of a serious shortage of skilled personnel. Indeed, there may be only one such person remaining, and he may be nearing retirement and the expected end of industrially-active life. This sort of (not unrealistic) situation is perhaps the 'text book' problem to be solved using a knowledge-based strategy. The characteristics of the problem would include :

1. Complexity. The engine itself may have many hundreds of thousands of interdependent components. Any one of these, by definition, could cause a system failure of some description if it alone failed.

2. Almost as a consequence of (1) above, the solution to a system failure is dependent on skill acquired through possibly many years of experience. Initially, that skill is the exclusive property of the craftsman.

3. Although numerical methods could be used in the diagnostic process, in reality, in order to effect a solution in a reasonable time, non- numerical techniques are often used in this situation. It is quite often the case that a successful, and repeatable solution may be found by listening to the sound made by a machine under specific loads. Other heuristics may be based on 'hot-spots' within the engine or even 'word of mouth' handed down from previous masters of the craft.

All these points, from complexity to the superiority of heuristic methods in the craft, would convince a knowledge-based system designer that this particular problem is eminently suitable for his favourite strategy. The main problem, as far as the system designer is concerned once the job has been undertaken, is the necessary interactions between himself and the domain expert. The immediate problems are at the personality level. Both individuals in the two-way communication process are experts in their own domain, but are basically incompatible. The domain expert may have a 'healthy' disregard for computers and their companions, or might be intimidated by their sudden presence in his world. At worst, the domain expert may even regard the new computer system and the KBS designer as some kind of threat to his superiority or even his job.

When meaningful communication has been established between the two individuals, the system building process can begin. It would start with regular consultations in order to gain a good 'overview' understanding of the domain, and would progress from there by attempting to extract the domain expert's knowledge in the form of a realistic information base structure and a knowledge base. The knowledge base would overlap the information base, but would concentrate on how the information encoded into the information base could be used in the diagnostic process, in response to a specific symptom. The rule base and control structure used to direct the application of those rules are obviously a main part of the knowledge base, and the design of these is totally dependent on the success of the knowledge elicitation process. In actual fact, the very size of the problem of knowledge 'extraction', or elicitation would tend to deter any reasonable person. However, the nature of knowledge-based systems facilitates INCREMENTAL DEVELOPMENT, i.e. a very much simplified system can be created initially, with further enhancements easily catered for as more and more information and knowledge becomes available. This does not mean that the initial ideas stage and outline algorithm stage can somehow be avoided. It is extremely important in the choice and eventual structure of the control system. It does permit the rapid implementation of a limited knowledge based system, which can thereafter form the basis for further consultation with the domain expert for reasons of system enhancement and tuning. The existence of an operational system, however limited in performance, has a dramatic effect on the morale of the system builder and the confidence and enthusiasm of the domain expert.

The process of elicitation discussed here is deemed so important that a completely separate discipline has come into existence: KNOWLEDGE ENGINEERING. A knowledge engineer would be responsible for the initial PROBLEM DEFINITION, the contact arrangements with the relevant domain experts, and the outline design of the knowledge base. Each new task for a knowledge engineer involves a mixture of psychology, adaptability and common sense. He may also be required to communicate, on a professional basis, with personnel responsible for the actual construction of the many functions which eventually become the expert system, i.e. the encoders.

Various attempts have been made, some more successful than others, to provide some guidance to the person responsible for system building, in the form of a computer program. A good system would probably be knowledge-based and provide some kind of explanation facility to permit dynamic debugging. It would also require a means of knowledge base modification and information base manipulation. The following methodologies could be of use:

1. Textual output of rules used along with suitable explanations and prompts for modifications.

2. Graphical output optimised for the particular information and rule base structure used. This could be in the form of an associative network, or part of one, in which both nodes and links can be dynamically altered to reflect the modified structure.

6.3 System Input

The knowledge elicitation problem involves, at some eventual stage, an optimised computer-user communication facility. Both text and graphics can be used for input and output. On the input side, this could perhaps include a diagram of the system model in use, with some interactive facility for modification on a global, or systems scale. In advanced systems, characterised by a large information and rule base, such a knowledge elicitation tool may even include a dynamic environment in which questions and answers occur automatically as the system grows. The need for a comprehensive model-building environment such as this becomes essential at a certain level of size and comple•ity, and in many ways, the usefulness of any knowledge-based system is dependent on the 'user-friendliness' of the user-interface and the 'transparent' power that lies beneath.

For the family tree rule-based system developed in this text, the user-interface need not be over-complex. The system itself is a rather simple one, with the problem being familiar to most people. In effect, a simple textual input facility, directed by meaningful prompts would be ideal. The input facility in this case could comprise :

1. An initial menu which lists all manipulation possibilities .

2. An input system to facilitate the choice .

3. A system 'supervisory' facility to direct program flow in the relevant direction as a response to the user choice selection.

The supervisory system is the most important feature of the above input facility. It is responsible for the correct selection of functions within the toolkit of such functions, and has the task of directing program flow in the manner required to carry out the information base manipulation processes demanded by the user. The menu and prompts merely provide a familiar 'front-end' to the system, thereby isolating the user from the details of all internal operations. Checks must, of course be made, on the validity of data input by the user, and some protection (warnings) should be incorporated to protect any existing data structure from possibly dramatic, and unwanted, damage.

A menu display, suitable for the family tree system described in this text, is shown in Figure 6.1. The menu shown in that diagram would be quite easy to produce with the use of TITLE, PRINT and READ. TITLE was defined earlier in this text and the other two functions are LISP primitives. In fact, utility functions are available for all of the options within the menu. For example, ADD1VAR can be used in some kind of iterative or recursive loop to add values to a list, which would first be initialised to NIL. Before this occurs, a check would be made on the previous existence of the list, perhaps using (NULL). If the list already exists, the function would be designed to provide a warning of that situation and prompt for further commands, which would be either continue or abort the current process and return to the menu. It may be recalled that ADD1VAR appends the new object to the tail of the list supplied as an argument. In addition to validity and existence checks, the system would also require some facility to detect the end of entry to the list. The second option in the menu of figure 6.1 is essentially an identical copy of option one. It has been added as a separate item in an attempt to clarify its meaning to the user. The list of property list variables is stored in the same way as the list of relatives in the family tree information base.

INFORMATION BASE MANIPULATION
MENU OF UTILITIES

1 ...... Initialise/extend list of objects

2 ...... Initialise/extend list of propeties

3 ...... Modify (rename) object in list

4 ...... Remove object from list

5 ...... Remove property

6 ...... Build information base

Input choice by number -

Figure 6.1 A proposed menu of information manipulation facilities

---

The third option in the menu of Figure 6.1 would be based on either REM-OBJ1 or REM-ALL. These functions cause permanent erasure of information and should, perhaps be used alongside a confirmation utility, i.e. "are you sure ?". The fourth option, again is identical, in essence to the third.

The fifth option in Figure 6.1 can be directly catered for by ALT-OBJ, which requires, as arguments, a list, the old object (spelling) and the new object name. It should perhaps be subject to the same verification process proposed for REM-ALL though.

The sixth and final option in the menu is the one to build the information base. This has already been developed in the text and incorporates BUILD and PLACE. Once this particular function (BUILD) has been successfully executed, a viable information base should be in existence, for use by the family tree rule-based system. Further modifications, which are almost inevitable, can be easily catered for by invoking the menu system on an existing information base.

One essential feature of any data structure manipulation menu system associated with a rule-based system is the facility of rule building and modification. Fortunately, in the rule-based system described in Chapters Four and Five, a standard, rigid rule structure was developed. Because of this, a fairly simple function could be developed, capable of creating a 'rule skeleton', i.e. an empty list structure in readiness for 'filling'. Such a structure would be of the form :

```
(IF source-list ((test1) (test2) ...... (test.n))
(THEN (action ...destination-list or function)))
```

Where the following information would be required :

1. *The position in the list of rules*, the new one to be placed.

2. *The source-list identifier*.

3. *The destination-list identifier*, or the function to be evaluated. If the destination device is a function call, this would be input in the form : (FUNCTION ARGUMENTS). For example, (INCLUDE INDIVIDUAL POSSIBILITIES).

4. For example, (MARRIED TO ONE OF THE OTHER POSSIBILITIES). In the rule structure used in the family tree example, only the head and the tail of each antecedent list, are significant. For this reason, it may be possible to incorporate some kind of automatic sentence-building facility into the rule-building process.

All these facilities could be incorporated into an initially simple system, capable of guiding the user through the potentially tortuous process of model building. The overriding development philosophy of this text; function (or procedure) abstraction, is present in its extreme form, in the menu system.

6.4 System Output

In most knowledge-based systems, the most suitable output form is textual. A conclusion, possibly supported by explanations is usually sufficient to satisfy the end-user. However, there are other situations where output is required in other forms. If a system were to be developed to control the shut-down procedure in a power station, or the various processes of a factory, the most important output would be in the form of direct action. In the problem alluded to in section 6.2 on knowledge elicitation, a theoretical problem was 'invented' to demonstrate the suitability of the knowledge-based approach and the role of the knowledge engineer. The problem was basically one of diagnosis and the output of a system developed in response to this problem could be assumed to be essentially textual. However, diagnostic information may be more useful if displayed on a schematic diagram of the target system. The use of high-resolution graphics would add a new and important dimension to the KBS, as it would be used by relatively inexperienced personnel.

A much more simple, but valid problem is the family tree builder discussed earlier in the text. The input to the system would, almost certainly be textual in nature, but the output would, again almost certainly, be required in graphical form, i.e. the familiar tree structure. The efficacy of the system can be demonstrated by merely displaying each list output by the function TREE as it appears in the deductive process. The output would merely be a list of 'conclusion lists'. Shown below is an example of the early stages of output of that system.

```
((MIKE-X STEVE-X))
((CHARLES-X GRAHAM-X ELSA-X GEORGE-X) (MIKE-X STEVE-X))
((DIANNE-X DAVE-X) (CHARLES-X GRAHAM-X ELSA-X GEORGE-X)
(MIKE-X STEVE-X))
(NIL (DIANNE-X DAVE-X) (CHARLES-X GRAHAM-X ...........)
(MIKE-X STEVE-X))

((MIKE-X STEVE-X))
((GRAHAM-X ELSA-X GEORGE-X) (MIKE-X STEVE-X))
((LISA-X JAMES-X) (GRAHAM-X ELSA-X GEORGE-X) (MIKE-X
STEVE-X))
(NIL (LISA-X JAMES-X) (GRAHAM-X ...........) (MIKE-X
STEVE-X))
```

etc. until the tree is complete.

It can be noted from the above lists that the list whose CAR is NIL represents a successful search to the end of one branch of the tree. Internally, the NIL represents an absence of children credited to all those individuals detected at that level. One other fact can be noted by comparing the two 'sets of lists', partitioned as above for clarity. In the second set, the CAR of one of the lists has been removed. In this way, the sub-list (CADR), which represents the youngest generation, always contains the children of the CAR of the next sub-list. For example, in the second list set above, both LISA-X and JAMES-X are the children of GRAHAM-X, whereas, in the list set above that, DIANNE-X and DAVE-X are the children of CHARLES-X. A structure is present and can be used to output the results in a meaningful way.

6.4.1 Output Formats

In order to facilitate the output of a family tree, based on the information available to us in the form of lists of objects as discussed above, the following considerations should be made :

1. Should the output include all the individuals in the family, or should it be restricted to the direct relationships (a more simple situation)?

2. Is the tree to be displayed in total, or will it be desirable to 'zoom in' on specified areas of interest? This would be a rather important consideration to make if the number of individuals in the structure is large, i.e. too large to fit into one display screen or window. If that is the case, then a much more complex and 'intelligent' output facility would be required to carry out the necessary scaling and data filtering.

In the interests of clarity and brevity, this section will be concerned with the development of part of a system to display part of the family tree. We will take point one above, and decide to cater for the more complex situation of full displayed relationships, i.e. the direct descendant and his or her spouse (if recorded). On point two above, in order to display enough data on the screen without overcrowding or the need for scaling, only one branch of the tree will be displayed. This significantly reduces the complexity of the problem, and therefore the number of functions required, but it also has the effect of demonstrating the inherent search methodology used by the second part of the rule-based system from which the source lists originate. Let us first consider options available to us for the purposes of display.

1. Use of arrays. Arrays are implemented in all versions of LISP, and represent a powerful data structure. They may usually be declared as either integer, long integer, floating-point or pointer types. In the latter case, any valid LISP object can be stored in array form and this could be the basis of an ideal vehicle for the display of the family tree either as a scaled-down and compacted 'full-picture', or any specified portion thereof. The very fact that a fixed structure which includes all interrelationships and relative coordinates exists, enables us to scale that structure according to some predifined relationship, or to scale and display any part of that array.

2. Use of lists. Lists are used exclusively in the rule-based system defined in Chapter Five, and the final output of that system as it appears in that chapter is, in fact, a series of lists. A display method which uses such lists directly has none of the benefits associated with the use of arrays, but does present an intriguing possibility for animation. That is, the tree may be seen to 'grow' as the system progresses.

Using the second of the above methodologies, and taking a subset of the overall problem, the algorithm is :

Problem :

To output the results of the rule-based system developed in Chapter Five as a family tree. The final output should include the descendants of ROOT as represented by one branch of his family tree. The construction of the tree will include some kind of graphics manipulation in order to demonstrate the relationships present.

Solution :

Each branch will be displayed separately until the tree is complete. For the purposes of demonstration, the output will cease when one complete branch has been displayed. Each list, characterised by a NIL at its head includes all related individuals in a branch, up to the youngest generation. Therefore, this list may be used to construct the bulk of each branch. Subsequent 'target lists' (with NIL at the head) may be used to complete the youngest generation level. Graphics utilities may be used at each level to 'join' each individual to their parent in the tree. Two status flags will be used: MAIN and DONE. MAIN will become true when the bulk of the branch in question has been displayed and DONE will become true when the tree is (eventually) complete.

INPUT :   KEYBOARD - None

            ENVIRONMENT -
            Status flags MAIN and DONE
            Conclusion lists output from the family tree rule-based system

OUTPUT :   DISPLAY -
            The display of one branch of the family tree, including spouse

            ENVIRONMENT -
            Status flags set to T at various stages in the construction

BEGIN
    Clear the display area.
    Display the person ROOT centred at the top of screen.
    Display the spouse of ROOT.
    Set the status flags to NIL.
    While the status flag MAIN is NIL, do the following:
        Position cursor at the next lowest generation level (5 down).
        For lists with NIL at their head, do the following:
            Display each individual other than the youngest generation.

Join each individual to its parent with a line.
Set the status flag MAIN to T.
Display the youngest generation within that list (CADR (LIST)).
Join each individual to its parent with a line.
Display the rest of the youngest generation in that branch.
Set the status flag DONE to T.

The algorithm above makes some generalities, but as an outline sequence, it holds the essence of the method to be used. The algorithm, as it appears above should be capable of producing the family tree structure of Figure 6.2.

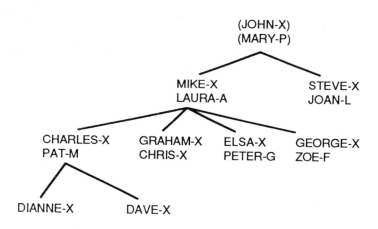

Figure 6.2 Part of the family tree as determined by the rule-based system of Chapter 5

The first function to be defined in the sequence of abstractions allowed in the algorithm, will concern itself with checking the status of both of the status flags. It will invoke one of two execution paths; either display the bulk of the tree branch or merely add to the youngest generation level of the tree. If MAIN is NIL, then the bulk of the tree branch has not yet been displayed. If MAIN is true (T) then the youngest generation level must be next. When DONE is true, then the display is completed to our (or the algorithm's) satisfaction :

154

```
(DEFUN DRAW (LAMBDA (STATUS)
   (COND ((NULL STATUS) NIL)
         ((NOT (NULL DONE)) NIL)
         ((NULL MAIN) (FILL-TREE STATUS))
         (T
           (EXHIBIT STATUS)))))
```

where FILL-TREE is responsible for displaying the bulk of the family tree branch and
EXHIBIT is responsible for the display of the youngest generation as it appears in the
CADR of each list of interest. FILL-TREE comes next :

```
(DEFUN FILL-TREE (LAMBDA (STATUS)
   (COND ((NOT (EQ (CAR STATUS) NIL)) NIL)
         (T
           (PROG ()
             (MAPC 'GENERATION (REVERSE (CDDR STATUS)))
             (SETQ MAIN T)
             (YOUNGEST (CADR STATUS)))))))
```

Notice that a check is initially made on the head of the supplied list. Nothing will
happen until the list supplied as an argument has, at its head, NIL. MAPC is used on
those parts of the list which contain all related individuals down to the list containing
the youngest generation and GENERATION is invoked iteratively on each element in
the list specified. Once that has been accomplished, the status flag MAIN is set
modified and finally, the youngest generation in that list is displayed with
YOUNGEST. GENERATION, therefore has the overall responsibility, albeit in a
supervisory manner, for the display of most of the structure of the tree :

```
(DEFUN GENERATION (LAMBDA (OUT-LIST)
   (COND ((NULL OUT-LIST) NIL)
         (T
           (PROG ()
             (VERT-MOV 5)
             (POSITION OUT-LIST))))))
```

where VERT-MOV is merely responsible for a vertical movement, the scope of
which is determined by the argument (5 in this case). The function is relatively
trivial :

```
(DEFUN VERT-MOV (LAMBDA (NUMBER-OF-LINES)
   (PROG ()
   LOOP
```

```
(COND ((GT NUMBER-OF-LINES 0)
        (TERPRI)
        (SETQ NUMBER-OF-LINES (- NUMBER-OF-LINES
        1))
        (GO LOOP))
    (T
        (RETURN NIL))))))
```

The function POSITION is much more important and involves double iteration in its quest to display the individuals in each list structure supplied in the correct levels of the family hierarchy :

```
(DEFUN POSITION (LAMBDA (DISP-DATA)
    (COND ((NULL DISP-DATA) NIL)
        (T
        (PROG (I J K)
            (SETQ DATA DISP-DATA)
            (SETQ I (LENGTH DISP-DATA))
            (SETQ J 2)
            (SETQ K (/ 80 (LENGTH DISP-DATA)))
        LOOP
            (COND ((GT I 0)
                    (PRINC (CAR DISP-DATA))
                    (SPACES (- K (LENGTH (EXPLODE
                    (CAR DISP-DATA)))))
                    (SETQ DISP-DATA (CDR DISP-
                    DATA))
                    (SETQ I (- I 1))
                    (GO LOOP))
                (T
                (COND ((GT J 1)
                        (SETQ DISP-DATA
                        (SPOUSE DATA))
                        (SETQ I (LENGTH
                        DATA))
                        (SETQ J (- J 1))
                        (GO LOOP))
                    (T
        (RETURN NIL))))))))))
```

The second, or outer iterative level has the effect of replacing the original list with a list of the married partners of each of the individuals in the original list. Once loaded, the new list can be output in the identical fashion to ensure that the married partners are displayed beneath the relevant direct relation on the display. A further level of

156

abstraction is required to actually produce a 'list copy', and that is catered for by the function SPOUSE :

```
(DEFUN SPOUSE (LAMBDA (DATA)
   (COND ((NULL DATA) NIL)
         (T
            (PROG (I SPOUSE)
               (SETQ I (LENGTH DATA))
               (SETQ SPOUSE NIL)
            LOOP
               (COND ((GT I 0)
                        (SETQ SPOUSE
                           (APPEND (WHO (CAR DATA))
                           SPOUSE))
                        (SETQ DATA (CDR DATA))
                        (SETQ I (- I 1))
                        (GO LOOP))
                     (T
                        (RETURN (REVERSE SPOUSE))))))))))
```

One possible problem could arise if one of the individuals in the original list supplied to POSITION was not married. A NIL partner would result in the spouse list being 'out of step', i.e. the wrong spouse. To eradicate this potentially embarrasing situation, the function WHO is called from within SPOUSE :

```
(DEFUN WHO (LAMBDA (SPOUSES)
   (COND ((NULL (GET SPOUSES 'MARRIED)) (LIST 'NONE))
         (T
            (GET SPOUSES 'MARRIED)))))
```

This function produces a valid entry other than NIL in the spouse list when any individual decided against the virtues of married life. In such a case the entry 'none' will be placed.

FILL-TREE has the added responsibility of causing the display of the youngest generation included in the list supplied to it. It does this via the function YOUNGEST :

```
(DEFUN YOUNGEST (LAMBDA (YOUNG)
   (COND ((NULL YOUNG) NIL)
         (T
            (PROG (I)
               (SETQ I (LENGTH YOUNG))
               (VERT-MOV 5)
            LOOP
```

157

```
(COND ((GT I 0)
          (PRINC (CAR YOUNG))
          (SPACES 2)
          (SETQ I (- I 1))
          (GO LOOP))
      (T
          (RETURN NIL)))))))))
```

This is a very simple function which has the task of initialising the lowest level in the tree with the children of (CAR (CDDR list)). Notice that two spaces are placed between each individual at that level, rather than attempting to equalise the spacings as done before. At this stage, it is uncertain how many individuals will eventually be placed at this level. The use of PRINC rather than PRINT has the effect of initialising the cursor position in readiness for the next list. EXHIBIT is invoked from the top level in this sequence: DRAW. Once the bulk of the tree branch has been constructed, DRAW sets the status flag MAIN to T and then invokes EXHIBIT :

```
(DEFUN EXHIBIT (LAMBDA (LAST)
   (COND ((NULL LAST) NIL)
         (T
            (PROG (I X)
               (SETQ X (CADR LAST))
               (SETQ I (LENGTH X))
            LOOP
               (COND ((GT I 0)
                         (PRINC (CAR X))
                         (SPACES 2)
                         (SETQ X (CDR X))
                         (SETQ I (- I 1))
                         (GO LOOP))
                     (T
                         (RETURN NIL)))))))))
```

The function selects the list, from the supplied list, which contains the youngest generation of that list. It then proceeds to PRINC those individuals at the correct level on the display, with a two-character spacing. The ROOT object has not yet been catered for. The function, however, is easy to define. It merely has to be placed, centred at the top of a cleared display screen with his married partner displayed immediately beneath him as before :

```
(DEFUN ROOTPUT (LAMBDA (ROOT)
   (COND ((NULL ROOT) NIL)
         (T
```

```
(PROG ()
   (TITLE1 ROOT 1)
   (SPACES (- 40 (ABS (/ (LENGTH (EXPLODE
   ROOT)) 2))))
   (PRINC (WHO (CAR ROOT)))))))))
```

and TITLE1 is a version of the previously-defined function which was designed to provide a title for the information building process. Its definition, with modifications is now :

```
(DEFUN TITLE1 (LAMBDA (TTL NUMBER)
   (PROG ()
      (WINCLR)
      (SPACES (- 40 (ABS (/ (LENGTH (EXPLODE TTL)) 2))))
      (PRINC TTL)
      (VERT-MOV NUMBER))))
```

The only remaining feature to be added to the display system at this point, is the use of graphics to join the relevant relatives to each other. There are many ways of accomplishing this, and the method depends to a large extent on the version of LISP in use. Some versions have a host of facilities, specifically designed for the production of graphs and for graphical interaction. In others, those facilities are severely limited if present at all. The version of LISP used in most of this text, IQLISP is supplied with three basic graphics primitives. The first of these must be used to select the IBM graphics resolution. The choices are 320 or 640 columns, representing medium or high resolution. If high resolution is selected, text may still be printed, but a noticeable degradation in output speed can be noticed. The other two graphics primitives are POINT and LINE. If a single pixel is to be highlighted at coordinates, say 300 along the horizontal axis and 10 on the vertical, then the following command can be used :

```
(POINT '300 '10 '1 NIL)
```

where the 1 represents a white dot internally and the NIL argument tells the system to overlay the display at that point. If the following function is called :

```
(LINE '300 '10 '300 '200 '1 NIL)
```

then a line will appear from the coordinates 300,10 to the coordinates 300,200. The two last arguments have a similar effect as in POINT.

A suitable graphics utility for the family tree problem would require relevant coordinates for each end of a joining line. This could be catered for within

POSITION, since that function includes a quantitative evaluation of the current position of each object at each level. Armed with this information, possibly on the property list of each individual displayed, it should be feasible to provide LINE with the information required to complete the tree.

6.5 Summary

All computer-based problem-solving systems, whether they are implemented using traditional stategies or knowledge-based techniques, require some form of user-interface. To the system designer, access to the internal functions that make up his system, is the ideal interface. All the power of the system is available to him and he is aware of the likely consequences of their use. The system designer is the domain expert and he has no real difficulties in relating to his system. As the system becomes ever-larger however, limitations in the inherent memory capacity of one or more human beings become apparent. The situation is made even worse if time elapses between computer system-to-designer interactions. We have all, I suspect, had some experience of this phenomena, and that is one of the main reasons for accurate, legible and complete documentation.

To the 'end user', the interaction problems can be acute. In most cases, the person given the task of using the system to solve problems is not interested to any great degree in the internal complexities and 'cleverness' displayed by the designer. The user merely wants reliable results with the minimum of fuss. To assist in this aim, the interface to the system would ideally be 'tailored' to that one individual, in order to provide for him the most acceptable assistant. The system should appear as a friend able to give advice and assistance, and not an adversary taking every opportunity to thwart progress and to misinform. Much work is underway into knowledge elicitation methodologies and this has been supported by cognitive scientists, who have been traditionally involved in most aspects of knowledge engineering.

Trends for the future will be the use of natural language interfaces incorporating graphics support. This, and the possibility of an extension to speech input are extremely attractive propositions, especially as complexity inexorably grows to almost unmanageable proportions.

Chapter Seven

Testing and Debugging

7.1 Introduction

This chapter has been deliberately placed after the discussion on knowledge-based system development. In this way, realistic examples can be used and referred back to. All LISP systems are supplied with some kind of facility to assist in the inevitable testing and debugging stages of system development and they are, to varying degrees, essential for the implementation of large-scale system design. Such facilities may include mechanisms to halt the process at specified places or to trace the execution of a particular function. However, test strategies for large, complex systems, usually require more facilities than present as utilities within the LISP environment. When this is the case, the whole design philosophy must be considered, i.e. whether to take a 'top-down' or 'bottom-up' approach. If a top-down strategy is employed, lower level functions may be simulated with STUBS. With a bottom-up approach, the lowest level functions are developed first, with the higher level 'driving' functions being simulated in some way. This latter approach was demonstrated in Chapter Three of this text, which dealt with the development of a list manipulation toolkit. All lowest level tools were developed separately, and tested as 'stand-alone' functions. Dummy driving functions were specially developed to test their effectiveness in a realistic, integrated system (TEST1 and TEST2). However, most of the following system development was carried out using a top-down approach.

7.2 The Editor

Most microcomputer implementations of LISP are supplied in the form of INTERPRETERS, and with such a system, the programmer interacts within a LISP environment. Each new function, list or variable bound and assigned, remain so assigned in that environment until it is either saved or shut- down occurs. As each new function is developed, it must be tested and inevitably debugged. In order to facilitate the manipulation of functions and lists within the LISP environment, an editor is usually supplied. In IQLISP, this takes the form of a STRUCTURE EDITOR which may be used to perform any necessary modifications, without leaving the current environment. Structure editors should not be confused with text editors. They appear, at first, to be rather complicated systems, but with use and experience, the serious LISP programmer soon begins to appreciate the subtleties of this type of editing facility. Structure editors provide a facility to edit a LISP-like function or list as a structure of atoms and CONS cells, rather than a sequence of characters which includes the structure boundaries (the parentheses). Once the function or list structure has been defined using DEFUN or SETQ etc., the editor maintains that structure whilst performing modifications to objects within it. In IQLISP, the following specialised calls to edit functions are available :

1. (ED 'Expr 'Cmmd-list)
     Where Expr = the expression to be modified
                 Cmmd-list = an optional list of commands which operate on
                                the prompts used by the system .

2. (EDF func)
     Where func = a LISP function. This is the function used to edit functions .

3. (EDV Ident)
     Where Ident = a valid LISP ident .

4. (EDP Ident Prop)
     Where Ident = a valid LISP ident
                 Prop = a property list variable.

All these edit functions would be useful to manipulate an information base as outlined in Chapter Three. In fact, these functions could have been invoked by the system builder rather than use the toolkit developed in that chapter. Only one of these functions was not duplicated in the system manipulation toolkit, i.e. EDF.

EDF is an extremely powerful tool for the manipulation of functions during the debugging stage. Consider the following function :

```
TEST-RULE (LAMBDA (RULE INDIVIDUAL)
    (COND ((NULL (CADDR RULE))
                    (ACTION (CAR (CDAR (CDDDR RULE)))))
             ((NOT (TEST-ANTECEDENT
                    (CAR (CADDR RULE)) INDIVIDUAL)) NIL)
          (T
               (TEST-RULE (LIST (CAR RULE)
                                      (CADR RULE)
                                      (CDAR (CDDR RULE))
                                      (CADR (CDDR RULE)))
                                  INDIVIDUAL))))
```

This function works well in the rule-based system of Chapters Four and Five. It can be seen to be a collection of function calls on specific parts of a list structure. In the development stage, i.e. algorithm to final encoding, the structure of this function and the list on which it operates, was decided. If the editor EDF is called, with TEST-RULE supplied as arguments, the following dialogue may result :

162

```
*  (EDF TEST-RULE)        - invoke editor

:                          - edit prompt

:PP                        - pretty-print TEST-RULE
```

The function TEST-RULE is then displayed, pretty printed. If the command P is used, the following dialogue might occur ;

```
:P                         - print TEST-RULE

(LAMBDA (RULE INDIVIDUAL) (COND & & &))
```

This gives us an indication of the structure of the function. In order to look 'deeper' into the structure, we could select the third object (say), the 'active' part of the function :

```
:3 P

(COND (& &) (& NIL) (T & ))
```

The editor always maintains its position within the structure being edited. In order to move back to the original outer structure, the 'up-arrow' key results in the following display :

```
(... (COND & & &))
```

and in order to examine the structure beginning with COND, the command :

```
:1 P
```

would be used. The summarised functions above tell us that there are two conditional clauses, the first one involving two functions and the second having, as its action part, NIL. The T clause of the COND statement is also indicated. Let us carry on with a typical dialogue :

```
(COND (& &) (& NIL) (T &))

:2 P                       - print the second expression
```

```
((NULL &)  (ACTION &))

:1  P                    - print the first expression

(NULL  (CADDR RULE))

:0  P                    - print the outermost level too

((NULL &)  (ACTION &))

:2  P                    - print the second expression

(ACTION  (CAR &))

:2  P                    - print the second expression

(CAR  (CDAR &))

:2  P                    - print the second expression

(CDAR  (CDDDR RULE))
```

At this stage, we have delved deep into the structure of the function TEST- RULE. It may be that (CDDR RULE) requires modifications in the light of testing. Let us assume that CDDDR is a mistake. The use of TEST-RULE has invoked an error situation and it has been traced to that source. It is realised that the expression should include CDDR. The following dialogue will resolve the matter :

```
:REP (2 1)  CDDR  P      - replace element positioned at 2,1
                           with cddr. Then print it
(CDAR  (CDDR RULE))

:X                       - exit to command level

(K)eep, (A)bort, or (C)ontinue? _
```

The command X is used to exit from the editor. Before final modification to the original function (as opposed to the copy produced by EDF), the system gives the user the chance to either set the modification permanently, abort the process leaving the original function unchanged, or continue with the editing process.

Although the ability to 'wander' through the function structure in this way is obviously a powerful editing feature, it would soon become a tedious process to find one object lying deep within a complex structure. Fortunately, the system used here has a comprehensive FIND facility. Using the example of TEST-RULE, we could invoke EDF and correct the erroneous modification made earlier to the expression (CDDDR RULE). Here is the dialogue :

```
*   (EDF TEST-RULE)

:F  CDDR  P                    - find CDDR and print it

CDDR

:0  P                          - move one level 'out'

(CDDR RULE)

:REP  1  CDDDR  P              - replace with CDDDR and print

(CDDDR RULE)

:X                             - exit the editor

(K)eep, (A)bort, or (C)ontinue? _
```

Some care must obviously be exercised, since CDDR may appear at other places within the function being edited. In IQLISP, F may be used with argument modifiers (wild-cards) to facilitate pattern matching. F searches for a given pattern towards the right from its current position (focal point), whereas FB can be used to search towards the left. Other tools available within ED,F etc. are :

1. NEXT Shift the current focal point (position) to the next element, at the same level in the object being edited ;

2. PREV Similar to (1). The focal point is shifted to the previous element, at the same level in the object being edited ;

3. IA,IB Taking as arguments, a position and data, the new datails are inserted either after or before the position specified ;

4. SA,SB With the same arguments as (3), data is spliced into the structure being edited ;

5. DEL   Delete an element specified from the structure being edited ;

6. REP   Replace old data at a specified position with new data specified

In addition to the essential facilities, others exist to move data around in the structure (MOV) and to make and place copies of that data within the structure being edited (COP).

The final requirements are those facilities to alter the structure itself. SL places parentheses around elements specified by their position, and UL removes them.

An editor of the type described here is not only desirable, it is essential for the orderly manipulation of possibly highly complex LISP functions. The nature of LISP demands this approach to dynamic editing.

7.3 Error Trapping

During the testing phase of system development, the time arrives when functions (once saved) must be tested on some predetermined data. Errors can and do occur in the early stages, and LISP systems have various methods of trapping some detectable errors, in the process passing control to some kind of dedicated error monitor. IQLISP has two error trapping routines; one available as a primitive function and one available as a library utility. The latter of these provides a very powerful means of debugging and can potentially save hours of work. When an error is detected in the LISP environment, control is passed to ERROR, which provides a great deal of information on the cause of the error and the sequence of events leading up to it. While in the ERROR MONITOR, the programmer has a good degree of manipulative scope for determining and correcting the cause of error. As an illustrative example, consider the following function, previously defined to remove all occurrences of a specified object from a specified list :

```
REM-ALL (LAMBDA (LIST NAME)
    (COND ((NULL LIST) NIL)
            ((EQUAL (CAR LIST) NAME)
                (REM-ALL (CDR ALIST) NAME))
            (T
                (CONS (CAR LIST)
                    (REM-ALL (CDR LIST) NAME)))))
```

The function will be operated on a list previously bound to the identifier NUMBERS :

```
(SETQ NUMBERS '(ONE TWO THREE ONE FOUR FIVE))
```

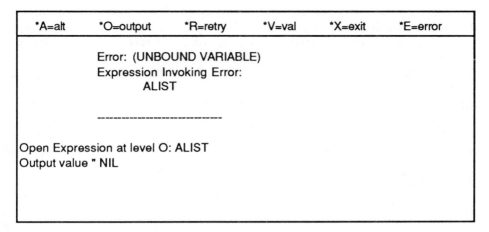

| *A=alt | *O=output | *R=retry | *V=val | *X=exit | *E=error |

Error: (UNBOUND VARIABLE)
Expression Invoking Error:
        ALIST

Open Expression at level O: ALIST
Output value " NIL

Fig. 7.1 A typical output in the error monitor

Therefore, when the function REM-ALL is invoked to remove all occurrences of TWO (say) :

```
*  (REM-ALL NUMBERS 'TWO)
```

the display shown in Figure 7.1 is produced. The display is partitioned into two 'windows'. The top window, which has a highlighted boundary, is termed the STACK CONTROL WINDOW, and contains within the highlighted top of that window, a list of function keys that are recognised as specific commands by the error monitor. They are :

ALT-X   This causes the stack to be unwound to the current stack level and exits from the error monitor. The action to be taken on exit is determined by the following :

ALT-R   RETRY. Evaluation will occur on exit, at the current stack level, on the expression at that level. This is useful for re-invoking modified functions automatically.

ALT-O   OUTPUT VALUE. All expressions below the current stack level are aborted and the curent exit value is returned.

ALT-V   VALUE. The last value returned by a programmer command is assigned as the next exit value.

ALT-E   ERROR. The primitive error routines are invoked.

Below the top line are two blocks of information. The first indicates the reason for the invocation of ERROR and the second gives the actual expression within a given function, in which the error has occurred. A line is drawn to separate this information from the rest of the stack control window, which holds dynamic information. The first line of information in the bottom half of the stack control window initially gives the expression at stack level zero, i.e. the actual expression causing the error. By repeatedly pressing the 'up-arrow' key on the IBM keyboard, the stack level is progressively increased and this has the effect of displaying previous expressions. For example, on pressing the up-arrow key once, the following information would appear within the bottom half of the stack control window :

Open Expression at level 1: (CDR ALIST)

and if the up-arrow key is pressed again :

Open Expression at level 2: (REM-ALL (CDR ALIST) NAME)

Figure 7.2 shows the complete screenful of information produced by the error monitor if the up-arrow key is pressed once again to inspect level 3.

```
*A=alt      *O=output     *R=retry      *V=val      *X=exit      *E=error
_____

           Error: (UNBOUND VARIABLE)
           Expression Invoking Error:
                   ALIST


           -----------------------------

Open Expression at level 3 :  (REM-ALL (CDR ALIST) NAME)
Output value " NIL
```

Figure 7.2 The error window after stack manipulation

As it happens, the open expression at level zero has the answer. By stepping up the stack, it would be realised that LIST and not ALIST was used in the function argument and as a local variable elsewhere in the function. However, it may not be quite so obvious in cases where there are many variables and many functions within an integrated system. There is one other, extremely significant feature of the error monitor, related to the scope of variables used in the function causing the error. One of the main design philosophies of this text, is the 'localising' of variables to specific functions. As a deliberate policy, as many variables as possible are bound and assigned as local variables in order to ensure generality. Although this philosophy tends to protect the system from unwanted and unpredicted identifier conflicts, it does have the effect of isolating the user from local changes in a similar way. The user can overcome this problem with the aid of STUBS (see 7.7), but this may present an unacceptable burden in terms of development time and added complexity. Fortunately, once a function has invoked the error monitor, all locally- assigned variables are available to the designer as if they were global free variables. For example, with the REM-ALL function execution situation as depicted in Figures 7.1 and 7.2, the value of ALIST can be checked :

```
::ALIST                              - check the value of ALIST

Error during EVAL : (UNBOUND VARIABLE) - not bound

::                                   - next action within
                                        ERROR?
```

Having examined the rest of the stack, possibly all levels up to TOPLEVEL, it is strongly suspected that LIST should have been used. This can be checked :

```
::LIST                               - check the value of LIST

(ONE TWO THREE ONE FOUR FIVE)        - correct value
```

Suspicion confirmed, it is now only necessary to edit the function REM-ALL. This can, if required, be performed directly from ERROR :

```
::(EDF  REM-ALL)                     - invoke EDF from ERROR

:F  ALIST  0  P                      - in EDF, find the offender

:REP  2  LIST  X                     - correct it and exit

(K)eep,  (A)bort,  or  (C)ontinue _  - choice on exit from EDF
```

The double colon tells us that we are back in the error monitor. In order to refresh the stack control window, that has by now been over-written by EDF, the command CONTROL-PRINTSCREEN (on the IBM keyboard) is input. The open expression (REM-ALL NUMBERS 'TWO) is accessed by pressing the up-arrow key. ALT-R is invoked to set the input mode to RETRY, and ALT-X is pressed to exit from the error monitor. If all is now well, the results of the execution of the now-corrected REM-ALL should appear on the screen :

(ONE THREE ONE FOUR FIVE)

7.4 Trace

It is useful, especially with recursively-defined functions, to be able to 'watch' the progress of a system. It may well be that certain suspicions exist as to the correct definition and execution of a function. The function in question may appear to execute without invoking ERROR, but even so, the final output of the integrated system is not as expected, and a fault is deemed to exist somewhere in one the system functions. TRACE allows us to view the invocation of a specified function by supplying a message on entry , e.g.:

ENTERING function

and a message, with the output or returned value on exit :

EXITING function VALUE = value

With the use of TRACE, we can check that the function has been called and we can verify its output value. The inner execution details are not available. As an example, consider the function REM-ALL applied to the list created in the last section (NUMBERS) :

(ONE TWO THREE ONE FOUR FIVE)

The following dialogue will invoke the required test sequence using TRACE :

* (TRACE 'REM-ALL)	- invoke TRACE on REM-ALL
OK.	- system confirmation
* (REM-ALL NUMBERS 'ONE)	- invoke REM-ALL with appropriate arguments

The results from the traced invocation of REM-ALL on NUMBERS are illustrated in Figure 7.3. With this display, it is possible to relate each output to that expected from a recursively-defined function such as REM- ALL.

```
ENTERING REM-ALL
   ENTERING REM-ALL
      ENTERING REM-ALL
         ENTERING REM-ALL
            ENTERING REM-ALL
               ENTERING REM-ALL
                  ENTERING REM-ALL
                  EXITING REM-ALL VALUE = NIL
               EXITING REM-ALL VALUE = (FIVE)
            EXITING REM-ALL VALUE = (FOUR FIVE)
         EXITING REM-ALL VALUE = (THREE FOUR FIVE)
      EXITING REM-ALL VALUE = (TWO THREE FOUR FIVE)
   EXITING REM-ALL VALUE = (TWO THREE FOUR FIVE)
(TWO THREE FOUR FIVE)
```

Fig. 7.3 Trace for REM-ALL applied to a list of numbers (NUMBERS) and a specific object to be removed from that list

In order to remove the trace from the function, the following command is required :

```
*  (UNTRACE 'REM-ALL)
```

This will ensure that the trace output does not occur on the function's next invocation.

7.5 Break

BREAK is perhaps the most powerful of the debugging facilities of IQLISP. It has a similar effect as the error monitor in that it provides access to locally-bound variables and their modified values within the confines of the local function environment. It has other benefits too. They can all be conveniently listed :

1. *Access to local variables,* plus the ability to modify them.

2. *Verification of invocation.* Sometimes it is extremely helpful to know that a function has been accessed. For example, in a compound COND expression, a given test should cause the invocation of function X (say), when that test is true. The very fact that function X is subsequently broken proves the validity of the COND clause and the test that goes with it.

3. *The ability to CONTinue to the next invocation of function X* (say). If a function is called repeatedly by another, via an iterative or recursive process, each invocation can be trapped and examined.

4. *The accessibility of all LISP's facilities during the 'break'.* It is even possible to use the IQLISP editing functions without exiting BREAK.

As an extreme example of this, let us consider the family tree rule-based system developed in this text. At the highest level of abstraction, we have defined a supervisory function called TRIBES. It carries out some initialisation, but is mostly concerned with controlling the sequence of events leading to the successful determination of the root of the tree and the subsequent tree itself. We will invoke BREAK on, perhaps the lowest level function, TEST-ANTECEDENT which you may recall is responsible for the antecedent match within each rule :

```
*  (BREAK 'TEST-ANTECEDENT)    - invoke BREAK on TEST-ANTECEDENT

OK.                            - system confirmation

*  (TRIBES)                    - start the rule-based system

TEST-ANTECEDENT BROKEN         - TEST-ANTECEDENT accessed

>>  _                          - prompt within BREAK
```

The function TEST-ANTECEDENT is now broken. Several choices are available to us at this point. From our point of view, we may actually want to remind ourselves of the absolute definition of the function in question. That presents no problem :

```
>> (PPF TEST-ANTECEDENT)              - pretty print TEST-ANTECEDENT

(LAMBDA (ANTECEDENT INDIVIDUAL)
    (*BREAK TEST-ANTECEDENT)
    (COND ((NULL (PROPS INDIVIDUAL)) NIL)
          ((NULL ANTECEDENT) NIL)
          (T
            (OR (EQUAL (LIST (GET INDIVIDUAL
                                  (CAR ANTECEDENT)
                        (LIST (EVAL (CAR (LAST ANTECEDENT)))))
                        (EQUAL (GET INDIVIDUAL (CAR
                        ANTECEDENT))
                            (LIST (EVAL (CAR (LAST
                            ANTECEDENT)))))))
```

```
                    (EQUAL (EVAL (CAR (LAST
                    ANTECEDENT))))))))))
```

OK.   - system prompt

>> _   - back to BREAK

Notice from the pretty printout that a call to BREAK has been inserted into the function itself. The next operation in the debugging process might be the verification of arguments and local variables. This is the first time in the present system execution that TEST-ANTECEDENT has been invoked. We would therefore expect ANTECEDENT to be the first one in the first rule of the rule list in use. Therefore, at the BREAK prompt, we might type in the following :


```
>>ANTECEDENT                                - examine the actual antecedent
(FATHER IS RECORDED AS (QUOTE NIL))         - the value for this BREAK

>>INDIVIDUAL                                - examine the value of
                                              INDIVIDUAL

JOHN-X                  - the value of INDIVIDUAL
```

Correct. Let us continue to the next invocation of TEST-ANTECEDENT :

```
>>CONT                                      - continue to next access

TEST-ANTECEDENT BROKEN                      - caught again

>>ANTECEDENT                                - re-examine the argument

(MOTHER IS RECORDED AS (QUOTE NIL))  - antecedent this time

>>INDIVIDUAL                                - check for the correct individual

JOHN-X                                      - individual this time
```


CONT can be used over and over to cause the system to 'step' between each invocation of the function to which BREAK has been applied.

Once the fault has been found, the structure editor may be entered from the BREAK prompt to edit any previously defined function. Once the edit session has been completed with the modifications either ignored or permanently set, the BREAK prompt will again appear, and the debugging process can resume. It is the availability of all the functions present in the LISP environment that gives this facility such potential power as a debugging aid.

7.6 Step

Although not available in either IQLISP or iLISP, some versions have the facility to step through a system execution session, giving helpful advice as it proceeds. As each function is invoked from the outermost, most abstracted level to the lowest level, each function identifier would be printed, with their arguments and output values in a similar fashion to TRACE. It would, of course, be possible to develop such a utility within the LISP environment.

7.7 Stubs

An approach to the sort of facilities found in step can be made by deliberately incorporating another function invocation into selected functions. This new function would have the responsibility of displaying, on the screen, all the relevant data associated with the calling function, mainly for the purposes of debugging. Stubs however, are very useful in the development process. If a top-down development strategy is employed, it is usually necessary to simulate as yet non-existent lower level routines. This is an extreme form of abstraction, but it does facilitate the verification of program flow and assist greatly in the rapid commencement of the encoding stage of system development. The stubs could be either simple functions with a single PRINT statement in the function body, or they could be more complex 'dummy' routines which carry out some simple numerical or object manipulation in order to verify a particular concept.

7.8 Summary

In any comparison with interpreters and compilers, interpreters always appear to provide a much better develop-test-debug facility. There is usually less of a need to resort to DOS-level editors to create and modify programs. The LISP systems discussed in this text are supplied as interpreters which have very good development aid facilities, which can be used during actual program execution. In IQLISP, each function can be saved within a previously-defined PACKAGE for later down-loading, or a complete environment can be saved, incorporating all those functions 'known' by the system at that time. Modifications can even be made to the TOPLEVEL process to provide for an even greater degree of 'customisation'.

Systems implemented in LISP tend to be large and complex. The language itself, plus its inherent facilities make it ideal for the implementation of problem-solving systems characterised by complexity. Knowledge-based systems have traditionally been implemented in LISP, and that will continue to be the case, especially with the advent of a standardisation and extension (COMMON LISP). However, complexity places a great strain on system debugging. Top-down design strategies and function (or procedure) abstraction help enormously in maintaining order, but eventually, testing with a sample problem (or sub-problems) is always necessary. The need for powerful and easy to use debugging tools is acute, and various approaches have been successfully made to cater for these needs. It must be emphasised that, although step-wise refinement is possible, and is perhaps the obvious methodology for knowledge-based system development, as each function is developed through the algorithmic process, every attempt should be made to render each function general. With this in mind, it may be noticed that most functions defined in this text include some error checking, even though the same error check may be seen to occur on several functions in a logical sequence. Every attempt is also made to ensure that as many variables as possible remain LOCAL to its function. Each function should be rigorously tested with dummy data, provided perhaps, by a dummy calling routine such as TEST1 and TEST2.

Chapter Eight

Other Strategies

8.1 Introduction

The strategies employed in the development of knowledge-based systems depend, to a large extent on the problem domain and possible extensions to the initial system. The problem addressed in Chapters Four and Five of this text was chosen for its simplicity and its suitability for the type of information base structuring typically used. The rule base was designed from the outset to address the specific problems identified and a great deal of care was exercised in arriving at a standard form. However, small experimental systems are usually found to be inadequate when scaled up to realistic proportions and implemented in the real world. The points covered in this chapter should be borne in mind and further researched before attempting a large-scale venture. Fortunately, knowledge-based systems are amenable to modifications, and maintenance is basically the same process as development. Therefore, most 'overlooked' factors can usually be catered for at a later stage, and anxieties about possible omissions should not be allowed to obscure and delay system development.

8.2 Goal-Driven Techniques

The family tree knowledge-based system described in Chapters Four and Five is defined as DATA-DRIVEN. This means, in effect, that the inference mechanism invokes an information base search, in which each rule is used, cause alterations to a temporarily-created data base via its action (or THEN..) part. Each rule, applied in turn, requires a certain premise to exist as a result of the previous rule application, and by this means, each rule can be seen to be 'driven' by the data made available by the previous one. The initial rule is driven by the data contained in the unmodified information base.

Using the information base previously built (RELATIVES), if the following question was to be asked :

```
IS LISA-X THE GRANDCHILD OF JOHN-X ?
```

then that question can be seen to provide a GOAL for the inference mechanism to address. It could be re-phrased :

```
PROVE THAT LISA-X IS THE GRANDCHILD OF JOHN-X
```

and many systems, called THEOREM PROVERS, have been developed with this type of problem in mind. Theorem provers find much use in mathematics, especially in areas of the discipline characterised by complexity and therefore amenable to the application of approximations in the form of some kind of heuristic sub-solution. Rule based systems applied in such domains are also able to prompt for further information required in the computation, or provide a justified 'impossible' conclusion.

The definitive proof of the specified relationship between LISA-X and JOHN-X could be catered for in our forward-chaining rule-based system. It would, for instance, be possible to supply JOHN-X as the ROOT for the tree- tracing routines, and success would be apparent if that search was able to find LISA-X at the lowest (youngest) level in the tree. However, the relationships would be implied, in this approach, by our own knowledge of the extent of the information base, and the methods of search employed by the control system. The final output of that system, if displayed as a recognisable tree, would allow us to 'work out' the correct relationship between any two individuals represented in the tree. In other words, this forward-chaining approach is not at all ideal for the problem in hand.

We could partition the problem in terms of reasoning. The following steps in the proof are typical of human reasoning in the solution :

```
IS  LISA-X  THE  GRANDCHILD  OF  JOHN-X ?        - the original request

DOES  JOHN-X  HAVE  CHILDREN ?                   - first level of inquiry

IS  LISA-X  THE  CHILD  OF  ONE  OF  THOSE ?     - the final goal
```

This may appear somewhat similar to the search process undertaken in the solution to the family tree problem, but the differences are significant. The ever-diminishing SEARCH SPACE at each search level is represented in the steps above as SIBLING GOALS. That is, the original request, or overall goal has the effect of producing a SUB-GOAL to investigate the children of JOHN-X. That sub-goal generates a further sub- goal to which, in this case, is the final goal. These steps can be represented another way :

```
IS  LISA-X  THE  GRANDCHILD  OF  JOHN-X              - the original request

IS  THE  FATHER  OF  LISA-X,  THE  SON  OF  JOHN-X      - one case
    OR
    THE  MOTHER  OF  LISA-X,  THE  DAUGHTER  OF  JOHN-X  - other case
```

This involves only two steps, and the test for the relationship is represented more fully. The first approach caters for the condition of JOHN-X actually having no children, in which case all further inferences would cease. This example is perhaps too simple to demonstrate the power and applicability of goal-driven strategies, even though the problem domain should by now be familiar. It could perhaps be made more suitable if the information base is extended to include individuals with various relationships, some uncertain. For example, the direct family of each of the married partners in the family of John-X could be present, or the direct family of Mary-P (his wife in the information base RELATIVES) could be included. There could be very many more generations to sort out than the limited number incorporated into the current version of RELATIVES (three). All these realistic extensions to the information base have the effect of increasing the search space, and the generation, by a backward-chaining control structure, of more sibling goals in the solution to a particular query. Each THEN clause in a backward-chaining rule represents a sub-goal which the control structure (strictly speaking, the rule interpreter) can recognise, and apply a rule or function to. In this way, the control system would use the action part of each rule to direct the search path through the knowledge base. For example, using the information base RELATIVES, we may wish to prove that members of one social (or professional) club are opposed, in their ideals, etc. to members of another. This could be incorporated into an outline rule of the form :

```
IF  INDIVIDUAL-1 IS A MEMBER OF CLUB-X
    AND
    INDIVIDUAL-2 IS A MEMBER OF CLUB-Y
THEN
    INDIVIDUALS 1 AND 2 ARE OPPOSED
```

where the individuals are contained in a list of two and supplied to the rule in the form specified in the rule-based system of Chapters Four and Five :

```
(IF list-of-2 ((INDIVIDUAL-1 IS IN A (CLUB))
               (CLUB IS (X INDIVIDUAL-1))
               (INDIVIDUAL-2 IS IN A (CLUB))
               (CLUB IS (NOT (X INDIVIDUAL-2))))
 (THEN
               (OPPOSED INDIVIDUAL-1 INDIVIDUAL-2)))
```

Four sub-goals may be generated by a backward-chaining system. These are:

```
(FIND (CLUB INDIVIDUAL-1))
  (IS-IT (X INDIVIDUAL))
```

```
(FIND (CLUB INDIVIDUAL-2))
(IS-IT (NOT (X INDIVIDUAL-2)))
```

The final outcome of the rule above is either OPPOSED or NOT-OPPOSED. On the basis of the results of this type of query, it is perhaps wise to ensure that future queries of this type, on these individuals, do not invoke the inference mechanism in this way, i.e. the fact should be included in the global information base. One main problem exists with this simple system. The individuals of interest may have many club memberships. Some of those may conflict, whilst others are compatible. In this case, the system should search for all those memberships associated with each individual and come to a conclusion on the basis of :

1. Opposition 'proportions'. Each individual may have, for example, five memberships. Two of those may have opposite beliefs to a given 'standard' and three may be compatible. Therefore, the conclusion may be :

    OPPOSED 0.6   where the value 0.6 has been arrived at via :

    $$\text{OPPOSED FACTOR} = \frac{(\text{Number of memberships} - \text{Number opposed})}{\text{Number of memberships}}$$

    Using this, so-called OPPOSED FACTOR (CERTAINTY FACTOR), it can be seen that a value of one denotes absolute compatibility (no opposite beliefs), whilst a value of zero indicates absolute incompatibility (no agreement on anything at all).

2. The degree of compatibility, measured against some standard, on the basis of 'type classification', i.e. religious, political, sporting,   etc.

    Care must also be exercised in cases where a sub-goal may invoke a function which requires execution of the sub-goal.

Goal-driven and data-driven inferences can be incorporated into the same knowledge-based system, as is the case with MYCIN, one of the first viable systems. The actual definition of the rule can be used to direct the control structure to operate either in the forward-chaining or backward- chaining mode. In such a system, rules would be declared explicitly to be either forward or backward-chaining (or in some cases, both), and the appropriate control structure executes them.

The system model can be conveniently illustrated in block diagram form as shown in Figure 8.1. With reference to this diagram, it can be seen that both parts of the control structure, the forward and backward inference engines, would add new data to the information base as the system executes. The diagram illustrates a system model in which two separate sub- systems exist. Each could be used separately with the appropriate rule base, or could be used as an integrated system with a common information base, interconnected by the links existing between each rule base and the identified goals. Specific commands could be incorporated into the system to direct control to either of the two inference mechanisms in order to facilitate 'switching' between the two inference engines, along with a kind of message passing scheme. With this kind of structure, the utmost care should be exercised in segregating the knowledge base into forward and backward chaining rules. By virtue of the nature of these two distinct types of rule, the possibility exists, in a system incorporating both types, of the occurrence of INFINITE LOOPS.

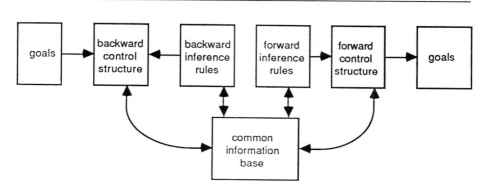

Figure 8.1 A system employing forward and backward chaining inference mechanisms

Goal-driven systems tend to require more steps in the solution to problems involving large search spaces, as the inference mechanism creates more and more sub-goals. In a problem domain such as the family tree builder described in this text, the forward-chaining method has been shown to be the most suitable, perhaps even obvious, choice. In any general overview involving a range of problems, it may be found that backward- chaining presents the better choice. Given a fairly complete information base, most problems will be associated with known goals. In this situation the goal-driven method is usually used, mostly because with this type of system, inference occurs at query time, not assertion time as it does with forward-chaining techniques.

In general, the following considerations should be made when deciding on the inference methodology to employ :

1.   *The actual type of system in question.* Is it, for instance, to be characterised by multiple queries? It has already been said that goal- driven techniques are more efficient for inference at query-time.

2.   *Forward-chaining would be more efficient if the search space was large and the goal is one of classification.* An example of this is the traditionally-used one of

classification in the animal kingdom, i.e. what is FIDO? In effect, this would appear as a more involved example of the type of system used in our family tree problem.

3.   *The speed of termination of inferences.* All these three points are interrelated, but do have some subtle differences. In some cases, there may appear to be as many steps involved in the inference process using both methods. It comes down to efficiency in terms of speed of termination. The extreme situation is one where neither method has a clear advantage. In such a case, the choice is more difficult to make, and considerations on possible future developments of the system need to be made.

8.3 Classification of Knowledge-Based Strategies

The use of the term 'classification' in the title of this section may be somewhat confusing as it is the name of one of the categorisations in our scheme. The scheme in question is in Figure 8.2, and includes three broad classifications of problems involving the requirement for knowledge and experience in their solution. Of course, any general scheme of this nature is bound to be bedevilled by 'fuzzy' boundaries and there are likely to be many which fall somewhere between the groups specified. They may even involve all three.

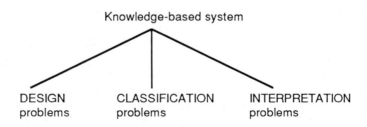

Figure 8.2 A classification scheme for Knowledge Based Systems

---

182

8.3.1 Design Problems

A typical example of this classification is the design of electronic equipment. The problem is characterised by extreme complexity and ultimately involves a process which includes the initial specification stage, the actual development and eventually, the testing of the system, perhaps by simulation. A design would begin from the specification stage, and an automated system would be responsible, in the first instance, for soliciting (or eliciting) information about the customer's intended application and would require specific details of the performance expected of the final electronic system. In fact, this process is perhaps the most important event in the whole development cycle, since it is the model- building stage on which the rest of the system is based, and against which the final design is compared by simulation and evaluation. As mentioned previously, the almost separate discipline of knowledge elicitation , which makes use of specific tools to create an optimal environment for this extremely important process, is receiving much attention in the AI world, for very good reasons.

The design assistant could incorporate three levels of expertise :

1. *Knowledge elicitation in the determination of precise requirements from the user.* The system would have access to engineering design knowledge and would be able to ask relevant questions in order to clear up anomalies and enforce 'structured thought'. It would be invoked in the creation of a structured information base which represents a model of the intended system. Libraries of existing designs would be matched against the model, or part of it, as the model evolves into a viable system (as the expert system sees it). Specifications would be validated through the vehicle of user- interaction, and these would be used later as the basis for a test and correct phase, under simulation. The system may also be responsible for an outline manufacturing capabilities evaluation, but this is considered such an important task in the determination of economic viability, that it would most probably be incorporated as a separate system.

2. *The design stage itself.* An interface to an existing computer-aided design package capable of, amongst other things, schematic capture and dynamic simulation, both in terms of logical correctness and hazard- free behaviour in the time domain (for digital hardware. Analogue systems would be subject to frequency-domain analysis). Such a system may have built-in 'intelligence' and could even be an expert system in its own right, responsible for enforcing good design practice. These practices would include the provision of facilities in the electronic design for later automatic test (ATE). This may well form a fourth 'arm' in the integrated development assistant package.

3. *Process simulation and evaluation.* The system would be responsible for the planning exercise required to set up the manufacturing process. This would involve process and manufacturing simulations, in addition to product

simulation in terms of functional behaviour and reliability. On the basis of these results, a critical design analysis can be carried out to identify design weaknesses and evaluate potential design improvements.

Only after these systems have operated successfully, each interacting with each other, would the recommended design be output as a conclusion of the entire design assistant.

In the process of electronics equipment development using this technique of design 'partnership', much user-computer interaction is necessary. It would be necessary to continually update the information and knowledge bases used by each part of the system as experience grows. Explanation facilities are obviously required, and a good knowledge- elicitation tool and general user-interface is desirable.

A model for this type of integrated system is shown in Figure 8.3 and incorporates the three levels of responsibility discussed.

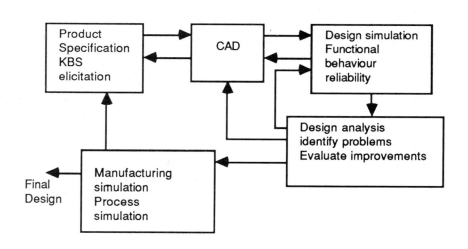

Fig. 8.3 An integrated IKBS manufacturing facility

An extension to this model, as shown in Figure 8.3 is possible. The experience of the production engineer could be incorporated into a manufacturing scheduler capable of simulating the manufacturing process, taking into account such diverse factors as the requirement and availability of skilled and unskilled personnel. It may also be capable of considering the changes required to the factory floor as a consequence of manufacture commitment; and perhaps it would be required to take into account the various related but separate tasks involved, and how best they could be managed in terms of efficiency. The whole task of project planning and expedition is receiving much attention at present, and is being supported by industry and government alike. The potential to increase efficiency in the manufacturing process by the application of expert system technology is overwhelming. The structured approach to project planning has, for some time, incorporated mechanisms to help the project manager in his difficult task: such mechanisms as CRITICAL PATH METHODS, BAR CHARTS, etc., and computer-based tools are available, based on graphics displays, capable of assisting in the creation and maintenance of those structures. Knowledge-based systems find their 'niche' in the management of complexity, and are ideally suited to the job of large-system planning. The availability of semantic networks (associative networks) gives the knowledge-based system designer an ideal representational tool for use, both in the essential model-building process, and also in information display. The display in question may be designed to show the path through the network chosen by the expert system in its expedition process.

Another extension to the system, as outlined in Figure 8.3, is perhaps the obvious one of direct manufacture integration. Computer Integrated Manufacture (CIM) is now used widely in advanced factory environments, and this facility would be an ideal candidate for integration into our knowledge-based system. With such a (successfully) integrated and interfaced system, the whole process of new product design, or even product modification and development is catered for. The steps identified in the process involve the initial specification level, where interaction with the potential customer occurs, the actual design stage, where the system provides guidance to the designer, the test and evaluation stage, where simulation takes place, and the final product. All these steps are traditionally undertaken by skilled personnel with different levels of responsibility, but all working to a predifined goal, i.e. the efficient and reliable development and manufacture of industrial or commercial products which meet strict quality control standards. An integrated expert system is capable of assisting in that corporate aim, and once installed, can only provide an ever-improving development environment.

8.3.2 Classification Problems

Problems falling into this category are also called DIAGNOSIS problems. The family tree building system comes broadly within this group in that the solution is bound up with a fairly rigid tree structure which has definite paths leading to a given query. The earliest knowledge-based systems were based on classification tasks and were designed for assisting in medical diagnosis (MYCIN, ONCOCIN, INTERNIST, etc.). In fact, the medical diagnosis problem remains one of the most widely used problem domains in which expert systems find use. They are characterised by the following factors :

1. The target system model is highly complex. Any information base in use is necessarily large.

2. Information and knowledge, although extensive, is severely limited by man's shortage of acquired knowledge about his own system. The situation is continually improving, but it will be many years before a complete 'system understanding' is achieved. In place of complete understanding, there exists well-tried heuristics, which become more reliable with experience.

3. An approach to a definitive diagnosis involves a sequence of queries addressed to the patient and specific clinical tests which become necessary as the diagnostic dialogue progresses to the point of hypothesis. On the basis of presenting sysmptoms, the medical practitioner will almost always begin the diagnostic process from the same starting point and carry on with the same sequence until one of the specialist clinical tests proves a hypothesis.

4. Documentation of previous cases is very good and abundant. Case studies tend to be made by medical staff keen on research, and patient records are meticulously kept. This detail and sheer quantity of relevant information makes the subject area ideal for mathematical processing via statistics. Diagnostic procedures can be designed on the basis of multiple occurrences of symptoms and the documented evidence of cause as the problem progresses and definitive investigations become possible.

In some instances, it would appear that a definitive diagnosis can be made on first consultation, on the basis of pure heuristics. However, this is usually verified by a limited range of tests, designed mainly to exclude other, less likely and possibly more serious problems.

One of the first medical diagnosis expert systems was concerned with the identification of micro-organisms responsible for certain patient systems. The system uses abduction to arrive at tentative conclusions, using an extremely large information base on known organisms and their likely effects. It operates with a mixture of a form of statistics and heuristics. Each tentative classification has attached to it a kind of conditional probability called a CERTAINTY FACTOR, with a range of 1 to -1. One signifies absolute certainty and -1 indicates the opposite. The system has the benefit of a large information base incorporating facts on the identity of a micro-organism in the form of TRIPLES. This is a common form of representation used in knowledge-based systems, and in the case of MYCIN, holds information in the order :

(CONTEXT PARAMETER VALUE)

In MYCIN, this type of triple is augmented with a certainty factor. The rules in MYCIN are fairly simple production rules of the basic form :

```
(IF ((THE GRAM-STAIN OF THE ORGANISM IS NEGATIVE)
     (THE SHAPE OF THE ORGANISM IS ROD-LIKE)
     (THE ORGANISM IS ANAEROBIC))
 (THEN
     (THE ORGANISM IS BACTERIODES)))
```

A rule devised for backward-chaining. In actual fact, the MYCIN rules incorporate probabilities as mentioned earlier, and a combination of evidence from various sources, in order to arrive at a reasonable conclusion. To cater for this, numerical values representing prior and conditional probabilities are incorporated in the system.

As the system progresses in response to a specific request, conditions arise where evidence is so uncertain that assistance is required. Heuristics play their part in the reduction of complexity by helping the system to make 'educated guesses'. However, even this ultimately fails, and a direct input of specialist information is required of the clinician. As each question is answered, new or empty triples become instantiated, thereby facilitating backward chaining and the building of a more complete information base. Great care was exercised in the development of MYCIN to provide an acceptable interface to the clinical specialist. The questions generated by the system reflect the search strategy employed, and without due care, the questions put to the user could appear to be very much unstructured. In effect, the logic of the inference mechanism would be apparent to the user, and this might appear to be somewhat convoluted. The whole philosophy of Knowledge Engineering would be contradicted.

MYCIN was one of the first successful applications of knowledge-based systems. It was successful by virtue of its acceptance by the users as a viable and usable aid to diagnosis in their particular domain. The control structure was necessarily domain-specific and this had the obvious effect of limiting the system to the identification of infectious diseases. Fortunately, there are significant similarities between the characteristics of the MYCIN domain and other diagnosis areas, and hence the general grouping of Figure 8.2 under the title of classification. This was recognised as new application areas were considered for the knowledge-based approach, and an attempt was made to extract the domain-dependent parts from MYCIN, leaving an essentially domain-independent control structure. The system resulting from this exercise is called Empty Mycin, or E-MYCIN and provides an empty expert system SHELL ready for information base building. Of course, with this system, the information base and the rule base must be produced in the strict format demanded by the MYCIN structure. This system has been successfully used to provide expert assistance in fields as varied as Engineering (SACOM), water resource management (HYDRO) and blood disorder diagnosis (CLOT). Other applications have been identified and are in the process of development.

The diagnosis classification need not be applied solely to question/answer dialogues, with input supplied direct from the domain specialist. It is too difficult to envisage a system capable of obtaining its information directly from some kind of 'sensory' device. In the case of medical systems, which depend ultimately on the results provided by laboratory equipment, it would seem reasonable to provide an elicitation path for that information to be input to the knowledge-based system without further interaction. Indeed, laboratories of all kinds have some sort of programmable interface to specialist equipment, and in many cases, well- documented interfaces exist on laboratory devices, specifically provided for computer control. As more and more essential parts to a viable diagnosis system come under the influence of computer control, the more it becomes possible to produce a completely integrated system, capable of efficient operation with the minimum of human 'interference'.

One area of diagnosis considered ideal for the application of knowledge-based systems is the general field of IMAGE ANALYSIS, or IMAGE INTERPRETATION. As an example, consider one very narrow technique used in medical diagnosis; Ultrasonic Imaging. If the system boundary is placed around the upper-abdominal area, the field of view would include, amongst other things, the liver, kidneys, spleen, gall bladder, and diaphragm. If the diagnosis is limited to just one of those organs, then the problem can be considerably simplified. If an ultrasonic imaging system is employed in order to non-invasively provide a 'picture' representing an appropriate cross-section of a patient's upper-abdominal area, the following factors are immediately pertinent :

1. Ultrasound is relatively safe to the patient if operated within strict limits. However, partly due to these safely considerations, the quality of the derived image is less than perfect. Other factors having an influence on image quality are related to the physics of ultrasound and the properties of the interaction of ultrasonic energy with human tissue plus its variation within the significant field.

2. As a result of (1), image interpretation and the diagnosis which results is largely the responsibility of experienced personnel. The diagnosis may become quite subjective in certain instances, and different people with similar backgrounds and experience will often disagree.

3. In order to provide a more objective diagnosis, more information may be necessary. This information could take the form of previous medical history, or it could be provided as the result of clinical tests indicated in the diagnostic process.

A system capable of diagnosing gall stones may require the following basic information :

1. The presenting sysmptoms, as interpreted by the medical practitioner.
2. The size, weight and age of the patient.

3. Previous medical history.

4. The coordinates of the 'target' organ within the field of view. This could provide the basis for a system able to guide the operator to the relevant position in order to obtain an appropriate image.

5. The characteristics of the organ in question. Its size, shape and characteristic appearance in the ultrasound field.

6. The characteristic appearance, within the ultrasound field, of specific abnormalities. An information base would be required on these alone.

These items would represent a starting point in the specification of a knowledge-based system capable of supplying some assistance in the diagnosis of specific pathology. The knowledge base would include normal data on the investigation cross-section involved, the relevant physical details of the equipment in use, and information on known abnormalities associated with specific symptoms.

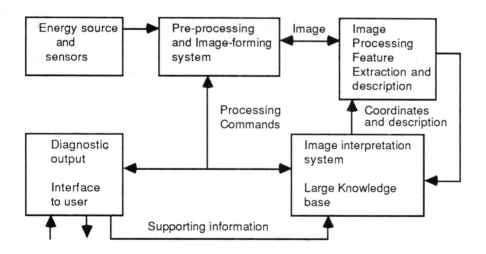

Fig. 8.4 An image interpretation system

A knowledge-based system designed to provide assistance to radiologists in the diagnosis of 'structural defects' evident in images produced by clinical imaging is shown in Figure 8.4. The diagram shows five basic components to the system :

1. *The energy source and sensors.* This incorporates the actual ultrasound energy transmitters and receivers and provides a 'raw' signal to the rest of the system.

2. *The pre-processing and image-forming system.* The signal derived from the receivers can be 'cleaned up' considerably by virtue of our knowledge of the physical interactions involved and their effect on the derived signal. This is not a knowledge-based system as described in this text, although it could be interpreted as a physical system in which knowledge has been 'embedded' into the electronics (see later). Pre-processing takes the form of signal filtering and weighting in order to provide information in a form suitable for the formation of an image.

3. *Image processing.* The image, as produced by conventional ultrasonic imaging systems, is basically limited to points 1 and 2 above. The pre-processed image is formed on a television monitor and presented to the investigator in just that form. The human response to this type of data is to attempt to identify structures within it, thereby extracting detail from all the surrounding complexity. An experienced radiologist will be able to recognise more clinically-significant detail, embedded in more artifactual information, than a less experienced person. This system would be responsible for deciding on border conditions and would provide specific descriptions of structures it is able to isolate in this way. It may even take some guidance from experts, either directly, or from some kind of knowledge-based system integrated into the equipment.

4. *The image interpretation system itself.* This would incorporate a diagnostic knowledge-based system such as E-MYCIN, and would take the information supplied by the image processing system as a basis for diagnosis. Textual information would also be used to guide and support the interpretation.

5. *Diagnostic output and user interface.* The interface to the user would take two forms. The first is the actual image produced by the conventional parts of the equipment, overlaid perhaps with tentative boundaries produced by the image processing system. The second is a textual input/output device on which diagnostically supportive information is initially given, and on which interaction is facilitated between the expert and the knowledge-based system.

It may be noted that several feedback paths exist in the system as outlined in Figure 8.4. The fact that communication channels exist between all separately-identified parts of the system, means that control can be exercised on a global scale by the expert system.

Diagnostic systems may be found in all domains and the nature of the requirements of such systems makes them ideal candidates for the expert systems approach. One domain receving much attention is the electronic systems area. As electronic hardware becomes more and more complex, due in part to the availability of CAD/CAM equipment, and more systems are made up of sub-systems, some being programmable, the need arises for built-in diagnostics. It may not be sufficient to wait until a, possibly catastrophic, failure occurs before the diagnosis-repair sequence is initiated. Self-test could be incorporated, capable of some kind of corrective action on the basis of 'test reports' generated by each of the sub-systems. The modularity afforded by the hardware development approach adopted results in the possibility of modular test. An expert system operating as a 'supervisor', perhaps making regular system performance appraisals, might even have the capability to switch-in a back-up module in case of localised failure. This topic is described as FAULT TOLERANCE.

8.3.3 Interpretation

The most striking example of interpretation can be found at the computer/user interface. It has already been said that knowledge elicitation is a crucial component of knowledge-based system development, and a good user-friendly interface to the system will ensure its acceptance and subsequent use by domain experts. With most expert systems (if not all), some input is required of the user and some output is given by the system. Input/output requirements can be decided on at initial development stage. For example, it may be decided that all input will take the form of single words in response to prompts :

```
What is the age of the equipment (in years) ? > _
```

or it may take the form of statements, again conforming to some rigid formulation specified in the prompt. Output can be accommodated by 'canned text', such as :

```
Object 2 was moved to behind object 10
```

where, in the above example, the canned text is OBJECT .. WAS MOVED .. OBJECT, and the remaining items are inserted as the program proceeds. While this provides an acceptable situation in some instances, for large systems characterised by large amounts of textual output, and also subject to incremental development and modification, it may cause problems. As the system extends and changes, the actual meanings of the canned text may become vague or even misleading. In such cases, it is almost essential to provide a better output facility than the basic one described here.

Eventually, as systems increase in size and complexity, some form of textual interface is required which is able to cope with subtle changes in system detail, thereby adapting to the changing interface needs. Unfortunately, for any individual attempting to create a natural language interface, all human languages are relatively terse in their nature. They are prone to ambiguity, which can be overcome with experience gained, both from our childhood learning process and from perhaps many years of 'translation' of varying degrees of language 'purity'. Traditionally, computer scientists deal with subjects such as PARSING of SYNTAX, using such techniques and devices as PARSE TREES, CONTEXT-FREE GRAMMERS, DICTIONARIES, FEATURE INDICATORS and AUGMENTED TRANSITION TREES. In fact, the whole field of parsing and language interpretation by computers is a major independent discipline within the domain of computer science. A solution to the problem was attempted in the late 1950s and early 1960s, very soon after the successful implementation of the first digital computers. Simple translators were demonstrated, based on a dictionary of approximately 250 words and using a syntactic rule base of three. In the late 1960s much work and finance was invested, mostly in response to the great enthusiasm and expectations of research personnel. However, in spite of this long-term investment, there exists no really good natural language interface. The enthusiasm remains, and with advances in speech processing hardware, the race for a natural language interface based on direct speech input, is on.

The output of information in a form suitable for the domain in question, and more important, the person using the system, has a high priority when considering the user interface.

Code conversion could be used to provide an output which appears more natural. In such systems, an English phrase may be associated with each entity in the representation of knowledge. Consider the following example of conclusive data, as it might appear internally before being output. The following list may be a conclusion or part-conclusion in a knowledge-based system :

```
(CONNECTED (MODULE-1) (SYSTEM-X))
```

This would be associated with a phrase such as :

```
MODULE-1 was CONNECTED to SYSTEM-X
```

It would take the internal representation and 'fill in' the more natural phrase according to given arguments. The control structure could be responsible for expressing this in a much more acceptable way :

```
MODULE-X WAS CONNECTED TO SYSTEM-X
IN THE MANNER PROPOSED BY SPECIFICATION-Y
```

Extra heuristics could be employed to produce an output which would give the user the impression that the system is very sophisticated indeed. For example, the following heuristic could be applied :

```
IF the MODULE is an AMPLIFIER
    AND the MODULE is the only one of its kind
THEN
    OUTPUT CONFIGURATION (MODULE)
```

The phrase might then appear as :

```
THE DIFFERENTIAL AMPLIFIER MODULE WAS CONNECTED TO SYSTEM-
                              X
    IN THE MANNER PROPOSED IN SPECIFICATION-Y
```

This approach to text generation is very useful in knowledge-based systems. As the details surrounding different objects within an output list change in some subtle, but semantically-significant way, the associations and heuristics involved in the text generation process maintain meaning. This technique has been successfully implemented in E-MYCIN, but it does tend to break down when the output list becomes too complex in terms of the number and type of objects involved. Consistency and fluency difficulties arise in such situations, due mainly to the very loose association with the rules of linguistics.

Augmented transition trees (or networks - ATNs) have been used in the formulation of grammatically-correct sentences. However, many advances have been made in the discipline, using large knowledge bases to accomplish acceptable results. These systems include MUMBLE, KAMP and TEXT.

8.4 Blackboard Methods

In an integrated system, which may include many knowledge-based systems, perhaps in some kind of hierarchy, it may be that some or all of the classifications shown in Figure 8.2 are implemented. As systems extend to involve expertise from more than one specialist discipline, and communication is required between each of these components, interaction becomes progressively more problematic. Knowledge-based systems and their knowledge bases are usually domain-specific. The basic problem can be visualised by considering the following analogy :

A bio-medical engineer is given the task of designing a piece of equipment to monitor and analyse oesophageal pressures as a function of time. In order to carry out the design of the hardware and software required, he needs to consult with specialist medical personnel. The gastroenterologist has specialist knowledge on the anatomy and physiology of the gastro-intestinal tract and the basic specifications of the project would probably originate from this source. However, in order to probe deeper into the underlying causes of a particular clinically-related problem, he might ask the advice of a bio-chemist. In the course of development, it is decided to incorporate information obtained from radiological investigations. For this, the specialised knowledge of a radiologist is sought. A meeting is arranged between all the individuals involved in the project. At that meeting, it becomes apparent that each individual has a wealth of specialist knowledge, and thought processes strongly influenced by their training and experience. In effect, communication becomes difficult, with each individual unable or unwilling to understand the minute details of the other specialities. After all, the requirements are for each person to understand fully, the problems associated with his domain. Each domain specialist should be equipped with his own user-friendly interface, by which other individuals can communicate at the level which best suits them in the context of the problem in hand.

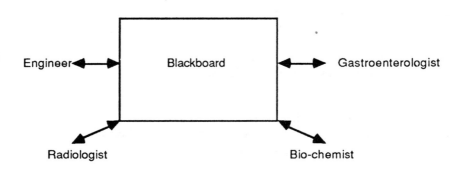

Fig. 8.5 A blackboard control structure.

In the block diagram of Figure 8.5, each of these hypothetical individuals are represented. As one individual requires information, he writes the request on the blackboard. The request is noted by the appropriate individual, and the solution is placed on the board. If, in the course of problem-solving, one specialist requires further information outside his 'sphere', then that request for information is placed on the blackboard. The use of a blackboard, or some other similar device in such situations, has the effect of simplifying otherwise complex interrelationships, and it facilitates communication.

It is not too difficult to visualise the same technique being applied to large 'layered' expert systems, and it is commonly used in such situations. Internally, a common area is assigned in which simplified messages are placed, in readiness for action by other parts of the integrated system.

8.5 Summary

In this chapter, we have explored additional strategies to the forward-chaining, data-driven approach of Chapters Four and Five. The goal- driven approach was discussed, and examples of its potential use were given. It should also be apparent at this stage, that both forward and backward rules and control systems would probably be required in any realistic system, the method being largely governed by the problem to be solved. Considerations on strategies should begin at the problem definition stage and should certainly be decided on before the final encoding phase.

Other factors, not specifically treated up to this point should be considered. They include BACKTRACKING, TRUTH-MAINTENANCE and STRUCTURED KNOWLEDGE BASES. The latter has been discussed in this chapter in a limited sense, and in a specific context.

8.5.1 Backtracking

If a particular information base can be considered in the form of the familiar tree structure, and if, in the search for a given goal or conclusion, the control structure has reached an inconclusive 'dead-end' in its quest, it should be able to BACKTRACK to the relevant node in the tree where that particular branch originated. These points are termed CHOICE POINTS. A good example of the need for such a facility can be found in a depth-first search algorithm. In any system employing backtracking, some facility must be provided to keep a record of previously passed choice points.

8.5.2 Structured Knowledge Bases

In the simple family relationships rule-based system, it could be seen that, within the inference mechanism (the control structure), rules could be identified. At the TEST-ANTECEDENT stage, a rule existed of the form :

```
IF  CONDITION-1  IS  TRUE
    OR
    CONDITION-2  IS  TRUE
    OR
    CONDITION-3  IS  TRUE
THEN
    ALLOW  THE  ACTION  PHASE  OF  THE  RULE  TO  CONTINUE
```

It can be seen that this part of the control structure could be replaced by a certain rule from a separate rule base. Such a rule base would form a CONTROL KNOWLEDGE BASE, and the provision of this extra flexibility at the control level could have a great influence on the system's inherent inference power. In the case of multiple knowledge bases, the separation and creation of layered, hierarchical knowledge structures is one method of dealing with complexity.

8.5.3 Truth Maintenance

In large knowledge-based systems in which the system produces conclusions as permanent facts, as a result of system execution, information consistency could become a problem. In the same way that LISP systems employ garbage collectors to 'clean up' the environment, facilities can be added to knowledge-based systems to effect truth maintenance. One approach would be to store a record of specific conditions which lead to conclusions (termed 'beliefs'). With this record, conclusions which no longer apply, as a consequence of a change in assumptions, can be identified by tracking down the source contradictions occurring when those beliefs are tested against current assumptions.

Chapter Nine

Dedicated Hardware

9.1 Introduction

One of the main criticisms levelled at LISP-based systems used in the general area of artificial intelligence is its speed (or lack of it). One other factor often quoted by its critics is the memory-intensive nature of knowledge-based system applications. These criticisms can be sympathised with, especially when one considers the structure of typical systems. These are :

1. *A possibly large information base*, characterised by richness and complexity.

2. *One or more rule bases*, possibly containing thousands of rules in some kind of hierarchy.

3. *A control structure* containing many abstracted functions. In more advanced systems, the inference mechanisms themselves may be structured in such a way as to incorporate control knowledge.

4. *A user-interface*, equal in nature and complexity to the 'main system'. This interface should also include an explanation facility.

All these essential system parts, plus the nature of LISP, tend to support the hypothesis that such systems do indeed suffer from lack of execution speed and excessive memory useage. In the laboratory, these considerations are secondary to the main task of concept-proving, even though large-scale successful applications exist 'in the field'. In most currently-used systems, speed is not 'sensitive', and in fact, the time taken to perform conclusive inference can sometimes be made more 'interesting' to the user by providing progress reports, or even perhaps by graphical animation of network traversal.

The importance of artificial intelligence is so great in many domains, that in the future, the technology will most certainly be applied at the instrumentation level. The medical imaging system proposed in Figure 8.4 is one example of the potential implications of this strategy. All parts of the integrated system shown in Figure 8.4 would, ideally, be incorporated into the same piece of equipment. For this to be successful, the user should not be expected to wait too long before a diagnostic opinion or identification is produced. It should effectively be 'transparent' to the user. The equipment may have the following features :

1. *Automatic diagnostic assistance*, in the form of textual output with image-highlighting graphical support.

2. *Automatic adjustment of analogue system parameters* in order to produce optimal image quality on the basis of diagnostically- significant information at its disposal.

3. *The possibility of connection to a large medical records data base*, in order to obtain medical details pertinent to the individual and the investigation. Results of the image analysis process, confirmed by the medical specialist, could be added to those records in a two-way communication configuration.

For a system such as the one outlined and discussed here, speed and efficiency would be major considerations.

9.2 Symbolic Processing Architectures

In the design of any new computer architecture, the 'architect' always has an application in mind. General-purpose computers cater for a broad range of applications, from the scientific domain, where numerical computations are the norm, to commercial applications in which the manipulation of text may be of equal importance to numerical calculations. The computational requirements of languages such as LISP and PROLOG impose a particular set of constraints on computer architectures. Symbolic languages are used in domains where the development of software capable of manipulating symbols is required, and as we have seen in previous chapters of this text, a heavy emphasis is placed on abstraction. Architectural mechanisms able to support abstraction is one of the requirements of suitable architectures.

In any discussion of hardware suitability to a particular implementation language, the salient characteristics of the language in question should be explored. For LISP, a list of the more important characteristics can be made, as shown below.

9.2.1 Data Typing

In LISP, an object's type is part of its value. For example, in the function to multiply two numbers together :

$$(* \ A \ B)$$

the * in the expression means that the function is about to multiply two values. However, the types of those values, and therefore the type of the expression, is determined at run-time by the variables supplied. They could be integer, floating -point, complex number, etc. This is known as LATENT DATA TYPING. This has a significant effect on LISP-specific architectures. In particular, it has given rise to a form of hardware-based memory storage system known as TAGGED MEMORY. In tagged memory, the type of the object as well as the object's value is stored in one memory word. With this direct form of typing, the possibility exists for rapid object accessing, generic operations and garbage collection. Speed of execution of code is influenced to a great extent, with this method, by the inherent facilities of data field and type-check processing in parallel.The ability to execute a multi-way branch based on an object's type can be achieved on a machine equiped with tagged memory. There are problems however. In any system in which more information is supplied in order to simplify and speed-up execution, there exists an increased memory usage overhead. Although this is a problem which can be reconciled in a dedicated LISP machine, it may impose too heavy a burden on processing power if conventional computer languages are to be catered for on the same machine.

9.2.2 Object Extent

The extent of an object in a computer programming language relates to its 'lifetime' in the execution time of the program in which it was created. In LISP, an object's extent is said to be infinite, in that it remains in existence for the lifetime of the program, once created. This imposes the one major overhead in LISP systems; that of GARBAGE COLLECTION. When an object becomes inaccessible, because all references to it have been removed, then it should be removed from the environment. However, because of the structure of the language, this does not happen automatically. Effectively, it remains within memory space until it is either deliberately removed or power-down occurs. The problem is solved in all LISP systems with the aid of a garbage collector, capable of identifying inaccessible and unused objects, and removing them, thereby freeing memory space. With regular use of LISP interpreters, the onset of garbage collection, automatically initiated by the system, becomes obvious, even irritating. In actual fact, the process may involve a combination of background stack manipulation and garbage collection.

9.2.3 Graph--Orientated Memory Structures

Relationships of objects are represented in LISP-like languages by object interconnectivity. The actual address in memory of each object is only important to the system CPU, or more likely, the MEMORY MANAGEMENT SYSTEM. Logically-correct solutions to specific problems are characterised by interrelationships between program variables as well as variable values, and it is rather efficient to represent these as interconnected graphs, using absolute memory addresses as links. This process of graph, or network traversal by virtue of memory addresses is one of the basic modes of memory interaction.

The concept of VIRTUAL MEMORY is important in this discussion. The facility to 'divorce' the basic task of memory management from the software system control structure has a major impact on the efficiency of the application. It addresses one of the main problems associated with knowledge-based systems using LISP as the implementation language. To further increase speed of execution, a single, uniformly -accessible memory address space is required. In other words, the device of memory SEGMENTATION should be avoided. If this cannot be achieved, then execution speed will suffer because of the overhead caused by segment register calculations at specific artificial boundaries. Graph, or network traversal is such an important task in knowledge-based systems, that the efficient memory management of an essentially uniform memory address field is extremely desirable.

One other factor, associated with the efficient use of memory, is the suitability of high-speed CACHE memory. Run-time data structures can be loaded and temporarily stored in this area of extremely fast memory in order to carry out searches at optimal speed. In fact, most dedicated systems will be found to have this facility since it provides a simple method of significantly increasing throughput.

9.2.4 Control

LISP systems used in knowledge-based applications are usually endowed with a rich and complex control structure. In the process of inference, there will be many function calls, arguments passed, intermediate results stored and results returned. Using traditional architectures, this operational methodology alone would impose a great burden on the hardware. Heavy use would be made of a stack which would have the potential, in LISP systems, of causing serious memory conflicts. Arguments might be saved temporarily either on some kind of stack, or in main memory. A suitable architecture would incorporate significant facilities to overcome these difficulties. Hardware support would be provided in the form of fast-access registers associated with the processor, and generalised hardware control mechanisms might be included to support non-blind backtracking etc.

Figure 9.1 shows the block diagram of a basic architecture along the lines discussed in this chapter. It shows a central processing unit (CPU), interfaced to RAM in an intimate way. This forms a local cache, or local registers which may be used to hold data temporarily and access them at maximum speed. The CPU would probably be a 32-bit device, clocked at a rate of at least 10MHz. It would incorporate some of the features of high- performance processors, such as hardware-implemented numerical manipulation, internal timers, large register arrays, pipelining, memory management and extensive interrupt capabilities. The internal and closely associated register arrays may be optimised for use in search and data structure operations, and the device would have extensive and powerful bit manipulation and branching capabilities. An interrupt control interface is shown in the block diagram of Figure 9.1 since it is considered an essential component in a system of this complexity. In addition to interrupts, a separate DEBUG interface is also shown. This would be essential in the test and debug stage of the type of system best suited to our class of application. It would be capable of providing a communication path between a supervisor system in a specific development environment, and would facilitate the kind of maintenance strategies outlined in this text. Figure 9.2 shows the block diagram of a typical outline development environment.

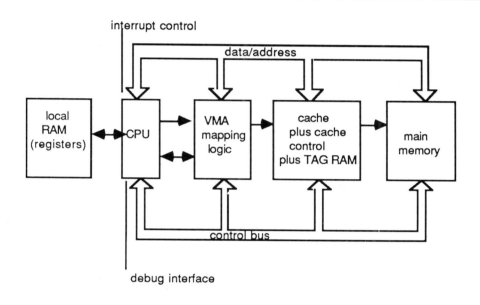

Figure 9.1 Simplified diagram of a symbolic processor architecture

In the final analysis, the architecture shown in Figure 9.1 has only a few architectural elements which distinguishe it from a state-of-the-art general-purpose architecture. Parallel computations are apparent in knowledge-based systems, but in simple systems, this can be accommodated with the aid of tagging and hardware control support. In some cases; image processing in particular, it may be desirable to perform inference at roughly the same time as image processing, and in such cases it may be prudent to consider architectures best suited to that narrow field. In general-purpose symbolic processing hardware, the emphasis will be on system integration on a 'chip scale'. Parallel architectures will find their use in knowledge-based systems employing multiple levels of knowledge, and in integrated systems in which each level of expertise can operate, to a certain degree, independently and at the same time as others addressing different aspects of the same problem. In such cases, replication of the single-level devices, synchronised in their behaviour by parallel control mechanisms will be found to provide the best solution.

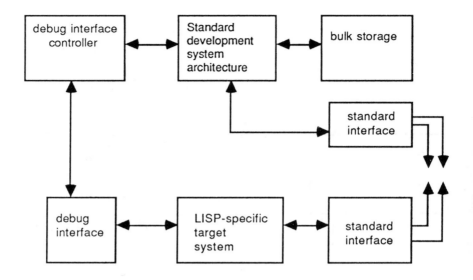

Figure 9.2 A development environment

9.3 Garbage Collection

This topic has been alluded to many times in this text, both in the discussion on LISP as an ideal implementation language for knowledge-based system development, and also in this chapter on dedicated architectures. The problems associated with the structure of LISP, i.e. the linked-list approach to maintaining association, are obvious. Unfortunately, the solution to the problem is somewhat more convoluted, especially when applied on large, LISP-specific architectures. These systems are characterised by large, virtual memory facilities, in which a scan of the whole of memory, essential to efficient garbage collection, cannot easily be made. The problems arise, of course, because not all of the environment is stored in directly -addressible memory space at any one time (as far as the processor is concerned). The algorithms used traditionally can be conveniently listed in rough chronological order, and a brief comparison of these, in the context of computational architectures will be instructive.

9.3.1 Mark and Sweep

This is the oldest and perhaps most obvious method used for garbage collection. It originated in the early 1960s. The method involves two phases: mark and sweep. Initially, the system examines each object in the environment and 'marks' the ones it finds to be accessible. In order to accomplish the identification of accessible objects, each pointer, one at a time, is followed to the object it references. The REFERENT object is then marked, and the pointers in the cells of the referent object are subsequently followed. The system has the facility to maintain a record of all the pointers yet to be followed. Once the mark phase has been completed, the second phase is initiated. The second and final phase is concerned with the deletion of unmarked objects. In actual fact, the process of deletion is merely the act of updating a 'free memory list' for use in subsequent allocations. This method is not used much in today's symbolic computer systems by virtue of its time overhead and unsuitability for virtual memory systems. Mark-and-sweep garbage collectors have been termed 'pausing' garbage collectors since, when the collection is underway, all regular processing is suspended. It may however be used in conjunction with other, more efficient techniques as a 'back-up'.

9.3.2 Reference Counting

With this method, a count of all references to an object is maintained. The algorithm used forces an object's removal when that object's reference count goes to zero. A major problem, however, is likely to occur when two or more objects have pointers to each other in a CYCLIC manner, but remain inaccessible to the system because no other pointers exist. In effect, they are isolated and inaccessible with a reference count of more than zero. Systems have been designed which make use of reference counting in the first instance, and resort to the mark-and-sweep algorithm less frequently.

9.3.3 Copying Collectors

These systems are currently very much in favour in dedicated computer systems. The basic theory is quite simple and can be seen to provide a garbage collection system which provides more 'housekeeping' than the previous ones. The memory system comprising the working environment is partitioned by the system into two identical halves, called the OLD SPACE and the NEW SPACE respectively. Old space may, at a given time contain objects which may or may not be accessible, and new space is considered free and available. In the process of garbage collection, all the objects in old space found to be accessible (by default), are moved over to new space. Once that has been achieved, all that remains to be done is to completely 'erase' old space. In realistic systems, both halves of the memory system are in use at any one time, in a dynamic fashion, and garbage collection effectively occurs in a time-shared manner.

In the quest for the ideal situation, in which real-time operation can be facilitated in symbolic computer systems, garbage collection has received much attention. All the previous systems mentioned have their advantages and disadvantages, but all have succeeded in some way to provide a satisfactory utility for the systems in use at the time. With the advent of dedicated computer architectures and the demand for real-time operation, there have been further developments in the inherently time-consuming business of garbage collection.

9.3.4 Generational Systems

It was realised in the early 1980s, that objects that had been around in the system for some time were likely to be more permanent (more stable) than objects more recently created. With this philosophy, objects could be classified in terms of GENERATIONS, with the older generations regarded as the most stable, and the youngest, the least. Under these circumstances, garbage collection is arranged to occur more frequently in the least stable youngest generation, and much less frequently in the more stable older generation. With this system, a significant amount of time is saved in the garbage collection process, and by cleverly partitioning memory space to accommodate these generations, it is possible to make optimal use of the hardware structures in use.

9.4 Embedded Systems

In the 1970s, a great deal of development work was carried out on creating 'smart' systems embedded directly into equipment. Microprocessors were utilised to provide a new level of programmability. Laboratory equipment was designed capable of being connected by buses, to supervisor systems, and by these means operational performance could be monitored and controlled. Problems of dynamic calibration and adaptability were addressed and solved. More and more of the characteristics of such apparatus came under the direct control of an 'intelligent' controlling system. Equipment sporting in-built computer systems were even able to carry out some kind of automatic self-diagnosis under fault conditions.

With the successful implementation of knowledge-based systems in the fields of medical diagnosis, geology and business planning, the concept of in-built intelligence, or EMBEDDED intelligence became fashionable. Instead of knowledge -based systems being implemented on large, relatively user- unfriendly systems, more suited to the academic profession than industry, the possibility of embedded expert systems becomes quite attractive. The actual computer hardware does not necessarily have to be radically different in such cases, it merely has to support a suitable implementation language and the large amounts of information associated with knowledge- based systems. Speed, as we have seen, is a major consideration, and this problem has been addressed in the latest dedicated LISP machines and dedicated chip -level architectures. For example, in 1984, Texas Instruments unveiled a computer system dedicated to LISP, called the EXPLORER. It was based on an earlier system developed at the Massachusetts Institute of Technology. The Explorer is essentially a 32-bit computer system and addresses most of the problems associated with knowledge-based applications discussed in this chapter. In addition to the Texas Instruments system, other symbolic computers exist. These may represent the state-of-the-art in tools designed to support knowledge-based system development and are rich in facilities to support knowledge representation and inference techniques. All these machines are single-user systems with powerful program development environments for symbolic computing, but none of them can be considered suitable for embedded applications.

In order to ensure the use of embedded expert systems, it will be necessary to considerably miniaturise the hardware aspects, and integrate the software aspects. It will, in effect, be necessary to integrate most essential parts of a dedicated system in a configuration involving very few, or perhaps one single chip. A single-chip system might incorporate such facilities as debug controller, tag control, cache memories, and automatic memory management. Additional supportive hardware may include high -speed array processors and dedicated interface controllers.

9.5 The Impact of VLSI

The type of embedded system which will exist in the next generation of 'smart' instruments will be made possible by the advent of very large scale integration (VLSI). VLSI implies single-chip architecture implementations, where space/power properties exact high prices from complex hardware features, which may be considered 'free' in systems employing small or medium scale integration (SSI, MSI). These features include increased critical path lengths and data routeing that might slow the basic machine cycle.

One of the most potentially significant recent developments in architecture, suitable for consideration as vehicles for the implementation of embedded knowledge-based systems is the so-called, REDUCED INSTRUCTION SET COMPUTER, or RISC. In these devices, the traditional approach to system improvements; an increase in the range and complexity of the processor's instruction set in response to equivalent increases in compiler complexity, has not been followed. Instead, the philosophy adopted has been influenced by research carried out into the behaviour of high-level compilers. In the case of the C/Pascal family, it was found that most instructions being executed were a relatively small number of the simplest instructions available. The added advantages of incorporating the complex majority of instructions poses a severe performance penalty. With RISC devices, the burden of implementational complexity falls firmly on the software. The philosophy is to optimise VLSI machine resources for execution, and rely on the compiler as much as possible for interpretation. The following RISC characteristics are considered ideal for knowledge -based system implementations :

1.   Each instruction in the severely limited instruction set is stored as a single machine word (if possible).

2. Each instruction can be decoded and executed in one machine cycle.

3. The use of memory move instructions are minimised. Almost all operations are performed in registers to simplify addressing modes and ensure maximum speed.

4. Pipelining and related devices are avoided whenever possible.

5. Interconnect-intensive structures such as globally-accessible resources are avoided if at all possible. These factors are 'expensive' in VLSI.

The most important aspect of the RISC philosophy is the inherent increase in throughput as a result of simple, fast instructions. The system complexity in these systems is largely a function of the implementation languages, and this would appear to be compatible with the programming methodologies associated with symbolic processing languages. The requirements of an ideal symbolic architecture, such as tagging, can be incorporated into a system based on the RISC strategy, and it is not too difficult to envisage a multi-disciplinary expert system based on parallel - implemented RISC architectures.

9.6 Summary

As knowledge-based systems move more and more out of the close confines of the research laboratories to the realms of industry and commerce, the shortcommings of prototype systems become apparent. In real- life situations, the domain specialist, who has been promised an expert computer-based assistant, will soon complain if the system appears somewhat less than reasonably intelligent. The first impressions gained by the customer may be further 'sullied' by advice which seems to take an eternity to arrive. Of course, clever user-interfaces employing a mixture of interesting displays and intricate heuristics can overcome some of these problems, but in the final analysis, the results are important. When the novelty of any new system fades, the utility of the processes involved must remain to ensure continual use, and in the case of expert systems, the actual system is extended and improved by virtue of the experience gained by its continued use.

In addition to dedicated systems, optimised for use by domain specialists in the field, the requirements specified in this chapter must also be satisfied, to a much greater extent in any knowledge-based system designed to operate in the embedded configuration. In parallel with on- going research into knowledge-based system methodologies and knowledge engineering, significant advances will be made in the area of embedded intelligence. The possibility of incorporating automatic operation systems into equipment, capable of inference by deduction, abduction and induction is intriguing to say the least. The feasibility of implementing supervisory systems capable of resorting to heuristics is established, and such facilities will eventually be common in all kinds of application domains.

Function Summary

1. Function name : ACTION (expr)

Arguments :   EXPR - A LISP expression to be executed.

Task : To cause the evaluation of the expression supplied. The expression is embedded in the THEN clause of a rule.

Side effects : dependent on the expression to be executed.

2. Function name : ADD-NAME (list name)

Arguments :   list - A list of objects bound to an identifier.
name - An object.

Task : To add a new object to the head of the list supplied. No attempt is made to control the order of placement. The new object always becomes the CAR of the list.

Side effects : None. All manipulation is local.

3. Function name : ADD1VAR (proplist new-var)

Arguments :   proplist - A list of property-list variables bound to an identifier.
new-var - A new property-list variable to be added.

Task : To place the new variable on the list of property-list variables. A check is made on the existence of 'new-var' on 'prop-list' before continuing. The new variable is appended to the tail of 'prop-list'.

Side effects : None. All manipulation is local.

4. Function name : ADD-VAL (name var new-el)

Arguments :   name   - An object within a list of atoms.
var   - A property-list variable.
new-el - A property-list value to be added.

Task : To append 'new-el' to the tail of a list of property-list values associated with 'name' and 'var'.

Side effects : The specified property-list is modified.

5.   Function name : ALT-ELEMENT (list old-name new-name)

Arguments :   list   - A list of objects.
old-name - A property-list value to be modified.
new-name - A property-list value to be placed.

Task : To modify a specified property-list value within a list. The function tests for a NULL list. It is designed for use by ALT-VAL, in which case 'list' is equal to the CDR of a multi-element list of property-list values.

Side effects : None. All manipulation is local.

6.   Function name : ALT-OBJ (list old-name alt-name)

Arguments :   list   - A list of objects bound to an identifier.
old-name - The name of an object to be altered.
alt-name - The alternative name.

Task : To alter the name of an object within the specified list. The function has the responsibility of transferring the property-list of 'old-name' to 'alt- name'.

Side effects : Property-list manipulation is global.

7.   Function name : ALT-VAL (name var old-name new-name)

Arguments :   name   - An object within a list.
var   - A property-list variable.
old-name - A value to be modified.
new-name - The new value.

Task : To alter the (atomic) value associated with a specified object (name) and a specified property-list variable (var). The new value is supplied as 'var'. The function will only operate on lists of two elements, i.e. one atom for variable and one atom for value. In the case of a list containing more than one value atom, a test within ALT-VAL transfers control to ALT-ELEMENT.

Side effects : None. All manipulation is local.

8.   Function name : BUILD (proplist relate)

Arguments :   proplist - A list of property-list variables bound to an identifier.
               relate   - A list of atoms.

Task : To build the information base which basically comprises property-list data.
The function steps through each atomic object in 'relate' and repetitively invokes
PLACE. The function returns NIL when all objects have been 'serviced', on the
condition of an empty list (all done).

Side effects : All side effects are due to PLACE

9.   Function name : BY-DEPTH (branch target)

Arguments :   branch - A list containing all objects in the search path.
               target - An object in 'branch'.

Task : To search a given branch of a search space for a specified target object

Side effects : None. All manipulation is local.

10.   Function name : CHANGE-ONE ()

Arguments :   none.

Task : To test the efficacy of ALT-OBJ. The function supplies a DUMMY-LIST, an
'old-name' and a 'new-name'. SETQ is used in order to effect global changes. The
dummy list must be set up first and some properties must be placed, possibly with
BUILD.

Side effects : DUMMY-LIST and the property-lists therein are altered.

11.   Function name : COLLATE-COUPLES (individual temp-list)

Arguments :   individual - An atomic object.
               temp-list - A list of objects.

Task : To collate and return a list containing two individuals who are recorded as
married to each other.

Side effects : None. All manipulation is local.

12. Function name : DO-JOB (rule-list list)

Arguments :   rule-list - A list bound to an identifier, which contains rules.
               list   - A list of objects bound to an identifier.

Task : To make a copy of the list of persons comprising 'list'. The function invokes rules in turn until all the rules incorporated in 'rule-list' have been serviced. The function checks for an empty argument list and always returns NIL.

Side effects : A copy of the original list is made (FULL-COPY).

13. Function name : DRAW (status)

Arguments :   status - A list of objects to be output.

Task : To control the screen output of a list of objects as a hierarchy. The status flags MAIN and DONE are tested, and on the basis of this, either FILL-TREE or EXHIBIT is invoked.

Side effects : None directly.

14. Function name : EXHIBIT (last)

Arguments :   last - A list of objects representing the youngest generation in a
               family tree.

Task : To print each object within the supplied list on one single text line, spaced two characters apart.

Side effects : None. All manipulations are local.

15. Function name : EXISTS (list name)

Arguments :   list - A list of objects bound to an identifier.
               name - An object.

Task : To check for the existence of the specified object on the specified list. If the object already exists, T is returned, otherwise NIL.

Side effects : None. All manipulation is local.

16.   Function name : FILL-TREE (status)

Arguments :   status - A list of objects to be output.

Task : To control the building of the 'main' part of a family tree on the display screen. The function uses MAPC to iteratively invoke GENERATION and the flag MAIN is set.

Side effects : The status flag MAIN is set. Other effects occur indirectly.

17.   Function name : FIND (list name)

Arguments :   list - A list of objects bound to an identifier.
               name - An object.

Task : To find the individual represented by 'name' on the list supplied, and if found, return that name.

Side effects : None.

18.   Function name : GENERATION (out-list)

Arguments :   out-list - A limited list of objects to be output.

Task : To perform some vertical screen alignment and to control the invocation of the basic display function POSITION.

Side effects : None directly.

19.   Function name : INCLUDE (individual temp-list)

Arguments :   individual - An object.
               temp-list - A list of objects.

Task : To include the object supplied to the head of the specified list.

Side effects : None. All manipulations are local.

20.   Function name : INIT-LIST (rule-list)

Arguments :   rule-list - A list of rules bound to an identifier.

Task : To initialise all 'working lists' used by the rules, in the supplied list of rules, to NIL. The function requires the rules to be in the form :

(IF list1 ((antecedent-1) (antecedent-2) ... (antecedent-n))
(THEN (.... list2)))

where 'list1' and 'list2' represent the source and destination lists of information relevant to the rule respectively.

Side effects : Each list is globally modified. Take care !

21.   Function name : LOOPS (list rule-list)

Arguments :   list   - A list of objects bound to an identifier.
              rule-list - A list of rules bound to an identifier.

Task : To cause the invocation of DO-JOB successively until the terminating condition of (NULL OLD-GEN), where OLD-GEN is a list operated on and tested within LOOPS. This function represents a forward-chaining 'primitive'.

Side effects : The lists OLD-GEN, NEW-GEN and ORDER are modified.

22.   Function name : MAKE (relations)

Arguments :   relations - A list of objects representing persons in an information base.

Task : To control the iterative process of family tree production, using one of the lists provided in the search for ROOT (FIRST-ONES). The function iteratively invokes the depth-first process until all branches are explored from the root condition.

Side effects : None directly.

23.   Function name : NEWPROP (list proplist new-var)

Arguments :   list   - A list of objects bound to an identifier.
              proplist - A list of property-list variables bound to an identifier.
              new-var   - A new property-list variable.

Task : To add a new property-list variable name to the property-list of the CAR of 'list'. A check is made on the existence of 'new-var' on 'proplist' before continuing. The function prompts for, and reads the associated value from the terminal and PUTs this on the property-list along with the new variable.

Side effects : Property-lists are modified.

24.   Function name : NON-NIL ()

Arguments :   None.

Task : To test for the existence of a property-list value assigned to a property- list variable.

Side effects : None.

25.   Function name : OLDER-PEOPLE (list)

Arguments :   list - A list of objects bound to an identifier.

Task : To control the invocation of DO-JOB iteratively, until the list OLD-GEN becomes empty. The function is part of the control structure required to produce a family tree on the basis of the existence of a ROOT object. For each iteration, a list (ORDER) is extended to include the next (younger) generation, the previous new generation becomming the older generation.

Side effects : None directly.

26.   Function name : OVERALL ()

Arguments :   None.

Task : To control the display of the family tree as it is built by the rule-based system. Screen initialisation is included.

Side effects : The screen display is modified.

27.   Function name : PLACE (props name)

Arguments :   props - A list of property-list variables.
name - An object which is to be the recipient of 'props'.

Task : To take a list of property-list variables, and step through each variable, prompting the user for the associated value information until all property- list variable/value information is stored on the property-list of 'name'. The function returns NIL.

Side effects : Property-lists are modified.

28.   Function name : POSITION (disp-data)

Arguments :   disp-data - A list of objects to be output.

Task : To output the objects in the list supplied in a 'justified' format, along with their married partners. Screen formatting is included.

Side effects : The display screen is modified.

29.   Function name : PROP-CHECK (relate)

Arguments :   relate - A list of objects bound to an identifier.

Task : To check for a NULL property-list on any object within the supplied list. If information is found on the property-list of any object, T is returned, otherwise NIL.

Side effects : None. All manipulation is local.

30.   Function name : RECORDED (prop list)

Arguments :   prop - A property-list variable.
               list - A list of objects bound to an identifier.

Task : To check for the existence, in the supplied list, of an object bound to the property-list variable 'prop'. The function invokes EXISTS, and on success, invokes INCLUDE to include the matched object in a list.

Side effects : None. All manipulation is local.

31.   Function name : REM-ALL (list name)

Arguments :   list - A list of objects bound to an identifier.
               name - An object.

Task : To remove all occurences of the specified object within the supplied list. Double recursion is used.

Side effects : None. All manipulation is local.

32. Function name : REM-OBJ1 (list name)

Arguments :   list - A list of objects bound to an identifier.
                name - An object.

Task : To remove the FIRST occurence of the specified object within the supplied list.

Side effects : None. All manipulation is local.

33. Function name : REMOVE (list1 list2)

Arguments :   list1 - A list of objects bound to an identifier.
                list2 - A list of objects bound to an identifier.

Task : To remove from 'list2', all the objects in 'list1' (if they exist).

Side effects : None. All manipulation is local.

34. Function name : REMVAR (list proplist var)

Arguments :   list   - A list of objects bound to an identifier.
                proplist - A list of property-list variables.
                var   - The property-list variable to be removed.

Task : To remove a specified property-list variable from each object within a list supplied. The function tests for a NULL 'list' and 'proplist', and does nothing at all if the specified variable does not appear on 'proplist'.

Side effects : Property-lists are modified.

35. Function name : ROOTPUT (root)

Arguments :   root - An object representing the root of the family tree.

Task : To display the root object and married partner centred at the top of the screen.

Side effects : The display is modified.

36. Function name : SPOUSE (data)

Arguments :   data - A list of objects.

Task : To collate a list of objects (persons) recorded as married to the persons in the supplied list. The function WHO is invoked at the lowest level to determine the spouse for each individual object.

Side effects : None directly.

37. Function name : TEST-ANTECEDENT (antecedent individual)

Arguments :   antecedent - A specific antecedent of an implication within a rule.
                      individual - An object.

Task : To test the antecedent in a specific way :

1. The property value of the individual represented by the first object in the antecedent, matches the last object in the antecedent ;

2. The property of the individual matches the result of the function call generated by the last object.

Side effects : None directly.

38. Function name : TEST1 ()

Arguments :   None.

Task : To invoke BUILD, giving the list of property-list variables created for the family tree problem and also the name of a dummy list of objects. The dummy list is called (appropriately) DUMMY-LIST and must be set up first. It is essentially a test routine designed for the building of an information base.

Side effects : Property-lists are modified.

39. Function name : TEST2 (new-var)

Arguments :   new-var - A property-list variable.

Task : To add the supplied new variable to the property-list of all objects in DUMMY-LIST, which must have been previously 'built' for test purposes. The function also assumes the existence of a list of property-list variables called PROPVAR. The new variable is permanently added to PROPVAR.

Side effects : Property-list modifications and an expansion of PROPVAR.

40.   Function name : TEST-RULE (rule individual)

Arguments :   rule - A strictly formatted rule.
             individual - An object.

Task : To control the testing of each antecedent in the list supplied as 'rule'. If all the antecedents are matched, then the function terminates by invoking an ACTION.

Side effects : None directly.

41.   Function name : TITLE (ttl)

Arguments :   ttl - A message to form a title (atom).

Task : To clear the display screen and output a centred title at the top. It provides a good level of abstraction for use by display driving functions.

Side effects : Display modified.

42.   Function name : TREE (list)

Arguments :   list - A list of objects bound to an identifier.

Task : To create an environment required to produce a family tree. The function checks for an empty list and the existence of a ROOT object. The function iteratively invokes LOOPS in order to simulate a depth-first search from ROOT to youngest generation. Each new list representing the current 'end branch' plus the immediate parents of the list are removed.

Side effects : None directly.

43.   Function name : TRIBES ()

Arguments :   None.

Task : To provide a top-level initialisation and invocation of the two distinct parts of the genealogy rule-based system. The ROOT is first determined, followed by tree-building.

Side effects : All temporary lists initialised to NIL.

44.   Function name : USE-RULES (rule-list list)

Arguments :   rule-list - A list of rules.
              list - A list of objects bound to an identifier.

Task : In addition to the usual empty list tests, the function inspects the binding of
the rule to be used. The function is responsible for calling another function to
evaluate specific rules applied to an individual.

Side effects : None directly.

45.   Function name : VERT-MOV (number-of-lines)

Arguments :   number-of-lines - The number of vertical movements.

Task : To provide a vertical 'tab' facility. The screen cursor is positioned according to
the number of effective line feeds.

Side effects : Screen display modifications.

46.   Function name : WHO (spouses)

Arguments :   spouses - An object.

Task : To obtain and return the married partner of the person supplied as 'spouses'.
The property-list variable 'married' is accessed.

Side effects : None.

47.   Function name : YOUNGEST (young)

Arguments :   youngest - A list representing the youngest generation in a family tree.

Task : To display the youngest generation of the family tree with a spacing of two.
The function invokes VERT-MOV first.
Side effects : Screen display modifications.

Appendix 2

References

Lisp

1. Abelson, H. and Sussman, G.J. (1985). Structure and Interpretation of Computer Programs. MIT Press, MA.

2. Allen, J. (1978). Anatomy of Lisp. McGraw-Hill, New York.

3. Bartley, D. (1986). A Production-Quality Lisp System for the PC. Texas Instruments Engineering Journal, Vol. 3, No. 1, pp 78-83.

4. Berk, A.A. (1985). Lisp: The Language of Artificial Intelligence. Collins, London.

5. Burge, W.H. (1975). Recursive Programming Techniques. Addison-Wesley, MA.

6. Daniac, I. (1983). Lisp Programming. Blackwell Scientific Publications, Oxford.

7. Ferguson, E. (1986). Using Scheme for Discrete Simulation. Texas Instruments Engineering Journal, Vol.3, No. 1, pp 83-92.

8. McEntee, T. (1986). Overview of Garbage Collection in Symbolic Computing. Texas Instruments Engineering Journal, Vol.3, No. 1, pp 130-139.

9. Pratt, V.R. (1979). A Mathematician's View of Lisp. Byte, Vol.4, No.8.

10. Siklossy, L. (1976). Let's Talk Lisp. Prentice-Hall, NJ.

11. Touretzky, D.S. (1984). Lisp - A Gentle Introduction to Symbolic Computation. Harper and Row, New York.

12. Winston, P.H. and Horn, B.K.P. (1984). LISP, second ed. Addison-Wesley, MA.

Knowledge-Based Techniques

13. Bledsoe, W.W. (1977). Non-Resolution Theorem Proving. Artificial Intelligence, Vol.9, No.1, pp 1-35.

14. Brachman, R.J. and Levesque, H.J. (eds.) (1985). Readings in Knowledge Representation. Morgan Kaufmann Publishers.

15. Brooks, R.A. Symbolic Reasoning About 3-D Models and 2-D Images. Artificial Intelligence, Vol.17, No.1, pp 285-348.

16. Bundy, A., Bierstall, R.M., Weir, S. and Young, R.M. (1978). Artificial Intelligence: An Introductory Course. Edinburgh University Press.

17. Charniak, E., Riesbeck, C.K. and McDermot, D.V. (1980). Artificial Intelligence Programming. Lawrence Erlbaum, Hillside, NJ.

18. Charniak, E. and McDermot, D. (1985). Introduction to Artificial Intelligence. Addison-Wesley, MA.

19. Clang, W.J. and Shortliffe, E.H. (eds.) (1984). Readings in Medical Artificial Intelligence: The First Decade. Addison-Wesley, MA.

20. Davis, R., Buchanan, B. and Shortliffe, E. (1977). Production Rules as a Representation for Knowledge-Based Consultation Program. Artificial Intelligence, Vol.8, pp 15-45.

21. Davis, R. and Lenat, D.B. (1982). Knowledge-Based Systems in Artificial Intelligence. McGraw-Hill, New York.

22. Doyle, J. (1979). A Truth Maintenance System. Artificial Intelligence, Vol.12, No.3, pp 231-272.

23. Duda, R.O., Hart, P.E. and Sutherland, G.L. (1978). Semantic Network Representation in Rule-Based Inference Systems. In Pattern-Directed Inference, ed. Waterman, D.A. and Hayes-Roth, F., Academic Press, New York.

24. Evertsz, R. (1983). Production Rule Methods in the Computer Revolution in Education. (eds. Jones, A., Scanlon, E. and O'Shea, T.), Harvester Press, Sussex, UK.

25. Findler, N.V. (1979). Associative Networks: Representation and Use of Knowledge by Computer. Academic Press, New York.

26. Harman, P. and King, D. (1985). Expert Systems. John Wiley & sons.

27. Henderson, P. (1980). Functional Programming. Prentice Hall, NJ.

28. Jacobs, H. (1985). Expert Systems: How The Inference Engine Works. Texas Instruments Engineering Journal, Vol.2, No.4, pp 135-156.

29. Lebowitz, M. (1983). Generalization From Natural-Language Text. Cognitive Science, Vol.7, No.1, pp 1-40.

30. Lenat, D.B. (1983). EURISKO: A Program That Learns New Heuristics and Domain Concepts. Artificial Intelligence, Vol.21, No.3, pp 61-98.

31. Lindsay, R.K., Buchanan, B.G., Feigenbaum, E.A. and Lederberg, J. (1983). Applications of Artificial Intelligence in Organic Chemistry: The DENDRAL Project. McGraw-Hill, New York.

32. Miller, R., Pople, H. and Myers, J. (1982). Internist-1, An Experimental Computer-Based Diagnostic Consultant for General Internal Medicine. New England Journal of Medicine, Vol.307, pp 468-476.

33. Pople, H. (1982). Heuristic Methods for Imposing Structure on Ill- Structured Problems: The Structuring of Medical Diagnostics. In Artificial Intelligence in Medicine, (ed. Szolovits, P) pp 119-190, Westview Press, Colorado.

34. Shank, R. Dynamic Memory: A Theory of Learning in Computers and People. Cambridge University Press.

35. Shapiro, S.C. (1979). Techniques of Artificial Intelligence. Van Nostrand, New York.

36. Shortliffe, E.H. and Buchanan, B.G. (1976). A Model of Inexact Reasoning in Medicine. Mathematical Biosciences, Vol.23, pp 351-379.

37. Shortliffe, E.H. (1976). Computer-Based Medical Consultations: MYCIN. American Elsevier, New York.

38. Schubert, L. (1976). Extending The Expressive Power of Semantic Networks. Artificial Intelligence, Vol.7, No.2, pp 163-198.

39. Siklossy, L., Rich, A. and Marinov, B. (1973). Breadth-First Search: Some Surprising Results. Artificial Intelligence, Vol.4, No.1.

40. Sleeman, D. and Brown, J.S. (eds.) (1982). Intelligent Tutoring Systems. Academic Press, London.

41. Vere, S. (1978). Inductive Learning of Relational Production. In Pattern-Directed Inference Systems, (ed. Waterman, D.A. and Hayes- Roth, F) pp 281-295. Academic Press, New York.

42. Waterman, D.A. and Hayes-Roth, F. (1978). Pattern-Directed Inference Systems. Academic Press, New York.

43. Winograd, J. (1972). Understanding Natural Language. Academic Press, New York.

44. Winston, P.H. (1975). The Psychology of Computer Vision. McGraw-Hill, New York.

45. Winston, P.H. (1984). Artificial Intelligence, second ed. Addison- Wesley, MA.

Architectures

46. Feustel, E.A. (1983). On The Advantages of Tagged Architecture. IEEE Transactions on Computers. C-22, N0.7, pp 644-656.

47. Hennessy, J. (1984). VLSI Processor Architecture. IEEE Transactions on Computers. C-33, No.12, pp 1221-1246.

48. Wilkin, M.W. and Wiederbold, G. (1984). Relational and Entity- Relational Model Database and VLSI Design. IEEE Database Engineering, Vol.7, No.2, pp 61-66.

49. Myers, G.J. (1982). Advances in Computer Architecture, second ed. Wiley Interscience.

INDEX

referent object 193
refinement, of an algorithm 4, 124
REP 164, 166
REPEAT 54, 55
REPEAT...UNTIL 98
repetition 54, 71
REPLACA 63
REPLACD 63
resolution, graphical 144
RETURN 78, 81
REVERSE 49
RISC 195
root 15
RPLACP 86
rule interpreter 101, 179
rule list 100
rule-based approach 93
rule-based strategy 16
rule-dependency 61
rules 13

SA 166
SB 166
SCHEME dialect 35
scoping, of variables 40, 47
search 98
search algorithms 136
segment register 190
semantic networks 184
SETQ 45, 47
side effects 51, 54
simulation 35, 183
single-pass 126
SL 166
special form 51
SQR 47
SQRT 41, 50
stack 57
standardisation 124
statistics 30
status flags 154
step-wise refinement 87
strategies, computational 1
strategy, rule-based 16
structure editor 161
stubs 161, 174
SUBST 49
supervisory system 148
symbolic information 37
symbolic processing 188
'Symbolics 3670' 195
symbols 38
system boundary 1, 2
system building 147
system, closed 1
systems theory 1
systems, intelligent 25

tabular representation 15
tagged memory 189

tail recursive 60
task classification 10
technology, enabling 1
terminating list 54
TERPRI 80
test-antecedent 109
test 101
testing 8, 161
theorem provers 178
top-down 5, 161
TRACE 79, 170
tree format 3
tree search 94
tree structure 69, 93
tree, searching 132
truth table 23
typing 188

UL 166
uncertainty 8, 16
universal quantifier 26
UNTIL 54
user interfaces 143
utility functions 143

variable, scoping 47
variable, loop control 113
variables 4, 19, 40, 47
variables, global 117, 169
variables, local 169
VASNET 30
verification 117
virtual memory 189
VLSI 195

WHILE...DO 98
wild-cards 165
WINCLR 80

Xerox 1108 195

ZEROP 52

226

This is a partial list of our professional-level computing books, including those due for publication in 1987. You can order them through your usual bookseller.

Title & Author	Subject	ISBN/ Publication Date

Artificial Intelligence

Designing Artificial Intelligence Software: A. Bahrami	This provides a collection of AI based programming techniques that can be applied to solving every day programming problems together with descriptions of frontier research.	1-85058-085-5 Winter 1987
Progress in Machine Learning—a European Perspective: I. Bratko & N. Lavrac	A collection of papers written by leading European researchers in many areas of AI with an emphasis on machine learning.	1-85058-088-X Spring 1987
Expert Systems for Personal Computers: M. Chadwick & J.A. Hannah	Emphasises the development of rule-based systems, written in BASIC or LOGO.	1-85058-044-8 Published
Build Your Own Expert System (2nd Edition for IBM PC and Compatibles): C. Naylor	Entertaining view of AI with programs completely re-written and tested for IBM PC, Amstrad PC1512 and compatibles.	1-85058-071-5 Spring 1987
Expert System Development in Prolog and Turbo Prolog: P. Smith	This is a practical book aimed at the development of real systems in the commercial and industrial fields.	1-85058-064-2 Summer 1987
Program Design for Knowledge Based Systems: G. Winstanley	There are very few books aimed at designers of AI systems; this book fills the gap, and will enable any AI worker (or persons new to AI) to produce reliable working systems in the shortest possible time, using LISP as the target language.	1-85058-066-9 Summer 1987

Operating Systems

UNIX—The Book: M. Banahan & A. Rutter	The title says it all!	0-90510-421-8 Published
Understanding dBase III & II: G. Burns	Packed with tested examples of dBase applications.	0-90510-475-7 Published
Parallel Processing— with Occam: Alison Carling	An introduction to parallel concepts for those with some knowledge of computers and computer terminology.	1-85058-077-4 Summer 1987

The Complete FORTH: A. Winfield	Long established book for beginners to this exciting language – faster than BASIC, easier than assembler.	0-905104-22-6 Published

Applications

The Desktop Publishing Companion: Graham Jones	Starts with a discussion of such computers as the Apple Macintosh and IBM PC plus aspects of how to plan a publication including typography, word spacing, selection and the positioning of graphics.	1-85058-078-2 Spring 1987
CAD on the PC – and Compatibles: H.S. Atherton	How to design and draft reliably with an IBM PC or compatible. Both 2D drafting and 3D modelling are explained and illustrated with representative software packages.	1-85058-089-8 Autumn 1987
Interactive Learning on the IBM PC: Graham Beech	Comprehensive guide to the methods and practice of computer assisted and computer -managed learning, with examples for the IBM PC.	1-85058-057-X Published
The SuperCalc SuperBook: E. Lee	Officially approved guide to SuperCalc 2,3 and 4. Complementary to the manuals and packed with examples to clarify advanced topics.	1-85058-080-4 Summer 1987
The PC Compendium, Vol. I: C. Naylor	A wide ranging collection of 50 articles on how to get more from the IBM PC and compatibles. Covers languages, operating systems, expert systems, obscure bugs and much more.	1-85058-087-1 Summer 1987
Interactive Video: E. Parsloe	The definitive book on videotape, disc and interfacing to computers. Particularly strong on design techniques.	0-905104-55-2 Published

Communications

Cost Effective Local Area Networks: S. Bridges	A complete guide to the theory and practice of local area networks.	0-905104-86-2 Published
Communicating with Microcomputers: I. Cullimore	Describes how to connect microcomputers to each other – and to just about anything else – using commercial packages or hand-crafted code.	1-85058-055-3 Spring 1987

A Programmer's Guide to GEM– on the IBM PC & Compatibles: *B. Howling & A. Pepper*	This is aimed at readers with a reasonable knowledge of high level languages who already understand the basic concepts of GEM.	1-85058-084-7 Winter 1987
Windows on the PC – fundamentals and applications of Microsoft's Windows operating system: *J.M. Hughes*	John Hughes provides users with an easy-to-understand but comprehensive survey of the Microsoft Windows operating system and compatible applications.	1-85058-082-0 Autumn 1987
PICK–Your System *N. Kitt*	Equally useful to managers and systems analysts requiring background or detailed knowledge of PICK.	1-85058-031-6 Published
Operating Systems: *A. Trevennor*	A practical guide to operating systems and how they work, illustrated with DEC systems.	0-905104-66-8 Published

Programming Languages

Prolog: Programming for Tomorrow: *J. Doores, A. R. Reiblein & S. Vadera*	Complete tutorial with numerous practical examples. Covers the Edinburgh/ICL dialect.	0-905104-52-8 Spring 1987
How to Solve it in LISP: IBM PC & Compatibles: *P. J. Hall*	Emphasises LISP in statistics, general business applications and simulations. Databases and expert systems are also examined.	1-85058-005-7 Summer 1987
Prolog Through Examples: A Practical Programming Guide: *I. Kononenko & N. Lavrac*	Takes a novel approach to the teaching of Prolog, by presenting a series of graded examples, which are solved in Prolog.	1-85058-072-3 Autumn 1987
Practical COBOL for beginners on Microcomputers: *K. Sullivan*	COBOL tutorial for use with inexpensive micros.	0-905104-60-9 Published
Big Red Book of C: *K. Sullivan*	Comprehensive tutorial on C with many complete listings of programs for business applications.	0-905104-68-4 Published
Applied Fourth Generation Languages: *J. Watt*	Introduces 4GLs and shows that the system designer must still use conventional design techniques. Examines potential application areas for 4GLs including sales, distribution, production and finance. Avoid wasting your time with unsuitable software.	1-85058-061-8 Spring 1987

An Invitation

Sigma Press is still expanding–and not just in computing, for which we are best known. Our marketing is handled by John Wiley and Sons Ltd, the UK subsidiary of a major American publisher. With our speed of publication and Wiley's marketing skills, we can make a great success of your book on both sides of the Atlantic.

Currently, we are looking for new authors to help us to expand into many exciting areas, including:

Laboratory Automation
Communications
Electronics
Professional Computing
New Technology
Personal computing
Artificial Intelligence
General Science
Engineering Applications

If you have a practical turn of mind, combined with a flair for writing, why not put your talents to good use? For further information on how to make a success of your book, write to:

Graham Beech, Editor-in-Chief, Sigma Press,
98a Water Lane, Wilmslow, Cheshire SK9 5BB
or, phone 0625-531035

2582